DRIVING TO CALIFORNIA

*An Unconventional Introduction
to Philosophy*

For Rosie
and those like her

DRIVING TO CALIFORNIA

*An Unconventional Introduction
to Philosophy*

COLIN RADFORD

EDINBURGH UNIVERSITY PRESS

© Colin Radford, 1996

Parts of the text were previously published by
Avebury (Gower Publishing Company Limited)

Edinburgh University Press Ltd
22 George Square, Edinburgh

Typeset in ITC Korinna
by Pioneer Associates, Perthshire, and
printed and bound in Great Britain

A CIP record for this book is available from the
British Library

ISBN 0 7486 0819 2

CONTENTS

To avoid circumlocution I have sometimes used masculine personal pronouns, rather than, for example, 'her or she' or plural constructions. I hope readers will accept that there is no sexist intent in this solution to a problem of style.

INTRODUCTION

WHAT IS PHILOSOPHY?

You are a philosopher. You may not have realised this, unless you are a fellow professional which, if only statistically, is highly unlikely. After all, what is philosophy?

This is the question I address in Part One, which is a philosophical autobiography. Your autobiography may be very different from mine, but my prediction is that it will be sufficiently like mine in the relevant respect for you to recognise the truth of my initial claim and, in so doing, come to feel more comfortable with the question 'What is philosophy?'

But why does it make people uneasy? Part of the answer is that, until very recently, philosophy was not taught and examined in schools, except in Europe, and especially France and Germany. And certainly the French are not embarrassed by this question for, among other things, they have read and discussed Descartes at their *lycées* and are proud of the father of modern philosophy.

However, this can only be part of the answer because no one (I hope) has been taught and examined in astrology at school, few now learn Latin, and many have not done any physics. But most of us have some idea about what astrology is, or purports to be, what studying in Latin would involve, and what physicists do. If you stoutly maintain that you have no idea what physicists do, because you carefully avoided this subject at school, my question would be 'And why did you avoid it? What was it that you thought you didn't want to study and be examined in?' When you made that choice, you were not clueless about physics.

Perhaps I protest too much? Perhaps by now you are beginning to protest that, yes, you do have some ideas about philosophy. Philosophers *argue*. They argue about very abstract matters, such as . . . well, whether God exists. But whatever they argue about, even if it's quite – very – concrete, like euthanasia, they never get anywhere. They never settle anything or make any progress. They still debate questions which they have been debating since philosophy started, whenever that was.

So often people feel *resentment* about philosophy. They are not entirely sure what philosophy is, or what philosophers do, but although philosophers seem to think, naturally enough, that what they do is very important, it's just talk. And that kind of activity does not commend itself to the pragmatic American, empirically-minded Briton, materialist antipodean. Ironically, however, Pragmatism, Empiricism and Materialism are all philosophical positions, and their professional supporters abound, especially in their countries of origin.

Some professional philosophers would agree that philosophy does not make any progress, does not get us anywhere, though they would not put it like that. They would say, perhaps, that philosophical problems are perennial, chronic, an unavoidable part of being human, which we should not regret but celebrate. My own view is not that this is not true, but that it is only part of the truth. Philosophy does make progress, it does settle some issues, and, what is more, some of these issues are of great practical importance.

In medieval times, animals were put on trial. Pigs were tried for killing and eating children, often found guilty, and put to death. We no longer do this. Why not? Because some brave and original persons began to ask whether a pig *could* be capable of murder. Surely no creature can be guilty of murder unless it knows what it is doing and knows that it is wrong? Could a pig have such knowledge, or such a 'guilty mind' (*mens rea*)? Once people realised that this made no sense, the trials made no sense, and after the more or less prolonged period required to make any change in the law, these cases were no longer brought. Or again: during the seventeenth century, many persons were tried for being a witch, found guilty and judicially killed. Eventually this horrible practice ceased. Why? I believe that a crucial factor in achieving this change was a philosophical argument. A witch was (by definition) someone who had sold his or her immortal soul to the devil in return for certain supernatural powers, such as being able to blight an enemy's crops, make a woman barren, cause sickness, generally to make mischief or engage in voluptuous and improper activities with their familiars, or with emissaries of the devil.

But how were they to be 'found', that is, identified? Obviously, any unpopular or unusual person was at risk, but more than unpopularity and suspicion were required. Some of these persons would, of course, confess to being witches; others, indeed, boasted that they were witches. But even then it was realised – because it must have been noticed in other cases – that some individuals confess to things that they could not have done, either because they are confused, or what we now call 'hysterical', or seeking attention, and so on. As to the boasters, well, some were no more than that. So what was required was a theory that would link certain traits and characteristics to being a witch. These would 'mark' them as the devil's own. In England, witches were thought not to drown, so the accused died whether they floated or sank. Another mark was the presence of physical abnormalities, such as supernumerary teats.

The reasoning which undermined the rationale for this activity was both obvious and philosophical. (Philosophical arguments are often of this sort, so that when they succeed, that is, are generally accepted, no one can see that the arguments are other than trite, obvious.) What reason or evidence was there for thinking that buoyancy or certain physical oddities were indeed marks of commerce with the Prince of Darkness? There seems to be no evidence, not even scriptural. Whether the question was raised by purely intellectual speculation, or whether it was prompted by humane considerations, the answer seemed to be that there really was no evidence against alleged witches which did not assume what needed to be proved, and trying and killing them was therefore unjustifiable and inhumane. The practices of 'finding' witches and trying them withered away, and with that, not only did belief in witches erode but so also did confidence that talk about witches made any real sense. (None the less, of course, there are places, peoples and churches where this way of thinking still persists.)

But all this was a long time ago. Surely philosophy has no such role to play today? I must disagree. Mrs Thatcher famously once insisted that poverty was neither a cause of, nor an excuse for, crime, not even theft. In so far as she felt it necessary to provide an argument for this view, it went something like this: many persons who are poor do not take up thieving; conversely, there are thieves who are not poor. *Quod erat demonstrandum*. But, by parity of reasoning, she can and, indeed, must argue that drunkenness is not a cause of driving accidents. For some drunks do not have accidents, and many accidents do not involve persons who are drunk. As I mentioned above, philosophical claims suffer from the fact that, once they are recognised and accepted, they seem too obvious to be worth saying.

Still, anxious as I am to avoid giving the impression that, however useful and effective philosophical argument or speculation can be, it is always *obvious* (after consideration, however prolonged), let us consider another issue, again taken from the law – a mine, if not a minefield, of philosophical questions. Most of us accept, as a platitude, that an adult, in his or her right mind, is aware of and responsible for what he or she does, and therefore, may properly be tried for, and found guilty of, behaviour which breaches a law – leaving aside the problem provided by 'absolute offences', where a person may be found guilty of an offence, even though that person did not know what he or she was doing, did not know that it was wrong or proscribed by the law. Now consider the law's treatment of minors. A minor is a person who, because of his or her age. cannot be held responsible for what he or she does, and so cannot be found guilty of any offence, and cannot, therefore, be punished for whatever it is that has been done. The philosophical questions are two: why cannot young persons be held responsible for what they do? And, at what age do they become responsible? These are questions which certainly do engage, and enrage, many individuals who would he startled, even perhaps offended, if I called them 'philosophers'.

I call them 'philosophers' because the questions which engage them are philosophical. But why do I say that they are philosophical? It is because it is not so much the truth of the claims which are the issue – for example, 'Minors are not responsible for their actions' – but what they mean and what evidence we have, or might have, for them. In other words, philosophers are not so much scientists of any sort, natural or social; they are rather persons who are exercised by, or critical of, some part or aspect of these and other activities. So scientists, mathematicians, doctors, lawyers, historians, teachers, even geographers, can wonder at, speculate about, be puzzled by some feature of what they do, when just doing, say, more history will not help to resolve the difficulty. (I had a geography master who revealed, only as a guilty secret, and only to his best pupils, that he was not sure that geography was a real, single, subject. What did we think? What do *you* think?)

I hope that a view – or, at least, my view – of what philosophy is is beginning to emerge from this introduction. But before trying to develop it one more stage, and then inviting you to read the rest of this book, I must mention one further problem in understanding what philosophy is. In my English fashion, I worked my way through college. That is to say, in the vacations between the three terms, I tried to find temporary jobs that would help me financially to get through the next term. I sometimes found work as a bus conductor. In those days, British buses had a driver, who did nothing but drive, and a conductor, whose task it was to take fares, give tickets and change to passengers, and ring the bell when a passenger wished to get off the bus.

Short-haul, double-decker city services could be exhausting, but they did have an advantage. At the end of every short trip, you got a turn-around rest. You had to wait at least five minutes at every terminus to allow passengers to board, and the bus in front to get a reasonable distance ahead of yours. But, at every turn-around, a time for relaxation and, in those days, a quick cigarette. the driver would come round to the back of the bus, sit down and have a talk. And, of course, every time I was on with a new driver, he would kindly ask, after I had told him that I was at university, doing or studying philosophy (I couldn't say I was reading philosophy, he would have thought that I wasn't writing any or talking about it), 'What's your philosophy, then?'

How embarrassed, disingenuous, pretentious I felt when I answered, as in truth I had to answer, 'Look I don't have a philosophy in that sense, *your* sense. At least, if I do, that's got nothing to do with what I do as a student of philosophy.' The point is that, for most laypersons, philosophy is something personal; it's *your* philosophy, and what that means is your way of coping with the problems and travails of life. So when I answered, as honesty or lack of imagination always compelled me to answer, 'I don't have a philosophy of life in that sense. And that's not what I do as a philosopher at university', the reaction was invariably that the driver felt snubbed. He would either go silent and roll a cigarette or, if more ebullient, proceed to tell me what his philosophy was. This often involved a belief in reincarnation or predestination, or both. At that point I could join him in conversation, asking him what *reason* he had for believing in reincarnation or what might lead him to abandon his belief that everything that was going to happen to him was determined in advance. And the invariable reaction to these challenges was a hurt silence. You don't debate your philosophy on its merits, but avow it and expect, as with religious belief, that it be received and accepted with respectful noddings and inhalations.

Let us return once more, and for the last time, to our question: what is philosophy? Philosophers sometimes say, in answer to this question and as an explanation of why it is so difficult, 'Philosophy is unlike any other intellectual discipline in that it has no subject matter. It is rather an *activity*.' Now because we are talking about the nature of philosophy and philosophers' answers to this question, it will come of no surprise when I say that not all philosophers would agree. In any case, even if the answer is broadly correct, it is not therefore terribly illuminating. Philosophy has no subject matter? Good. But what then is it? *What* activity?

I will try my readers' patience no further. Read Part One in which I try to show what Plato meant when he said that to lead a philosophical life was to lead an examined life, and why he thought no other was worth living. Plato, I believe, was right about philosophy. But he could not foresee – how could he – how it would develop and effloresce. Philosophy has become professionalised. It is taught, as it was in his time, as an academic discipline, but its being professionalised has changed it almost out of recognition. It is not just that there are so many more intellectual enquiries and disciplines than there were in the days of the Greek academy, each with their attendant philosophies, which muse upon and sometimes confuse the practitioners of whatever it might be: history, science, law, the arts, morality – today, supply-side economics or positive discrimination, it is also that, being professionalised, every contribution to the philosophical debate must be referenced and tied to what someone else has said. Professional philosophers will know from the nature of this book how much I regret the professionalisation of what I believe is not only a chronic feature of being human, but – *mirabile dictu* – a spontaneous and often playful, wonderful thing.

In Part One of this book I will show you and remind you of what it is to be a reflective human being and, hence, a philosopher. In Part Two I will provide you with accessible examples of what philosophers do professionally – or, rather, with some of the things that I have written as a professional philosopher. Each is prefaced with an attempt to explain what the issue is, and why philosophers have been exercised by it. All, with one exception, are pieces of writing which have been published in academic journals.

Part Three is very different. I am a philosopher through and through, yet I have never been able to believe that philosophy, the philosophical question, the problem, an attempt to answer it or even display it and examine it, can be addressed only in the professional article or book. Philosophical issues are often dogmatic, or funny, absurd, essentially linked to some situation which cannot be characterised except in terms available to the narrative writer. So, instead of suppressing this irregular and unprofessional work, I decided to do the opposite, but I have added postscripts to each piece in which I identify and briefly discuss some of the philosophical problems raised in it or by it.

A final word: you may be someone who is wondering whether to 'read' Philosophy at university or college. So you may be at school or a freshman – a first-year – student. You might be someone wondering whether to take a course at an evening class. As a result of reading this book you may decide that philosophy is not for you. The examined life is all very well but too much is more than enough, or vice versa. You should not regard this as a failure, and I would not see it as a failure on my part. The tendency to raise philosophical questions is, I believe, present in every human being, but the desire to pursue them, frequently or at length, and especially as a profession, must be regarded, if only statistically, as an aberration. There can be no examined life without a life to examine, and, for most of us, reflecting on it is an unavoidable, integral, yet transient and small part of that life.

PART ONE

THE EXAMINED LIFE

THE EXAMINED LIFE

I was 5 when it first happened, newly arrived on a farm in Gloucestershire, where my father had moved his family to escape the German air raids on Bristol. (He commuted to the Bristol Aeroplane Company, and continued to be at risk, but the rest of us were safe.) Having been brought up on a council estate, where I had found plenty to be terrified by, besides bombs, I not surprisingly fell in love with life on the farm. But I was rather nervous of the larger animals, especially the cows. Cecil, aged 8, a government evacuee, who had been on the farm for *ages* – about six months, I should think in retrospect – sought to put my mind at rest. 'Cows have got magnifying eyes,' he said. 'So you look very big to a cow, and that's why they're frightened of *you*. Look!' He picked up a stick, climbed the stile, and started to shout and wave his arms. Two cows that were browsing the hedgerow tossed their heads and obligingly lumbered off. 'See!' he said, vindicated and triumphant. See I did, and rushed off to tell my mother. (Even then, I loved to be able to tell people things, to *inform* them, especially my mother. And if I didn't have the information I wanted, I would simply make it up. She was very patient with what, given Cecil's behaviour, can't be all that uncommon, but my 'romancing' as she kindly called it, went on – and on – and caused me a variety of embarrassments, which I can still feel today. I think I'm over it now.)

As I hurried home, sneering at distant cows, excitedly pondering what Cecil had said, it happened. I suddenly felt – dizzy. There was something wrong, something *terribly*, *profoundly*, *wrong*, with what Cecil had said, but although I had stopped, and was grimacing and gritting my teeth in my effort to work out what was wrong, I could not do so. The shock and then the strain made me dizzy.

This was the first occasion that I can recall on which I was struck, seized, almost literally, by a philosophical problem. It has happened since, but the dizziness was never as strong as it was then, and I can't remember the last time I experienced it. I suppose that, as I grew up, and then became a professional, the excitement and tension have been diminished – after all, one has learned a technique – and, unhappily, one encounters the new, unbidden problem less frequently.

Well, what was wrong with what Cecil said? It seems so obvious now that I would be reluctant to retell this story, had I not told it to lots of my students over the years, and many of them cannot see what is wrong. 'How could Cecil have known?' is the most common response from those who are pressed for an answer. But the more aware of these look shifty as they say it.

What is obvious is that if cows have 'magnifying eyes', these eyes magnify everything, not only Cecil and my younger self, but other cows as well, and the cow itself. So if I looked 'very big' to the cow, she and her companions must have looked very much bigger. Our relative proportions would not be altered by her having 'magnifying eyes' and so it couldn't be our looking very big to her which explained her timidity.

But what does it mean to say that cows have 'magnifying eyes'? This may seem obvious. Cows' eyes have lenses which, if they were removed, would magnify anything seen through them. This could well be true, but if it is or were true, do or would cows see everything bigger than it really is, or bigger than we humans do? Again, the answer must be 'No.'

Cecil's remark sounds as if it makes perfectly good sense, and could well be true. But it doesn't make good sense, and it cannot be true. Cecil was guilty of confusion; the philosophical task was to spot this, and sort it out. I do not claim that all philosophical problems are 'conceptual confusions' – they seem too diverse for any monolithic account to be helpful, correct, or even meaningful – but the capacity to spot them, a willingness to suspect that they may occur even when no one else seems puzzled or confused, and a desire to uncover them and sort them out, are, I think, traits of the philosopher. In which case it is not surprising if others find us difficult, irritating, nit-picking, ignorant of the facts, and ourselves confused. All of which is sometimes true.

I have, no doubt, improved this story in its many tellings, but I cannot remember when I succeeded in working out what was wrong with Cecil's explanation of the timidity of cows; it was not for many years, I am sure. Nor can I remember what my mother said when I got back to her. ('Yes dear. Would you like a cup of tea?' is highly likely. It was what she invariably said to me when I burst home with my latest bit of information. It was what she said, thank God, when, after the first week of term at boarding school, I banged on our front door, and desperately rattled the knocker, and said when she opened the door at last, 'I've run away from school!') But I think I might have forgotten this childish episode entirely had I not, some twenty odd years later, read in a book on El Greco that perhaps the characteristic elongation of his (vertical) figures could be explained by his suffering from an irregular astigmatism. We probably never shall know if El Greco suffered from an irregular astigmatism, but even if we did, this could not explain the feature which had intrigued the critic and to which he had done no more than drawn our attention – otiosely, no doubt. Cecil's sort of confusion can be perpetrated by an intelligent, educated man or woman, working on a topic about which he or she has unusual knowledge, and escape not only his or her notice, but that of his or her publisher's reader. We shall never know how many of the art historian's readers were also untroubled by his 'explanation', but my guess is that they were a large majority. The 'obviousness', 'childishness', of conceptual confusions, is how they strike us *after* we have noticed them. We may then forget, and not wish to be reminded, if the confusion has to be pointed out to us, and those who do so are seen not as confused or ignorant, of course, but trading in the trite.[1]

I have also noticed that art critics and historians remark that the palettes of many artists redden and darken as they grow old, and hazard that this could be due, at least in part, to a deterioration in their retinas. I am less clear here that the explanation is just another confusion. It looks as if it should be, but if artists, as they grow older, not only suffer a retinal deterioration but go outdoors less often and work less often in full sunlight, it could I think be correct. In just the same way, and for just the same reason, a man who suffers from irregular astigmatism *will* misperceive the shape of objects when the object is isolated from others and he doesn't know what shape it is (which is how eyes are tested by the optician), so he would be likely to produce distorted drawings if he did not draw from life, and drew in a room where he could not compare his drawing with other things whose proportions he knows. These other things include, of course, what he painted on, his canvas, or paper. So unless El Greco never painted anything but murals (on unsquared, blank, uniformly coloured walls), working in a dim light that illuminated only the wall, and without models of any kind, that is, purely from memory, the explanation of why he elongated his figures is, in fact, incoherent. But I cannot even begin to imagine what unlikely hypothesis could save Cecil's explanation from being incoherent.

Colleagues of mine who are friends but not philosophers, would not be surprised by my discussing philosophical problems which arise in connection with perception. They know that philosophers are obsessed by it, and in very strange ways. One, a literary critic, said to me quite recently, 'I did philosophy once, you know? When I was an undergraduate.' I didn't know, and felt the surprise he expected. 'Yes. I went to this class. At the first class, the bloke came in and put a tomato on the desk. He said "What's this?" Ha! Ha! A bloody *tomato*! Well, everyone was embarrassed and didn't say anything, so I said "It's a tomato." He said "How do you know?" I ask you? I said I could *see* it was a bloody tomato. He said "Are you sure?" So I walked up to the front, picked it up, and bit it and said, yes, I was sure! Ha! Ha!' Dr Johnson's spirit lives on.

Obviously, my friend could not see what question – what

real question, what genuine issue – could have been raised by what the poor philosopher was trying to do. And though he generously volunteered that perhaps the chap had been getting at *something*, though he couldn't tell what, his glee and self-congratulation was unqualified when he ended his short story by saying the meeting broke up in disorder and he dropped the class. Now there are good philosophers, like J. L. Austin, who would agree that no real question had been raised, so I forbore to point out that, even having done what my friend (said that he) did, namely, bitten into something that looked like a tomato and tasted like one, the conclusion that it was a tomato might none the less be false or unwarranted. What then could settle the matter? We were now changed and ready to play football, and I did not continue by trying to explain either A. J. Ayer's views or, more sympathetically, Wittgen-stein's and Austin's.

Trying to do philosophy with non-specialists can be hell for all, and I find it best to try to show such persons how philo-sophical problems are raised by their own specialisms and may well have exercised them without their realising that they were engaged in philosophy. The questions about the tomato which the teacher was trying to raise with my friend are too abstract, too underdefined, too theoretical, to illuminate the nature of philosophy or persuade a sceptic about philosophy (rather than a sceptic philosopher) of its point, reality and, indeed, profundity. Immediacy and practicality are what's wanted. So let me return to philosophical problems concerning perception that are, I hope, less likely to confirm the preju-dices I wish to change.

I was about 14 or 15, sitting in a chemistry lesson in which our excellent chemistry master, 'Tricky' Williams, was talking about colour. In those days, as he told us, women doing the week's washing would put a 'blue-bag' in with their bed linen. Did anyone know why? A girl was allowed to answer. 'Yes!' agreed Tricky, 'To bring up the white, to make them look whiter', and he went on to explain that detergents achieved even better results, and how they did so. As he talked on, to a mildly interested class, he made the following remark, 'White things don't look white. They look yellow.' I flinched and sat bolt upright. I cannot remember what else Mr Williams said, because I was too exercised and too excited to listen to him. Once again I felt dizzy as I tried to work out what on earth what he said meant – for how could it possibly be true? Surely, white things are things which look *white*, and if they look yellow they are *yellow*; or at least they are yellow if they look yellow to people with normal eyesight in normal, that is, white light! So, wasn't he saying that white things were yellow? Or was he saying that very light yellow things were white? I just couldn't work out what he was saying, and felt myself brimming with intellectual excitement, tinged with a nervousness that I might be about to make a fool of myself, and not for the first time.

I asked Mr Williams my question when the class had ended. He grinned, chuckled, knowing I wasn't a scientist but pleased with my interest. He explained to me that when a scientist, speaking scientifically, describes something as white he means that it reflects all the colours that together make natural light. When a layperson describes something as white, he or she means that it looks white to him or her and normally sighted persons in natural light, but in fact such objects don't reflect as much of the light as objects that are white in the scientists' sense. They absorb some of the yellow light. So, to achieve that effect, women washing their whites add a tint of blue to them. Detergents work, not by reducing the amount of yellow light reflected by the sheets and shirts, but by affecting the material in such a way that it grabs the ultraviolet light and emits this as visible blue light. This corrects the yellowish tinge of white objects by jacking up the amount of blue light they emit and their overall reflectivity. So sheets washed in detergent are not just white in the layperson's sense, but even brighter than white in the scientist's sense. The ad-man's claim is true in this case. Did this not answer my question – and had I been paying close attention in the lesson? He had seen me with my eyes closed.

Tempted to reply that I had felt blinded by science and, I confess, chagrined that my master had sorted me out, I stumbled away. I did not return to these questions until years later, when I was a postgraduate student in philosophy, and my feeling that all had been made clear collapsed. I reasoned thus: it seems that there are two concepts of 'white' – the scientific and the non- or pre-scientific, the ordinary, layperson's concept. According to the latter, something is 'white' if it 'looks white' to normal observers in sunlight. Now this is supposed to be a definition, an account of the meaning of the layperson's word 'white'. But if 'white' means 'looks white to normal observers in sunlight', what does 'white' mean in 'looks white to normal observers in sunlight', and (so) what does 'looks white to normal observers in sunlight' mean?

Three or four years later, I was now in the second-year sixth and many of my friends were being called for medical examinations to determine their fitness for National Service. As an asthmatic, and anxious in case I should pass the medical, I deferred taking it, choosing to go straight to university. Others were anxious to get their National Service out of the way, but many looked forward to, and hoped for, a short-service commission in the RAF which would enable them to train to become jet pilots. But if they were less than A1, they could find themselves in the service for two years, serving as clerks or mechanics.

I was standing in the boy prefects' room, when one of them came in. He had the looks, physique and physical abilities that the rest of us envied, and the girls adored, and, quite unlike his usual cool, somehow always bronzed, self, he was white and trembling. I asked him what was wrong. 'I'm colour-blind', he said, and bowed his head to hide his tears, I think. 'I can't tell red from green – not on their tests. I can't . . . *believe* it!'

It was not until I was travelling home on the bus that evening that I was struck by the thought 'How could Billy not have known that he was colour-blind?' After all, if you're colour-blind, you can't tell certain colours from others. How could he have not known this? I tried to find out, and read that colour-blind persons judge the colour of things by relying on knowledge that they get second-hand. So although they may not be able to tell, say, green from blue, they know that the unclouded sky is blue, that grass is green, and so on. Relying on this and more particular bits of second-hand knowledge, and on various cues and clues, they are able to make correct colour judgements. That is why special tests have to be devised to identify their defect, which eliminate the extraneous information that normally guides their judgements.

This seemed to solve the problem, and it also seemed to explain how the phenomenon of colour-blindness could have been 'discovered' by scientists, though, astonishingly, it was not described by them until the time of Dalton. However, I was a bit disturbed to read that 'colour-blindness' was a layperson's term for a variety of conditions, some of which are so gross that the sufferer *does* know without undergoing special tests that his or her colour vision is defective. Why wasn't Bill among their number? After all, he couldn't tell red from green. And why hadn't scientists at least recorded the existence of persons who couldn't tell their colours, and knew this, well before the nineteenth century?

But it was another difficulty which niggled, though I could not quite formulate it. It niggled for years without my being able to say quite what it was. Finally I did get so far as to be able to at least make a verbal gesture towards doing so: it had perhaps been explained how Bill and others like him learned to make (mostly) correct colour judgements. But how could he and his fellows avoid knowing that they were not making (many of) them on the basis of their perceiving *colours*? Surely they could *see* – could not help seeing – that they couldn't see that the shirt was green and the shorts red, though they might know that they were, and could tell this visually in some way. But surely they knew the difference between a colour's *colour*, that is its hue, and its brightness or, possibly, saturation? So weren't they guilty of deception? Surely not. Were they then guilty of confusion or inattention?

When I reflected further on these questions, it struck me that I was assuming that hue and brightness would identify themselves, as it were, as different features, and perhaps this was a mistake. After all, the Ancient Greek vocabulary for colour seems to distinguish as different 'colours' what we should identify as one colour, as it shows different brightnesses and sheens or glitters, and collects together as one colour what we should distinguish as several.

Perhaps if I could talk to people like Bill, I would be able to get clearer about this matter, and doing so might help to reveal if there was some further question, as yet unidentified and unformulated, still niggling away?

My few subjects said no, of *course* they hadn't *known* that they were colour-blind until they had been told, although some agreed that they had, perhaps, suspected that something wasn't quite right, though this suspicion had grown slowly and reluctantly, and one, who had a colour-blind father, had been pretty certain that he had inherited his father's condition. When I asked them if, once they knew, they could see that they couldn't see that, say, red things looked a different colour from green things, though they looked *somehow* different, no doubt, they tended to say things like, 'Not usually. It takes effort and concentration to see that they don't really look different or, if they do, that they don't look a different colour.'

Though not unexpected, the answer to the second question is a very interesting result. For it suggests that the red-green colour-blind not only can't tell red from green, that is, they can't perceive these colours as different, can't distinguish their hues, but also that at least within these parts of the spectrum, *their making correct colour judgements depends on their conflating hue with* (what tests reveal to be) *luminosity/ brightness*. (After diagnosis they presumably just continue to use differences in luminosity to indicate the differences in hue which they cannot see.) So an undetected colour-blind subject might live his entire life without knowing that his sight was defective and his visual experiences were different from normal, and he would attach different meanings to 'red' and 'green' from most of the rest of us.

If this is correct, and if we make a further assumption, we can apparently get a very interesting result indeed. Let us suppose that some persons have an aberrant retinal structure and physiology. (Perhaps the colour dyes in their eyes are different from normal and are dependent on a recessive gene.) Despite the aberrant condition, their colour discriminations are just as good as, indeed just the same as, those with normal eyes. Wouldn't their physiology suggest that their visual experiences might be very different from ours and that although their colour judgements match ours, they attach different meanings to the colour words from us?

Since they talk and behave exactly as we do, a behaviourist might make either or both claims if he or she were persuaded that the alleged differences could never be revealed behaviourally. Many Wittgensteinians would also say that the hypothesis was incoherent, confused, or empty, because 'meaning is use', and the aberrant use the colour vocabulary normally, and because the hypothesised difference in experiences, being purely private, that is, uncharacterisable and undetectable, is illusory.

Now it may be that we could devise ways of testing this apparently untestable hypothesis. But if this couldn't be done, the hypothesis would still seem to make sense, and might even be true. Behaviourists might deny this, but that is not surprising because ontological behaviourism seeks to acknowledge and characterise experience solely through behaviour. As for the Wittgensteinians: Wittgenstein only said that in *most* cases, meaning is use – and as for the private experience or private object, he did not say that it was nothing; he said it was not a *something*, but not a *nothing* either! (*Philosophical Investigations*, §304).

The assumption that these persons with the unusual eyes may attach different meanings to 'red', 'green', and so on, *is* odd just because it is primarily, and perhaps solely, *things* which are coloured, not visual experiences; and these persons make, as independently as we do, judgements about colour, which match ours, and do so, like us, on the basis of their visual experiences. We find ourselves saying things like 'I should know if the hypothesis made sense and was true, if only I could have the experiences of one of these hypothesised persons – or of a colour-blind person.' But then we are struck by two thoughts. One couldn't have another person's experience in the required way, because if, *per impossible*, one did, it would not be his but one's own. Secondly, if we try to imagine – although of course it is impossible – that we did have another's visual experience or sensation when we looked at something, that is, if we, as it were, swapped experiences, or – and this seems to make more sense – if we had the same *kind* of experience he has when he looked at the shirt or the shorts, we would say 'How different from my own!' ('That's the kind of colour impression I get when I look at those shorts' or 'I've never seen this colour before!') But saying this would seem to make the experience something which is *itself* perceived or experienced, and which may be perceived and experienced differently by different persons, or the same person on different occasions. But experiences aren't experienced or perceived, they are had, enjoyed, suffered; and they could not be experienced differently without either *not* being an experience or by being a different experience!

Perhaps something has gone wrong with the argument? If it has, it involves treating the visual experience as a thing, that is, as something which can itself be perceived. This mistake in turn depends on assuming that the visual experience is determined by, and solely dependent on, physiology or neurology, and then rejecting that assumption. And the assumption is mistaken, because visual experiences, that is, the kinds of experiences which, for example, guide and inform judgements about what colour something looks, depend not just on physiology and neurology, but on a person's culture, language, general background information and beliefs, more particular bits of knowledge, and so on. As we shall see, neurophysiological determinants of experience, and so judgements, may come within an ace of playing no role in determining the content of the experience or of the judgements made! In which case Wittgenstein's gnomic judgement would be true. I shall return to this question.

The mistake, if it is a mistake, *is* tempting. Just how tempting it is, can be seen in examining the following case. We may assume that many 'primitive' painters have normal colour vision. Some of these when painting, say, an expanse of grass, will lay on paint of a single hue (and, of course, of uniform saturation) because they know that the grass itself is of a uniform colour. But in fact the grass does not all look the same colour, does not present a uniform appearance. At least it does not all reflect the same light. For the further away the grass, the less of the green light that it reflects reaches the eye. The proportion of blue light increases, its luminosity also drops, and its saturation may be altered as well. So the distant grass looks a different colour from the grass near to the painter, or it *should* do so. Constable sometimes adds white, lamp-black and yellow ochre to his green, and will then add several layers of glaze to capture this, and an earlier, conventionalised technique was simply to add in blue for distance. But the primitive painter is unaware of these physical facts, or has not learnt the conventional skills used to convey them, or simply doesn't look hard and carefully enough. *Knowing* that the grass is a uniform colour, he or she represents it with paint of a uniform colour. The result may be charming, but it is not convincing or realistic – which, ironically, is often exactly the effect which the painter wishes to achieve.

But suppose that a primitive painter says that is the effect that he wishes to achieve, and, proudly, that he thinks he has done so – he is particularly pleased with the grass, it's come out very well. (We don't have to imagine these cases; talk to 'Sunday' painters, read some of the remarks made by 'Le Douanier' Rousseau.) Assuming that this is a considered claim, and a sincere one, we are presented with a dilemma. Either we say that the grass looks different to the primitive painter from the way it looks to the rest of us – or, at very least, to those of us who find his painting of the grass inaccurate, unconvincing, and so on. But this is not only contrary to our assumption, but most implausible. Or we must say that the primitive painter is unaware of how the grass looks to him, indeed, that it doesn't look to him as he thinks it looks to him. Once again we are led to hypostasise looks, appearances, visual experiences, for we are saying that the look of the grass, its appearance to the primitive painter, how it appears to him, and so on, is something he gets wrong, and so it is itself (like) something that he looks at.

Again we find ourselves wanting to say that, however we should characterise what the primitive painter is doing, if only we could have his or her visual experiences then we should know what to say.

We talk in just this fashion when we engage in what must be one of the most common philosophical speculations which occur to non-professionals. We wonder if others see what we see when we look at the same objects; in particular, we wonder if they see the same colours as we see, or if they see them as we do. We pass remarks like 'I wonder if when I see something red, I see something which, if you were to see, you would say was blue?' But convinced that there is no way of answering the question, we soon abandon it as idle though intelligible.

There are many professional philosophers who see this question as not just unanswerable and idle, but meaningless. They establish this using the following dialectic: 'Look over there. Do you see the pillar box?' 'Yes.' 'What colour would you say it was?' 'Red.' 'That's right. Now what colour does it look to you?' 'Well – obviously, it looks red to me.' 'It looks red to me too. Now what was your question, your specula-tion?' Laypersons characteristically feel cheated. The dialectic hasn't revealed a flaw in the reasoning, but strikes them as a forensic device which prevents them saying what they're trying to say. They are forced to realise that it is at least very difficult to say what they had thought could be said without any difficulty whatsoever, but they tend to remain convinced that their thought is clear, and might be correct, and the philosopher understands it really.

Perhaps the philosopher and the layperson are both wrong in assuming that the speculation could never be put to the test. In an endeavour to do so, I once tried the following story on a well-known philosopher. 'Imagine that after a very heavy night's drinking, followed by a fall and a blow on the head, a man wakes one morning, gets up and staggers straight into this all-white bathroom. As he starts to shave he notices that he looks very unwell, his pallid face has a blue-green look about it. He then cuts himself shaving, and the blood – is blue! Horrified, he flings open the bathroom window to call his wife whom he can hear in the garden. The clear unclouded sky is blood red! What has happened? Well, it turns out that, perhaps as a result of the blow, his optical neurophysiology has been affected and in such a way that his reactions to the ends of the visible spectrum has switched. That is, when he looks at, and sees, red things, they look to him as blue things did before the accident, and when he looks at and sees blue things, they look as red things looked to him before the accident. Only white things, black things, and the colours that are roughly in the middle of the visible spectrum, that is the yellow, greeny-yellows, yellowy-greens and greens retain their old, familiar appearance.'

Now there seems no a priori reason why such a thing might not happen, even though physiologically perhaps, it could not. But if it could, the story makes sense, and therefore, so does the layperson's idle philosophical speculation. We can never have another's visual experiences but we have our own, and we should be struck if they suddenly changed in the way suggested in the story. Other persons' visual experiences may differ from our own in just the same way as the experiences of the man in the story differed before and after his accident. And so despite the fact, if it is a fact, that if these persons' colour judgements always concurred with ours no matter what the test, we could never test our hypothesis, it is none the less meaningful and could be true. The 'private object' exists, for we can never communicate this possible difference and, moreover, it plays a crucial role, for it is on the basis of these private experiences that we make our public, concurring colour judgements. If they were suddenly to change, our judgements would go haywire.

The famous philosopher was not impressed, and the way in which my story continues may help to explain why she was not impressed. What would happen with the man after a while, and supposing that he did not recover his old way of seeing colours? Having accepted that the change lay in himself, he would try to talk with the rest of us. If he owned a red car, he would say that his car was red, and look for a red car when he was looking for his car – though he would at first find that tricky and unnatural. 'Look for a blue one', he might say to himself initially. But – after a while – his re-education would, I think, become so complete that his colour judgements and behaviour would become as automatic and unthinking as they were before the change. Once this was achieved, I think he would not only say, for example, that the unclouded sky was blue, and that it looked blue, but that it (now) looked blue to him (once again). I think he might find it very difficult to remember how differently things looked before the accident. He might even wonder if it was a dream, or he had made it all up. Perhaps he had been hysterical!

If this is what would happen, then it shows that although the 'private object', that is, our private, incommunicable visual experience of colour, plays a crucial role in enabling us to make colour judgements, and in determining which ones we make, it also shows that the character of the experience – how it 'looks' to us – is itself determined 'publicly', that is, by the colours of objects, and hence by true judgements about the colours of things.

So the private aspect or dimension of our colour experience is not an 'idle cog' in the machinery of our description and explanation of colour perception. Moreover, although its character – or, at least, how we are able to describe it – is determined by, and describable solely in terms of public phenomena, it is not wholly determined by these factors, or may not be. Which means that we can point to its existence, with the help of stories like the one I told above, but of course we cannot *describe* this dimension. If we try, we want to use such words and phrases as 'green', 'looks red', and so on, and there is no other vocabulary, but we realise that it must transcend any language, pass through its net, however fine. Wittgenstein, who was a philosopher of genius with a methodological scepticism towards the private, was led therefore to say that the private object was not a something but not a nothing. I want to say that it is more of a something than he could allow.

A parallel can be drawn between what I conjectured would happen to the man in my story and what happens to the subjects of experiments with inverting spectacles. Inverting spectacles are goggles which invert the image on the retina (incidentally, thereby turning it the 'right way' up) or transposing it laterally, and the subjects wear the goggles continuously until the experiment is concluded. What happens? At first, the subjects see everything upside down or laterally inverted. As a result they may not be able to stand up or perform even the simplest tasks, without closing their eyes. But gradually, painfully, and clumsily they learn to function. In a few weeks they may even re-learn such skills as riding a bike. Finally, they become so practised in learning to cope with the effects of the goggles, that they begin to do things as easily and automatically as they did before the experiment started. At this juncture, their visual experiences 'flip' back to the way they were before the experiment. Everything looks normal once again. (Whereupon the goggles are removed and the poor subjects go through the same process all over again, until once again they can see normally.)

In these cases, we see how the character of the visual experience, and how it is described, is determined 'publicly'. And there seems nothing left over for what is private or ineffable. If anyone is tempted to say 'But perhaps even there is, or there might be . . .' let him or her suppress this thought. Because we can say, in the case of the experiments with inverting spectacles, that this is not surprising. For left and right, top and bottom, upside down and right way up, are structural features of reality and our experience of it, and what is quantitative and structural can be specified linguistically without residue, without the possibility of differences occurring between people's experiences which cannot be described and which may never reveal their existence (though not their nature) in language and behaviour. But in the case of colour, there is also and essentially content, and it is this which has an ineffable dimension, even if its nature is a function of the (public) colour of (public) objects.

Could the claims I want to make about our perception and experience of colour be put to a real test, or do we have to rely on invented stories and *gedanken* (imaginary) experiments? Perhaps they could, and I am indebted for the following suggestion to Austin Radford: scientists could devise 'inverting' spectacles for colour. (I have discussed this suggestion with scientists, and they say that it is feasible, though it would be difficult and expensive and since the wavelengths of light which are visible to human beings only occupy a portion of the electromagnetic wave band which is light, they demur at calling the projected device 'colour-*inverting*' spectacles.) The spectacles would transform or substitute for the light reflected by blue objects, light reflected by red ones, and vice versa. Or the spectacles might shift the whole spectrum, so that the light reflected by red objects would be substituted for or transformed into that reflected by yellow objects, and the same would be done for green objects, and so on, and finally, perhaps, the light reflected by blue objects would replace that reflected by red ones. Or they could arrange a shift of two places along the spectrum, and so on. Again, subjects would be fitted with the goggles. What would happen?

My prediction is, of course, that initially things would look the wrong colour but, after a while, the subject would accommodate to the change until, finally, everything would look as it did before the experiment started. The pressures to achieve this accommodation are not as great as they are with the spatially inverting spectacles but are, I feel sure, sufficient to bring it about.

But doesn't just this result show that there is nothing potentially idiosyncratic, yet private and so incommunicable about the (normally sighted's) experience of colour? No, although it gets within an ace of doing so. For although everything ends up looking as it did before the experiment began, if the goggles are removed, everything changes its colour appearance once again. And despite the subjects having accommodated to the first change, they might say with relief, either immediately the goggles are removed or after a while, 'Ah! That's better. That's how things used to look, how they really look. I'd forgotten', and so on.[2] And that there are parallel differences between subjects, though an hypothesis and perhaps an untestable one, remains intelligible. (In fact, if these spectacles were invented and used, we could know that differences must sometimes exist between different persons, but we still wouldn't be able to say between whom.)

In my original story, I concluded it in the following way: 'So the man almost forgets that anything did once happen to his colour vision. And yet – whereas he used to like to see his wife in cool colours, blues, he now encourages her to wear reds and oranges and yellows!'

Does the story establish that, contrary to what so many professional philosophers have said, at least some of our experiences have, and have essentially, a private, incommunicable dimension? The famous philosopher thought not, my story was 'Too bitty.'

As I recall, the second occasion in my life when I encountered what strikes me now as a philosophical problem, was very different from the first. This time I felt not *dizzy*, not that something was wrong – but what? but, 'This is crazy, impossible!', totally bewildered, in despair, and humiliated.

I was now aged about eight. The threat of German air raids lessened, and we had returned from the countryside to a northern suburb of Bristol, Filton, a dormitory for the BAC workers: I had started to attend Shields Road, the local primary school. Many of the workers at 'The 'Drome' were very ambitious for their children, and, partly in consequence, academic standards were high at Shields Road. At first, I was behind the other children in reading, writing and arithmetic, and I hated this. I'm afraid that I felt I was at least as clever as any of the rest of them, and wanted to show this – simple vanity was the motive, but behind that lay ambition.

Even at that age, I wanted to be a 'writer', but saying that gives my early ambition a false clarity. I was a working-class child; wanting to be a writer meant, I think, in as far as it meant anything at all, that I wanted a future in which I worked with words, in which talking was as important as writing, in which I told people things, and they paid attention! To achieve this I had to get an education, and that meant passing the 'scholarship'. If all this sounds repugnant, perhaps it was, but perhaps it was not as repugnant as it sounds. I wanted to be top, but I thought that everyone could get on and do well through education. And, in fact, when I took the scholarship, out of my class of fifty-one, all but three of us passed. And in the following year, 1947, all the top class passed and went to local grammar schools, and six children who couldn't get into the top class also passed. We were a working-class meritoc- racy in which everyone was a winner. (That of course was not true. There were children who were already identifiable as losers, and I knew that. Somehow I managed to suppress that knowledge when thinking about these things – which raises another philosophical problem of which I was then not aware either, namely, 'How is such suppression possible?') As for pressure; I was anxious to learn and do well, but not unhappy, because I thought I should succeed.

Yet here I was sitting by myself, in an empty classroom, staring at my exercise book. It was playtime, and the other children were rushing about, shrieking happily outside the huge windows that formed one wall of our modern classroom. Miss Davies, our young, pretty, needless to say Welsh mis- tress, into whose class I had recently been moved, and with whom I was in love, had gone to her own break, leaving me with the command that I was to remain in class until I had finished my work. And I could not.

The stumbling block was the last question in a set of ten examples in simple arithmetic. They were all 'taking away'. I had breezed through the first nine, confident that, as usual, I would be going more quickly than most of the others, when I encountered something entirely new. I can – or I believe I can – recall the precise numbers involved. Thirteen take away forty-eight. After puzzling over this briefly, I had thought it must be a mistake for forty-eight take away thirteen. Miss Davies, perhaps annoyed by my confidence that she must have made an error, told me brusquely that that was right, thirteen take away forty-eight.

It was impossible! You couldn't take a bigger number from a smaller one! But Miss Davies had told me to do it – so presumably it could be done. But how? After some ten minutes I had tried to apply my normal techniques to this abnormal example. Eight from three. You can't do it – there! So borrow ten. Eight from thirteen leaves five. Carry the one. Five from one. Can't do it. So borrow ten. But there was no number to borrow ten from. So you can't do it! By now I was sweating and in a state of anxiety and despair. Should I write 'Can't do it!' by the side of the sum? But I knew you weren't supposed to write anything by sums. You just did them, or didn't, because you couldn't. But this was new. *It* couldn't be done. But Miss Davies said do it. All right. So borrow ten, though there's nothing to borrow from. Five from eleven leaves six. Carry one. One from – nothing, nought. Now what? Despair! Tears now. Come on! What to do? Well borrow another one. From nowhere. One from one leaves nought. But I still owe one! If I borrow another one this will go on for ever! My answer will be nought, nought, nought, . . . , six, five. Suppose, somehow, *somehow*, that comes to sixty-five – which it can't! But suppose it does? Apply the usual checking procedure. Forty-eight add sixty-five equals . . . three . . . oh, this looks promising . . . carry one, six and one, seven, and four, equals one . . . oh, yes . . . carry one. Oh – no! Forty-eight plus sixty-five equals one hundred and thirteen. I was a hundred out! If you tried to take a bigger number from a smaller number, which you couldn't, it just seemed to generate numbers from nowhere, which wasn't surprising exactly, although that too was impossible.

I wrote 'Can't do it' by the side of the problem and burst into frantic sobs. Miss Davies found me with my head on my book, which I had soaked with tears. 'Oh come along, Colin', she said, and half picking me up, cradled my face against her bosom. 'There, there!' she said, stroking my hot, throbbing head. I burst into a further paroxysm of sobs, which allowed me to nestle into the exquisite, warm, firm softness of Miss Davies's right breast.

Miss Davies asked me why I was so upset, and I tried to explain. Thereupon, she taught me the trick which she had taught the rest of the class, before I had joined them. 'When you have to take a big number from a smaller one, turn the sum upside down. Take the smaller number from the big one – and just put the take-away sign in front! Forty-eight take away thirteen is thirty-five. So that's thirty-five with the take-away sign in front. We say "That's minus thirty-five." See?'

I thought I had grasped the technique, the trick, and when Miss Davies tested me with another example, sitting with me, in my desk, with her arm round me, I had. The comfort it gave me was not less than the comfort of her warmth. But she did not merely teach me a technique, or trick, she gave me an explanation for it. 'Imagine, Colin,' she said, 'imagine that you have thirteen shillings, but you *owe* someone two pounds, eight shillings.' 'Forty-eight shillings', I said, to show my understanding. 'Good boy. *Now* – how much would you have to *borrow* from your mam to pay your debt? Well, you give the person your thirteen shillings, and you still owe . . . ?' 'One pound, fifteen shillings?' Yes indeed; and my grasp of mathematics had been extended.

I say that my grasp of mathematics had been extended, because I had learned a new technique. Also, my concept of what was possible was extended, and with it, my concept of a number. I had learned the concept of a minus number, a negative number, not just a number that was to be taken away from another but one which was, in itself, negative. If one thinks of the series of numbers one, two, three, and so on, as ranging along the x-axis on a graph, I had learned to extend it through the point of intersection with the y-axis, O, backwards.

The irony of this story is that up until Miss Davies showed me how to take bigger numbers from smaller ones, my model for what I did when I did sums, was operations with counters. To add two numbers, take one number of counters and the other number of counters, put them together, then count the result. Subtraction involved a slight extension of this technique. Take the larger number of counters, and from this remove the smaller number of counters. The residue is the result. Now I prided myself on not needing to use counters to do sums, as some of the other children did. But when you have to take more counters away from a pile than you have in the pile – you can't do it! To model this process with counters, it would be necessary to introduce counters of, say, a different colour, and the pupil would have to learn that blue, say, meant a negative number. But what is that?

Miss Davies was wiser. She got me to understand, to learn to do the sums in question, and to use the new terms correctly, by explaining them in terms with which I was already familiar, namely, a debt; and that was a phrase I already used when doing sums. My philosophical problems with mathematics only became insurmountable when I could not be provided with a model for what I was trying to learn to do. But this did not finally happen until I was doing mathematics in the sixth form.

I have discussed this elementary problem in mathematics at length because everyone who reads this will be able to work it out; it is indeed elementary. My difficulties will seem childish misunderstandings, but what I hope to have demonstrated is that the solution requires extensions of techniques and concepts. So my difficulty was not just a consequence of stupidity, or a blind spot for maths, it was philosophical. I did not find it natural to go on, to take the right approach here, on the basis of what I already knew and could do. Good mathematicians do, that is, they do find it easy and natural to go on to new areas of mathematics as other mathematicians do. One consequence of this is that good, natural mathematicians are not naturally good teachers of maths, precisely because of their talent. It is only when they have done higher maths, which explicitly involves philosophy of maths, and where, perhaps for the first time, they encounter difficulties themselves, or after experience of teaching the rest of us, that they come to an awareness of the discontinuities in maths, and the source of some of the conceptual problems this can raise.

Until we find maths puzzling, we see it as Descartes saw the whole of knowledge. Starting with clear, distinct, simple, primary 'ideas', we feel that the rest of mathematics can be derived by reasoning that is itself simple, clear and inescapable. But this is an illusion. When the illusion is shattered we are then likely to think that we are simply being stupid, precisely because it shows that we have failed to understand. It is sometimes that, but sometimes our problems are conceptual, we are being philosophers.

Readers will be able to think of their own examples and ask themselves what was involved. They may remember being taught that multiplication is really – and is reducible to – addition; conversely, that division, 'sharing', is really – is reducible to – subtraction; that the product of a positive number and a negative number is negative; that you 'cannot' divide by nought; that any number raised to the power nought or zero is one; that the Romans had no numeral for nought, '0', and in consequence found quite simple arithmetic exceedingly difficult; that the Romans had no concept of the number nought (which is much more contentious); that a quadratic equation always has two solutions (if it has any at all), even if these are the same; that a tangent to a circle touches a circle at two places, which coincide; that a circle is simply a special case of an ellipse; that a line can be divided at a point outside itself; that a line has no breadth, and so on, and so on. Difficulties with these claims can be philosophical, which is not to say that they are not sometimes also and *eo ipso* failures of understanding. But philosophical failures of understanding often amount, I think, to the philosopher's intuitions and instincts about what is the same and what different failing to match those of the mathematicians.

After my episode with Miss Davies, I floated along, easily and buoyantly on the stream of school maths. If I threatened to sink at any time, it was only because I was away from school so much, but I became expert at establishing if the class had learned a new technique in my absence, in which case I would plead with friends to coach me. My first taste of real trouble was with calculus. I could not understand the way in which Miss Walker introduced it, though I learned to perform the more elementary operations. I was much later gratified to discover that my difficulties were 'genuine'; at any rate, they had been felt and expressed some 300 years earlier by a philosopher, Berkeley.

Maths in the sixth form lost the crystalline purity, the self-evidence that to me it had seemed so often to have up until then. I had never really liked maths, though I had done well in it, and it required very little swotting, because if things went wrong in maths they went completely wrong, and the fear that that might happen, especially in the next exam, always haunted me. They went wrong with increasing frequency in the sixth form. Series seemed completely artificial, arbitrary, pointless and impossible to remember. I had to learn masses of new formulae, and try as I might, I did not have the time to work examples in coordinate geometry, starting, as one of its inventors or discoverers would surely have approved, from first principles!

But what finally destroyed my appetite for maths and proved I was not a mathematician, were imaginary numbers. I will very briefly discuss my problem because it is easy to show why they are puzzling to anyone who knows that the product of two negative numbers is positive, and what a square root is. Given this knowledge, what is the square root of any negative number? To keep the case simple, consider: what is the square root of minus four? It cannot be two, because two times two yields four, and it cannot be minus two, for that square also yields four. Now to me, a number had to be either positive or negative. And if somehow a number could be neither positive nor negative, I couldn't begin to see how two such numbers when multiplied together could yield a negative number. Mathematicians do not feel these difficulties are insurmountable. They need negative numbers to have square roots, so – it seemed to me – they just invent them and call them 'imaginary'. So the square root of minus four is 2i. If you ask what that is, they just say 'It is the square root of minus four' and, as such, has the properties listed above.

Once again I felt as I had done with Miss Davies. This was impossible. And this time, even though I learned to operate with imaginary numbers, I could not get over my feeling that the idea of an imaginary number was incoherent, and their invention was a cheat! When I asked for a model to make sense of them, the teacher and my friends who could do maths talked in terms of a new axis of numbers at right angles to the other axis of numbers that I could accept. But this seemed to me at least as arbitrary and artificial as speaking, as the physicists did – self-consciously, I thought, and with self-congratulation – of time as the 'fourth dimension', and it was even less intelligible!

It will be clear to any professional philosopher reading the above that my thinking about mathematics and philosophical problems about mathematics, has been influenced by Wittgenstein. But I must reiterate that philosophical difficulties with mathematics – or, indeed, any other institutionalised activity – do not necessarily consist in misunderstandings. I believe that some philosophical problems with maths can properly be construed simply as misunderstandings, but others not. And although the mathematician does not need justification for what he does – and if he did, he has it in virtue of its acceptance by other experts – that does not mean that what he does is *inherently* unproblematic. The moves, leaps, extensions he makes may indeed defy sense, and their general acceptance among the *cognoscenti*, that is, among the practitioners of the art, no more guarantee that what they accept does make good sense, than it does in religion, magic, fortune-telling, psychoanalysis, phrenology, or any other practice.

My third encounter with philosophy was different yet again. I was about 9 or 10, standing in the playground at Shields Road, waiting for it to be time to go into the hall to eat my school dinner. Graham Harrison passed me, making for the gate. 'Are you going home?' I asked – he lived at the top of 'my' road and I knew him quite well. 'Yes', he said, grinning. 'Are you going home for *dinner*?' I asked, since I did not and was surprised that he did. 'Yes', he said grinning more broadly. Was it in slight embarrassment, I wonder in retrospect? 'Why don't you have school dinners?' He edged away from my impertinence, heading for home, his grin a frown. 'They're terrific!' It did not occur to me then, as it would have done a few years later, that perhaps his parents could not afford the two and a penny a week that five of these excellent three-course meals cost, and in fact I am sure that this was not so. He stopped and faced me. 'No', he said, and paused, then grinned. 'I go home for dinners. Well –', he looked at me squarely, 'you only see your mother once. Don't you? Really.'

I was so struck by what Graham said that I cannot remember what happened after that, except that I went around repeating it to myself, told my mother what Graham had said when I got home myself that afternoon, and then made his remark my own. It seemed such a beautiful thing to say, and so clearly true, and its truth and beauty seemed not two things, or even two aspects of one thing, but one and the same. Is that what Keats meant?[3] And yet what Graham had said *also* seemed – was; was, perhaps even more clearly – *false*, though it seemed to be vulgar and insensitive even to notice this. How puzzling! I was certain that his remark was true, and my certainty was not second-hand. But it didn't mean what it should have meant, because in that case it was false. And although I not only was certain that it meant something else, I was certain I knew what else it meant, and what he meant; but I could not say what this was! After much further thought, and discussions with my mother – I felt too shy to ask my teacher about it, or my father – I decided regretfully that I didn't *really* know what Graham's remark meant, yet I remained certain that it was true. And how could that be? Try as I might, I could not solve any of these problems, all of which are philosophical.

Of course, it will occur to everyone reading this, that Graham's remark is a metaphor, and I didn't realise this. But did Graham? And how much does realising this help to solve

my problems? Well, as some philosophers say, speaking
metaphorically when they do so, metaphors can be 'cashed',
that is, they can be expressed literally. So I should have translated the remark into one or more literal statements, whereupon all the problems would have disappeared. But how you
cash a metaphor depends on what you think it means, and I
could not say what it meant, and reluctantly came to the
conclusion that I did not know. I thought it none the less true,
but whether one thinks a (powerful, profound) metaphor is
true depends on its striking one as beautiful. (Keats again.)
And when you cash the metaphor, you destroy its beauty, and
lose the truth – as well as that part of its meaning which matters. Seeing that the remark is a metaphor solves none of my
problems.

So what should I say now about Graham's remark and the
problems it generated for me? Certainly one can say *something* in literal terms about the meaning of his remark, why
he said it, and what he was trying to convey. Equally certainly,
one cannot entirely reduce to, or translate the metaphor into,
literal statements – at least, not if the metaphor is any good;
and if philosophers' talk about cashing metaphors implies
that this can be done, it is simplistic. The living metaphor is,
in this way, ineffable, that is, one cannot say what it means.
As to its truth: there is no test, no criterion, no procedure for
establishing this – either the metaphor touches or strikes you
as true, and *eo ipso* beautiful (profound, powerful, disturbing,
and so on) or it does not. One doffs one's hat to a metaphor,
both as a human being and as a philosopher, and by the latter
I mean 'someone' who tries to give an analytic account of its
meaning and truth. And that, I think, is the literal truth about
Graham's metaphor.[4] In which case, though I have not exactly
solved the problems it raised for me, I now see that not much
more can be said in answer to them.

I am not primarily a moral or political philosopher, but
these thoughts about metaphor seemed helpful when, more
recently, I have tried to think about such declarations as 'We
hold these truths to be self-evident, that all men are born free
and equal', and about how philosophers react when confronted

by them. Those who framed the American Declaration of Independence (1776) and the Universal Declaration of Human Rights (1948), Article 1, held it to be true, perhaps self-evidently true, that all human beings are born free and equal, and many of them would concur. But philosophers have puzzled about just what is being asserted and whether it is self-evident, or even true. For, construed literally, these declarations seem patently false. It is simply not true that all human beings are equal legally, socially, or economically, neither are they all similarly endowed with respect to health, vigour, temperament, intelligence, appearance, which crucially affect the quality of human lives. So what is being claimed? Is it just pious nonsense?

Faced by this difficulty, many philosophers have a ready-made solution to hand. These statements are not descriptive but normative: they don't say what is the case, but what ought to be the case. And since such statements are logically independent, the fact that the declaration, construed as a description, is false (if and when it is false), is no bar to its being true when correctly construed as normative. In so far as normative statements 'describe' anything, they describe an ideal world, our vision of which provides sufficient guide for what we should do – or, if we are helpless, a guide to how we should feel about the one we inhabit.

Given this account, it has to be admitted that the grammar of the declaration, and of other similar statements, is misleading, or could be, for they are in the indicative mood. But philosophers have grown used to the thought that grammar can be misleading and have examined many examples where this thesis seems true and illuminating.

None the less, one of the best-known difficulties for a philosophical view remains. If it is *not* literally true that men are born free and equal, and if normative statements cannot be derived from descriptive ones, the normative claims may be true, but how is this to be established? If someone were to disagree with the founding fathers, what could be done to show him that he would be wrong? *Ex hypothesi*, it would be irrelevant to point out any facts to him, since the philosophers in question hold that facts are what answer to true descriptive statements.

The slightly desperate answer that is most usually given is: nothing by way of demonstration. All that those who share a moral position can do is to talk round the normative claims and hope that the doubtful and the dissenting will come to 'see' what they 'see'. And we may helpfully remind ourselves that regarding the extract from the declaration, many already do. (The rest have to be seen as callow, silly or vicious.)

This consequence of what moral and political philosophers have said about normative statements is very like one of the consequences of my account of metaphor.

A further question emerges from reflecting on metaphor. I was certain that Graham's remark was true, but I came to the conclusion that I didn't really know what it meant (at least, I could not say what it meant.) The problem was: how is this possible? Unless I knew what it meant, how could I be certain that it was true? Surely it is generally the case that we cannot know of our own knowledge that a statement is true without knowing what it means?

This is a real difficulty, and also seems to provide a difficulty for a time-honoured philosophical thesis about the relation between the meaning of a proposition and its truth or falsity. According to this thesis, to know what a statement means – to understand it – is to know in which circumstances it is true or false. This view, however briefly sketched, is appealing. After all, if we did not know in what circumstances a statement was true and in what false, we could not understand it, for we would not know what it asserted, what it stated to be the case or what it denied obtained. But isn't this plausible thesis faced with the difficulty that faced me concerning Graham's remark?

The obvious reply would be to distinguish between knowing when a statement is true or false, that is, knowing and being able to say in which circumstances a statement would be true or would be false, and knowing *that* it is true or is false, that is, which circumstances *actually obtain*. Once this distinction is made, it is easy to see that the thesis allows that we can understand a statement, know what it means, without knowing its truth-value (that is, whether it is actually true or false). The theory correctly notices a conceptual connection between the

meaning and truth of statements, without inappropriately or
even impossibly committing itself to the claim that we (first)
have to know whether a statement is true or false in order to
know what it means.

This reply is fine as far as it goes, but it does not go deeply
enough. For although in some cases, perhaps – or even, most
– we could know what a statement means without knowing
whether it is true or false, could this be true of all the statements we understand, and could it be true in all those cases
to which the thesis is intended and needs to apply? The answer
must be 'No.' And this is not because there are at least some
necessary statements, namely, the very simple ones, such as
'One and one make two', which we could not be said to understand unless we know their truth-value. Nor is it because, if
the thesis were quite generally applicable, we would have to
both understand that we might not know the truth of any
statement we understand, and not know that this statement
was itself true! The difficulty is rather that in a condition of total
first-order ignorance, that is, a condition in which a person did
not know the truth of any statement about how things are
(though he may know the truth of certain statements about
statements about how things are, and so on), individuals
could not know the meanings of many words whose meanings
they do know, and must know, if they are to understand the
statements they do understand.

This is because we are sensitive creatures who have to
learn the natural language that we speak. We rely on our
senses to do this, and, in particular, we learn the meanings of
many words via examples of that to which they apply. For
creatures like ourselves, learning an application for a word
and learning its meaning are not always two distinct lessons
or achievements, and could not always be separable. Which
means that coming to know the truth of 'Water boils at 100°C
(at sea level)', 'Water freezes at 0°C (at sea level)', 'The
unclouded sky is blue', 'That is blue' (together with a gesture
towards something blue), 'This is a syncopated rhythm', 'That
chap is scoring the runs, but, as a batsman, it is the other who
has *class*', 'Madeira is lighter than port', 'Here is a classic

example of scissors gait', and coming to understand these remarks are, on occasions, one and the same achievement. And this claim is not threatened by the facts that they need not always be, learners must already possess some linguistic knowledge, teachers should normally not be mistaken or perverse in their choice of examples, they should be recognised as having some authority by the learner, and so on.

Again this view might itself be challenged. It might be said that it depends on assuming that the individuals we have been speaking of have *learned* to use the words they utter, and that is a provincial assumption. If we suppose instead that an individual is insect-like, and his capacity to use language is innate, he will know how to use words, and have the capacity to understand what might be said to him, before he has learned anything of the world he is perhaps about to enter. So although no doubt it *is* in fact true that human beings cannot understand the statements they do understand without also knowing that some of the factual ones are true, this need not be true of every language user.

Although this defence of the philosophical thesis about statements might be thought to concede all the attack really requires – for we are not insect-like – it can be attacked. For although an insect might use, say, the word 'blue' as we humans do, that is, it might use it as a colour word and agree with us as to which things are blue, we *identify* its meaning differently from the insect. 'Blue' is defined in dictionaries as 'the colour of the unclouded sky'. For the insect this would be just another brute, contingent truth, which it might not know, while being able to use the word. But because we cannot give an 'analysis' of the word, that is, a perspicuous paraphrase which would teach someone how to use the word without the help of examples, dictionaries contain instructions for giving their readers an 'ostensive definition'. Their example is the unclouded sky – presumably because it is a stable example and a widely, easily available one. And it is in comparison with the unclouded sky that *other* things are adjudged to be blue or not.[5] So 'the unclouded sky is blue' does not have the same kind of status or play the same kind of role for the insect as it does for us – or can do for us. It is for us what Wittgenstein has called a 'grammatical' remark.

If this is correct, that is, if there are words whose meanings we could not learn without being shown examples to which they apply, either in fact or 'grammatically', there will be and must be occasions on which learning the meaning of a factual statement and learning its truth will be one and the same, or at least inseparable, and in these cases it is not true that we have first to understand them before we can determine if they are true.

Since I am trying to convey what philosophy is, and is like, and since it so often involves minute and protracted debate, I make no apology for acknowledging that what I have just said can also be attacked, and will show how.

It might be objected (a) that those things which are used to teach the meanings of certain words (call the representative example '*x*') need not in fact be *x,* and the learner could still learn the meaning of '*x*', and so could come to know this without there being actual *x*'s, and so without knowing *that* there are, or, *if* they are, which things are *x*. For example, the learner could learn the words 'dodo', 'unicorn', and so on, by being shown pictures, holograms, models, and so on. This point must be granted, but if it is to yield the desired conclusion it would have to be possible that all ostensive teaching could be done with examples to which the word whose meaning was being taught did not really, literally apply. But how should we then teach the meanings of such words as 'blue', or, for that matter, 'picture', 'example'? I shall simply say that the general conclusion needed by this objection cannot be reached.

It might be objected (b) that where '*x*' applied 'grammatically', as, it has been claimed, 'blue' does to the unclouded sky, and 'one metre long' does (or, rather, *did*) to the standard metre bar, they apply merely conventionally to these examples. So it is not a fact about the world that the sky is blue, or the standard metre bar is one metre long. These statements may be used to teach the meanings of 'blue' and 'one metre long', but they do not tell us what colour the sky is, or how long the metre bar is, only what the sky colour is called, what the length of the standard bar is called. (I think Wittgenstein would agree with this point; or perhaps it would be truer to say that he seems to be saying something like this.)

However, I think this view mistaken. These remarks do *not* merely tell us what the colour of the sky is called, and so on, and it *is* a fact that the unclouded sky is blue. (After all, it might have been another colour.) For although it is true that the exemplars provide standard examples by means of which other things are measured or compared, 'feedback' occurs. The other things which are blue, and are judged to be blue, on the basis of a comparison with the unclouded sky, are the same colour as the sky. (So it is blue.) But the sky might change its colour, and be adjudged to have done so in comparison with these other things. No exemplar is immune to this kind of possibility. But since this *is* a possibility, it is then a *fact* that, for example, the sky is blue. The role which the unclouded sky plays both as a standard, and as an example by means of which the meaning of 'blue' can be taught, does not mean that 'the unclouded sky is blue' is not a factual, contingent statement – albeit a true and reliable one. If the objector never says 'Well, in that case, the standard examples which are used to teach the meaning of '*x*', need not actually exemplify the qualities we call '*x*', we return to the first objection and my final reply to that. Still, it is true that there is no difference in kind, only of degree, between examples used in ostensive teaching and the so-called 'standard' examples.

Now what I have just said, allows one point to the objector. He or she can now say that although it may be true that we don't define 'blue' and other words in the same way as the insect, it doesn't follow and it isn't true that the objector and we attach different meanings to 'blue'. If it *is* a contingent truth that the sky is blue, then 'blue' doesn't mean 'the colour of the unclouded sky' for the objector *or for us*. For this is not a semantic equivalence, that is, it doesn't assert that 'blue' and 'the colour of the unclouded sky' have the same meaning, or, to put it another way, are the same concept. What it asserts is that 'blue' applies to the colour of the unclouded sky; that is what we call it. (And if it changed, and we continued to say it was 'blue', 'blue' would have changed its meaning, but 'the colour of the unclouded sky' would not.)

Is the objector correct? I think so. What does this mean? It means that my criticism of the traditional thesis concerning the relation of a statement's meaning and its truth is an epistemological one, not a logical one. That is to say, my claim that there are and must be cases in which we could not *learn* the meaning of a word without learning the truth of the statement in which it is used, does not mean that such statements as 'The unclouded sky is blue' are necessarily true, or even necessarily true for those who simultaneously learn the meanings of these statements and that they are true. The claim is instead hypothetical and epistemological, namely, that unless these statements are true, language users would not know the meanings of words whose meanings they do know, and would not learn them as they do, and must, learn them.

Although this discussion may help us to understand how we learn to make certain aesthetic judgements – consider, for example, Leavis's judgements concerning 'particularity'[6] – I do not think that it greatly helps regarding the problem presented by Graham's statement. For in accepting its truth, I was not learning anything approaching a general rule about how to use 'seeing someone once' or even 'seeing your mother once'. The use of that phrase to say something meaningful, true and profound is still virtually restricted to the particular statement that he made. In fact, I wish to use the result for quite different purposes.

Graham and I, and many other children in Kipling Road, went to Sunday School. It was simply something which children in our road *did,* by which I mean that attendance was not a decision of faith, but a practice or custom. You joined in when you were big enough to walk with the other children in the road the mile or so to the corrugated iron chapel in Wordsworth Road. This 'tin heaven', as I later heard such places called, was attached to the Church of St Gregory's, Horfield, whose architecture was so admired by Sir John Betjeman – which, needless to say, is also something that I discovered very much later. There were children who did not go to Sunday School, but they were either Catholics or Methodists, odd and alien, at least on Sundays, or they belonged to families that were not really or fully 'respectable'. I am sure that that was what I then felt, even though I very much doubt if I would have expressed it like that, or could have expressed it at all. So far as I can remember, none of the parents who dressed their children in their Sunday-best clothes, gave them their collection money, and sent them off, went to church themselves. But this did not puzzle us, or cause us to doubt Christianity. Perhaps this was in part because they sent us not just cynically, that is, so that they could have some time to themselves on a Sunday afternoon, but because they clearly thought it right for children. Even my father seemed to think this, although I knew that he did not believe in God. Parents simply didn't go to church on Sundays. But then they didn't have prayers at work either. But grown-ups got married in church, and the old ones got buried at church, and they took babies to be christened, and were surely christened themselves.

I can make that last claim partly because of an incident which took place years later when I was in my early thirties: I bumped into my mother who was walking up the splendidly named Eden Grove. Where could she be going? I couldn't imagine what would be taking her in that direction. She was flustered and embarrassed, but admitted that she was on her way to St Gregory's to be christened. She was ashamed to admit this, and I was astonished that she hadn't been christened as a baby. Of course I teased her about feeling that she ought to be christened, that this was proper and wise, but I wasn't surprised that she felt like this.

At any rate, every Sunday, a group of children would set off up Kipling Road, up the rather seedy Eighth Avenue, past the big tree and change of road surfacing that marked the Bristol boundary, into Wordsworth Avenue. This was council-house country, and when I was there by myself on my way to my grandmother, who lived in Emmerson Square, I was worried that the council-house kids would set on me (which they sometimes did, and the girls were as aggressive and frightening as the boys), but on Sundays there was safety in numbers. Past Eden Grove on our right, up into Wordsworth Road, until we got to the chapel.

What happened there was unremarkable. We sang hymns, we prayed, we listened to a sort of sermon by the superintendant, but paid more attention to the accompanying drawings he did on a blackboard. We divided into classes, where we were taught the Bible, and concluded with a hymn and a prayer. As we got older we giggled more, and misbehaved, and were warned by the superintendant. Then we went home, feeling virtuous, making arrangements, if we were old enough, about what we should do with the rest of the day, and all of us thinking about our teas. Going to Sunday School was a bit like going to school, except that it was shorter, going made you feel virtuous, especially because it was in some sense optional, it wasn't difficult or demanding in the ways that school could be and, in my case, I never felt I had learned anything. In fact I had. I had learned about Christianity in a way in which my children have not, and I find their ignorance shocking.

When you reached the age of about 12, Sunday School began to press you to go to church, to St Gregory's. The superintendant would take you aside for a chat, and children who would have continued were made to feel that they were being babyish. At that point most children ceased to be active members of the Church of England. They would attend St Gregory's perhaps once or twice and then not bother any more. It was too far away, not enough of their friends went, the high church services were too formal, their parents did not insist, they were growing up themselves and ready to join the ranks of the non-attenders. They had other things to do on Sundays. But they did not cease to be Christians. They became Christians like their parents.

I started to attend St Gregory's regularly, and ceased to be a Christian, like my father. Why did I go? Because my best friend Peter was in the choir, and I wanted to be with him in the choir. To become eligible I had to serve an apprenticeship of church attendance, and I would sit in the very front pew where I could see Peter. The services were stunningly boring, and worst of all was, of course, the sermon. During the sermon Peter and I would try to catch each other's eye, and make the other laugh. Peter would bite the pew to stop himself laughing, and I would try to turn my laughter into coughing. My paroxysms of coughing, snorting and yodelling made me leave the service on two occasions, my handkerchief stuffed in my mouth, tears streaming down my cheeks. A curate was solicitous. The organist who watched everything through his mirror was suspicious.

None the less, the choir master allowed me to join the choir, and that meant going to choir practice. I enormously enjoyed walking to practice, and coming home. It was winter and as Peter and I walked to and from St Gregory's we played a marvellous game. We would run across Eden Grove and leap up and into the large privet hedges that gave the houses privacy. You 'won' if you could stay up in the hedge balanced on the bent branches, and 'lost' if you were pushed back into the road. But the real excitement occurred if you leapt too enthusiastically and fell through the ravaged hedge into someone's front garden. This excitement was heightened on the way home by the fear, which sometimes proved a reality, that an angry householder would be lying in wait for you.

Choir practice itself was boring and, when you had to sing by yourself, embarrassing and fraught with the fear that one might collapse into laughter. Although I joined the choir, swung a censer, and swung one at the services at the stations of the cross, it was not long before my behaviour, and my bad influence on Peter, and complaints from people who lived in Eden Grove, resulted in my being thrown out of the choir. The choir master told me that I would have to serve a second term of probation at services, and if I could behave there, he might permit me to rejoin the other boys.

I attended St Gregory's once more, at evensong, the following Sunday. I sat in the front pew, but Peter carefully avoided my eye. I felt disappointed, let down, improperly rejected, resentful, bored and contemptuous. I did not sing the hymns but read the words, which seemed hollow and silly. I had never before bothered about the meaning of the chants, but now they struck me as meaningless. The prayers suddenly seemed pious and empty. The sermon was as boring as ever, even though this time I listened. Suddenly it seemed to me that not only did I not believe in God, and was not a Christian, but that really I had never believed in God. I longed to get out of the service, and when it ended I rushed past the prelate in the porch with eyes averted. I was perhaps too young for him to offer me his hand, but I did not feel that I could even accept his 'Good night' or wish him one, without insincerity.

As I walked home, and on many subsequent occasions, I remembered the many occasions on which I had prayed. But had I really *believed*? I remembered that when I was very young I had heard that faith could move mountains. I understood this to mean that if you believed hard enough, you could do anything. So I had closed my eyes, concentrated fiercely, and tried to will a chair to move. When nothing had happened, I decided that I could not have had sufficient faith. How silly it now all seemed to be! And when I prayed again, as I did, I knew why. I wanted something desperately, or was terrified. Prayer was evidence of human weakness, not of God's existence.

Though I went to church no more, I still had to attend services. There were 'prayers' every morning at school. How angry I felt as I stood in those meetings feeling that I could not pray, could not sing the hymns, could not bow my head. How wrong it was to force these observances on those who did not believe. I did not want to worship God, I wanted to debate his existence. I was a zealot in my disbelief. But I found to my surprise and self-righteous anger, that almost no one else wanted to do this. Most of my class-mates simply seemed not to be interested. I could not understand how they could not be interested, but just had to accept that they were not. But, I felt, those who clearly were Christians had to be interested. For they had a position, or should have one, they presumed it right, and their practices presumed on me and my acceptance.

I harried the believers, and quickly learned that they felt that even to raise the question of God's existence was deeply improper. But why? Well, they said, you must have faith. But why? The Bible said so. But surely to appeal to the Bible was to suppose just what I wanted to debate! Most of the arguments I succeeded in having are so commonplace that there would be no point in describing them. What emerged was that those who believed, believed. They wanted to say that they knew that God existed, but they did not believe that they could prove this – though some were quick to point out, I couldn't prove that he didn't exist either. They believed, they had faith, I should have it too, and it was a pity and proof of my pride and arrogance that I did not have faith. But why, oh! why, should I have faith, I wanted to know? It seemed to me that faith was either unnecessary or improper. It was unnecessary if you could prove that God existed, and if you couldn't, why ought you to believe? If God really did require us to believe in him without reason, that was unreasonable. If I would be punished for not believing in him, and I was frequently warned of this, that was morally improper, and if that was what he was like I wouldn't want to worship him even if he did exist! What infuriated me was that they, the Christians, seemed to think that it was I who was immoral and even mad.

When I was in the sixth form, I heard that the mother of another boy in the year ahead of me, the school captain and a lay-preacher, was putting it about that I was mad and bad and dangerous to know. Furious about this, and with him since I was sure that he was the source of her views, I cornered him in the prefects' room and asked him if the story about what his mother had been saying was true. Shamefacedly he admitted that it was. He explained that his mother was not well, was frightened, was shocked that anyone could not be a Christian and be proud of this, as she had heard I was, and she felt sure that if you weren't a good Christian you couldn't be a good person. I told him that I felt sorry for his mother, but her views just confirmed my views about Christianity and Christians. He then got angry, and in response to that, another difficulty with his position occurred to me. The requirement to have faith was not only improper and irrational but impossible! 'Why,' he wanted to know and he was intrigued – this seemed to sound a new note in an old song. 'Because', I said, 'I said, 'belief isn't something you do – or fail to do. It's something you have – or don't have.' He ruminated on this, and, as I watched him with interest, all our anger dissipated. Finally he said that if you prayed, and went to church, if you walked with God, belief would come. I had to admit that belief probably could be induced in this way, so that once again we were back to our old disagreement.

Now of course, I do not have to admit, it is evident, that I was proud, arrogant and aggressive in my disbelief. But, it seemed to me, they, who were in a great majority, were complacent in their belief. They presumed to be sorry for me. But they were not conspicuously cleverer, or wiser, or better than me – in fact it seemed to me that being a Christian seemed to have very little consequences for a person's character. And though I had to withdraw my too crude assertion that Christianity had caused wars, deaths and tortures, I felt able to insist that Christianity, like so many religions, had legitimated such evils. So, they replied, had communism. But, I said, I am not a communist, as you seem to assume, but a socialist and a free thinker. (How antiquated that phrase now sounds!) What evils have people like myself perpetrated? I would not suppress *them,* but they would suppress me if they could. They assured me that they would not.

Memories of other incidents from this aspect and period of my life return. Once, when I was about 15, and had been arguing in class about God – it was a religious-instruction period – a girl had rounded on me and said 'You think you are so clever, Radford. But a lot of people a lot cleverer than you are Christians!' The class agreed, and what she said was true, and to my chagrin I could not think of how to reply. Only later did it occur to me that a lot of people cleverer than her and me were not Christians and I said that in the next period. But the victory was hers.

On another occasion, after someone from the BBC had sat in on the headmaster's current-affairs class, I was invited to take part in a schools programme on religion. The headmaster felt this reflected well on the school and told everyone at prayers to be sure to listen. In retrospect, I am not sure what he hoped for or expected. At any rate, I went eagerly to the BBC studios at Bristol, and got angry during the lunch we were given before the discussion, because I felt that we were being primed about what to say. When we got into the recording studio I got even angrier when I realised that the only adult participant in the debate was a vicar. Was that fair? I got angrier still when he was allowed to embark on a long rigma-role, a sort of parable, about men being like children, and God was the father, and we were frightened because leading one's life was like entering a dark cellar, and God helped and guided us as a father would lead his child by the hand. I asked him why, if God was omnipotent, he didn't do what any father would do, and turn the light on? He spluttered and said finally that God couldn't turn the light on. We had to find our own way, albeit with his assistance. I said that we had to find our own way without his assistance, and what we had to do was turn the light on ourselves.

I felt thoroughly pleased with myself and hoped that I had impressed the very pretty girl who had been sitting next to the vicar. But, no sooner had we finished, and were drinking tea, and as I returned from the plushest lavatory I had ever used, an executive told us that there had been technical problems with the recording and we should have to do it all again. And could we sound more animated, please? We had all sounded rather dull! This made me almost speechless with rage, and I had dark thoughts about why we had to perform again. This time the vicar did not produce his fatuity, but as I was about to get stuck in none the less, I glanced down and saw that my flies were undone. I said virtually nothing in the ensuing recorded and broadcast debate. The headmaster, while not

displeased, asked at morning assembly why I had been so
quiet. I mumbled something incoherent, and he and others
were rather amused. And though I got out of the BBC taxi
when the pretty girl did, she forestalled my attempt to ask her
to go out with me by suddenly getting on a bus.

I do remember being impressed on one occasion by a
member of staff talking to me as we watched a football
match. Life, he said, was a mystery. That, I agreed, was true,
as I watched and envied the players their strength, skills and
beauty. It is a mystery, the master said, that anything exists.
That expressed something I had, up to that point only felt.
And, he went on, however much we find out and explain, some
things will always be unexplained. That seemed to me not
only true, but true and profound. 'That', he said, 'is why I am
a Christian. Can't you swallow your pride, admit the mystery
in life, and join us?' I literally stepped back and away, in horror.
'But that', I said, 'is simply to add to the mysteries and explain
them in terms of another. I can't do that.' He shook his head
and walked away.

As many others have done, I philosophised about Christianity
before I knew what philosophy was. At first I was a practitioner,
then I became an atheist. Later I became a professional
philosopher. What do I think now?

I ought first to say that many professional philosophers
would find that my thoughts here are still crude. None the less
it seems clear to me that the existence of different religions
means that they cannot all be true. Many practitioners themselves agree with this and have characterised each other as
'heathens', 'infidels', 'idolaters', and so on. But all religions
could be *false,* and each religion *is* false if its God or gods –
if it has any – do not exist. And it seems clear to me that it
is confused and obscurantist to argue that the practice of a
religion, even together with the faith of its practitioners, neces-
sitates that the God or gods to whom the faithful pray exist.
Even practitioners of religion don't believe that. But is
Christianity the true religion? Is there a true religion? What I
am able to offer here is a parable and a comment.

Like many parents, including sceptics, I went along with my young children's belief in Father Christmas. In fact I did more than that, I encouraged it by joining in conversations about him and what he might bring them, if they were good and fortunate. Why? After all, I did not believe in him. I suppose because I did not wish to shatter their childish belief, which seemed to give them so much pleasure and excitement, which added to the magic of Christmas, and which I expected would naturally erode with time anyway. I noticed that the attitudes of the two older children were different almost from the very start. The oldest, a girl, was a natural believer. She uncritically and enthusiastically accepted tales about Father Christmas and talked about him to the next child, a boy. He did not seem to be so enthusiastic, but for one Christmas both were simple, uncritical believers. On the Christmas Eve, the Lions Club sent a float round the area, lit up with fairy lights, on which sat a great fat, jolly white-bearded man with a sack of presents. Their open-mouthed awe was a joy to behold, and to have told them that Father Christmas was really Mr Evans, and there was really no such person as Father Christmas, would have been – I almost want to say a sort of sacrilege, and certainly unthinkable.

The next Christmas my wife and I took the children shopping. They were taken into the 'grotto' at one store, and were sat on Father Christmas's knee, and so on. But at the next, though we tried to avoid its happening, Austin noticed that there was another grotto, with, presumably, another Father Christmas. He was immediately suspicious, but Catherine was not. I tried to palm him off by saying that Father Christmas was very busy at this time of year and had to have helpers. He did not seem wholly convinced. Catherine was untroubled.

We managed to sustain Austin's suspension of disbelief that Christmas, though we lived in a house without chimneys, and I had to say that we always left the front door unlocked on Christmas Eve.

The next Christmas, Austin was aggressive in his disbelief. He noticed that we were buying presents, and told Catherine this. At this point I am afraid that, partly to sustain the belief of the third child, and partly because I wanted to see what would happen, I 'explained' this too. Father Christmas gave some parents money to buy their children presents because there were now so many children he could not make all of their presents in his factory at the North Pole. Indeed, parents who could afford it, were asked by him to buy presents. Catherine accepted this. In fact, her belief was not disturbed when she saw me taking presents into the children's bedroom that Christmas Eve. By now, Austin thought it was a lot of childish nonsense, and had to be persuaded not to air his views to his little brother.

It is obvious how this story could go on. As fresh difficulties appeared, I might have been able to explain them away to Catherine. I could have told her that although it was always parents who provided presents, they were agents of Father Christmas, who carried out his work. I could have explained that though young children did not understand, really Father Christmas was invisible, that he was a spirit, the spirit of Children's Christmases, and so on. At no point *need* she have given up her belief, instead each new difficulty for it could have been treated by her as adding to her knowledge and understanding of Father Christmas. And Austin could have not disproved any of this, though he would have been absolutely impatient with it.

In fact I did not do these things. I thought it about time Catherine gave up the belief and told her that Father Christmas did not exist. She seemed rather disappointed, but perhaps a bit relieved. Austin was gleeful, and I told him not to be so pleased with himself. I warned both of them to say nothing of this to their infant brother.

Of course, the analogy between belief in Father Christmas and belief in God is not perfect, and to draw it without noticing these differences would be to misrepresent and diminish the latter. The Father Christmas story is just a story. (But do we know that, and if it was made up as a fiction, could it not, none the less, be true?) More importantly, belief in the Christian God is so much richer and more profound than any belief in

Father Christmas. And if God is thought of as being all wise, all powerful, everywhere, the creator of the world, all good and the source of all goodness, not only can difficulties for belief in him easily be explained away, but those explanations do not always strike reasonable men and women as being *ad hoc* remedies but as providing insights which extend their imperfect understanding of him. The filigree of religious belief can be so much finer and more highly wrought than that of other beliefs, and strikes many as very beautiful. To me it seems ornate and suffers from an 'aery thinness'. Of course, religious belief can also be crude or, more charitably, simple. But its existence is no more surprising or impressive than the continuance of belief in popular astrology.

Like almost every other child, my childhood was suffused by fears and terror, and, if memory serves me right, these fears and terror, and the shame they caused me, reached their awful peak when I was about 12.

Twelve-year-old boys climb trees. But I was frightened of heights and humiliated when I would not do so. My best friend would walk across the outward-sloping, ten-inch wide parapet of the bridge across the railway at the bottom of our lane. He only encouraged me to do the same, and did not jeer when I could not, which somehow made it worse.

Twelve-year-old boys fight. Sometimes they do so to establish their place amongst their friends, or because they are to be used for that purpose and are too brave – or cowardly – to turn down the challenge. As a 12-year-old I happened to be the youngest and smallest boy in the gang in my street and when there was nothing better to do, I was often used by another boy to demonstrate that he was a better fighter than me. The punches hurt, the humiliation of being beaten and reduced to tears was worse, and the thought that this might happen when I went out to play was always with me. (By the time I was big enough and old enough to beat another boy in the gang, I was 15 and both young enough and old enough to see and feel exactly what I was doing to the cocky 12-year-old who provoked me. Once again I slunk home, hangdog and ashamed, and this time also worrying that Mrs Organ might come round to see my mum about what I had done to her Tony.)

But these were rational fears; my *terror* was reserved for what by then I knew to be unreal. Again like many other children I had always been 'frightened of the dark'. What a forgiving phrase! I mean that, as long as I could remember, I had been frightened to go to bed at night, frightened to be alone – not merely resentful that I was not downstairs, listening to the radio, drinking Camp coffee and eating toast tasting deliciously of hot coal and dripping with melting margarine – even more frightened if my bedroom was lightened only by the light from the landing or, worse, from the lamp outside in the street. I would plead to be allowed to stay downstairs and, after winning one or two delays, would finally be sent to bed. There, when I could bear the terror no longer, I would shout for a glass of water. I would ask my mother to come to bed with me, which kindly, puzzled and wearied, she often did. What relief! What bliss! What guilt! And what embarrassment when, ignoring my protests that I wasn't frightened, she would ask me what I was frightened of.

I could not say. The way the street light fell through the window with the coloured fanlights, so it looked as though a huge owl was perched, immovable, unblinking at the foot of my bed? That frightened me, but it was not what I was frightened *of*. Something. But I could not name it, and had I known it to name it, I would have been ashamed to do so. Why? I don't know why. All I know is that the terror was terrible, and so powerful that when my own children betrayed night fears, and despite my wish to be rid of them, I would let them fall asleep on the sofa in front of the tele. and then allow their mother to carry them to bed. (My children deny this.)

But by the time I was 12 I knew and believed that ghosts were not real. There: ghosts! And I knew and believed that there was no man and no ghastly thing inside my room, or on the landing, or outside the window, that was going to get me. It did not help.

Indeed, as a 12-year-old my fears, though I now knew them

to be groundless and irrational, got worse. This was because I had started to go to the pictures with my best friend, Peter. With my mother I had seen Bette Davis films to keep her company and she Tarzan films to keep me company. With Peter I saw *The Beast with Five Fingers.* Or, rather, I half-saw it because I spent at least half the film with my eyes closed, slumped in my seat, out of sight of the screen.

Being frightened at the pictures was bad enough. Being frightened on the way home, and in bed, and for years afterwards, was in every way worse. The fact that Peter was sufficiently understanding and frightened himself to say 'Cheerio' to me as we parted on dark winter nights at the top of my street after a night at the pictures, and then yell 'The Beast!' when we were invisible to each other, didn't help either. So what if he, and others, were frightened like me? That I was terrorised was burden enough. That I knew there was nothing to be frightened of made the terror humiliating and embarrassing. It was only in broad daylight that I could fully appreciate that my fear was puzzling. How *could* I be terrorised by things that I not only knew but believed did not exist and, therefore, could not harm me?

I believe that these thoughts and experiences partly inspired the paper, 'How can we be moved by the fate of Anna Karenina?'[7] which I wrote some thirty years later. And they may explain why I am so convinced that many of our responses to fiction are irrational that I have defended this view against attack after attack.

At any rate, childhood, whatever else it is, was to me, whatever else it was, a time of fear and terror (just as my early manhood was a time of anxiety and frustration). How comparatively happy it is to be middle aged! I do not think that I ever go to sleep at night by myself without being conscious of the fact, and luxuriating in it, that I am no longer afraid.

Sexually my childhood was normal, by which I mean that from about the age of 7, when I went into Miss Davies's class, it was riddled and redolent with sex. Rousseau's *Confessions* provide a precedent for a philosopher's examining his sexual life, but I do not wish to discuss the details of my sexual history: the episodes, excitements, longings and guilt; or at any rate I shall avoid this as much as I can to avoid embarrassment and improperly invading others' privacy. My interest is to show how sex raised what I see in retrospect to have been philosophical problems.

When I was in the first-year sixth form I was seriously in love, with two girls. That may strike some readers as a joke, others as not only improper but impossible. But it was, and is, no joke, for I still love them both. And by that I mean, in part, that each continues to preoccupy my thoughts, each continues to be an object of desire. I am faithful in my fashion, but for me fidelity means constancy rather than exclusiveness. So I satisfy one of the generally accepted tests of being really and truly in love. But the first philosophical question I shall raise here, though it was not the first that occurred in my life, is: is either really a requirement; why should it be? Why should real, true love be both exclusive and permanent? Why shouldn't the feelings in question have more than one focus, and sometimes disappear? Isn't it just romanticism – or puritanism – to insist that either possibility is really an impossibility?

A philosopher of love might make the following reply: if love were neither permanent nor exclusive, someone might be in love with hundreds of others and for no more than five minutes with each. For he or she could have the intense feelings, or some of the intense feelings, that are part of being in love for each of them for a very brief period, and simultaneously. But being in love is not just a matter of having these intense feelings, but of moral concern and commitment. To be in love with someone is to care for him or her, but you do not care for him or her if your concern for the other is transient and fickle.

But of course I do not have to deny this richer account of love to allow that love need not be permanent or exclusive. Perhaps being morally concerned with and for someone *is* part of being in love with him or her, but that does not mean that one cannot be morally concerned with and for more than one other person. It is only in sexual love that exclusiveness is thought to be a requirement. We do, or can, and no doubt should, love all of our children. And when the problem of jealousy arises here, we say that it is they who should not be jealous, not that we should restrict our feelings to one of them. As to falling out of love: the feeling of moral concern for that person may none the less remain, and even if that feeling doesn't remain, no doubt the moral concern should – though of course the one no longer loved may no longer want it.

A difficulty with the view of true love which exercises me is that, like belief in God, it is sometimes assumed to be subject to the will. I remember being struck by the solemn majesty, power and beauty of the burial service, and have later been appalled and angered by the meaningless mish-mash now offered in its stead. I then read the wedding service and was struck by the vows. I have in mind, not the marvellous line, 'and with my body I thee worship', which again has now been omitted or watered down, but the vow to love and to cherish until death. This too is very beautiful and moving, and no doubt expresses how many brides and grooms feel, or how one hopes that they feel. But how can one promise to continue to love someone? It makes *sense* to promise to cherish someone in so far as that involves continuing to look after the person, as long as he or she wishes it. But feelings! – surely all that one can do is to hope (and pray) that they will continue, and do what one can to sustain a situation in which they are most, rather than less, likely so to do?

All this connects up with and takes me back to one of the problems that puzzled me about my love for one of my loves whom – like the other – I shall call 'Margaret'. I loved Margaret. But I tortured myself with the questions: why do I love her, what do I love, whom do I love? These undoubtedly confused but real and obsessive agonisings would often present themselves like this: I love Margaret so much! She is so beautiful! Ah – but then would I not love her if she were not beautiful? Suppose she were – fat! Suppose she did not have, as she did, such – *breasts,* that were such and about which my feelings were such that I could barely utter the word, even to myself under my breath. But this was terrible! I didn't – I couldn't – love *part* of Margaret, I loved her. Indeed, I couldn't love Margaret for anything that might change, for even if it changed, she would still be Margaret and it was she I loved! So it seemed I couldn't give any reason *why* I loved her, without reducing my love, and I couldn't say who or what it was I loved, except that it was Margaret. The object of my love had to be what philosophers call a 'bare particular'!

While these musings may strike one as ridiculous, I think they do express what many have felt, and which have sometimes been expressed in poetry. But they mystified me, seeming both unavoidable and yet simply not true. In some moods, it seemed clear to me that my love for Margaret depended on the most particular and exquisite details of her looks, her movements, her voice, her laugh. Under the pressure of these observations, this realism, as I covertly watched her one day in the library, a solution suddenly burst on me. Of course! If any of these things were different, Margaret would be different, but it is Margaret, this Margaret, my Margaret that I love.

The relief and exultation that this solution gave me must explain why I accepted it, because clearly it is no good at all. For I loved Margaret, and Margaret was a person, and persons change, but when they change they do not become a different person, though if they change greatly in certain ways we will say that they have become a different sort of person. And I still love Margaret, though she has changed.

But a problem remains. We do love persons, and persons change. But we love one individual rather than another. So to begin with, we must love them for what they are. (It is irrelevant in this context for anyone to object that we should love everyone. Most of us do not, and even if we did, the moralist cannot mean that we should sexually love, and be in love, with everyone.) But persons change. We may love them for what they are now, or what or how they were then. So if our love continues, it must also change. Its object, the individual, is the same individual, but the content and nature of, and reasons for, our love must change. Perhaps we don't like to recognise this because it seems to suggest that even – or, rather, *especially* – the truest love suffers a certain inconsistency? Which may explain why we tend to brush aside the question 'Why do I love her?' with an impatient 'I just do.' Perhaps an even deeper and truer source of our unease here is that when we recognise that love which continues must change, we may then suspect that it is irrational that it continues? *Is* this aspect of love, its momentum, which is such an important part of its moral character, irrational? If it is, reason will not destroy it, and there is nothing about which we should be more glad than that we can have such irrational feelings and receive them.

I fell in love with the other Margaret, if not at first sight, then on the first occasion that I noticed her, as she walked into assembly one morning. Her back was so straight, her neck so slender, her head so neat and thoroughbred, her look so demure, and so much else. The problem that arose was not only philosophical but – and much more importantly at first – moral. For as our clandestine relationship developed, I gradually came to recognise and be appalled by the desires I had for her. I was naive and did not know then that anyone else felt the sorts of terrible feelings I felt for her. My problem was: why did I, and how could I, feel as I did? It seemed to me then that even if there were, and perhaps there had to be, some explanation in terms of my seemingly quite ordinary history, or, as seemed more likely, in terms of my peculiar and pathological constitution – I tended to think in terms of some massive and unbalanced hormonal outburst – this would still not give me an understanding of my feelings. They, and this problem, hunted me for years.

Let me try to convey the problem with a fictitious, and so anodyne, example. Suppose that you know a foot fetishist, and wonder what he feels and why he feels as he does. Suppose further what is almost certain to be false or at least doubtful in any real case, that he knows why he feels as he does. He tells us that his father used to kick him when he was a child – and we know (but how?) that had he not done

so, the fetish would have never developed. We might still feel
that we did not understand, and he might feel this too. What
then would give us understanding? What is it that puzzles
us?

I shall examine a philosophical attempt to answer these
questions by considering next a real example. A boy I knew
at Shields Road had gone on to Bristol Grammar School, and
when he was about 14 he took the part of one of Shakespeare's
young heroines in a school play. Until then I had no understanding of homosexuality. I had engaged in homosexual
activities, but even on the occasions that I had chosen to do
so, they had always been for me a substitute for what I really
wanted. (The masculinity of my mates had always been a
barrier to, and substitute for, my true desires. I managed desire
and satisfaction, felt some curiosity, did not feel nauseated or
disgusted – at the time – but often felt most strongly how
ludicrous it all was.) David appeared, as Juliet or Ophelia, I
forget which. He turned and looked at the audience, causing
a commotion amongst it. As he did so, suddenly I understood. Now I could understand how and why some people felt
as they did.

Understanding here is empathy, or its illusion. It is to see
and feel what the other sees and feels, or to appear to do so
and in such a way that no problem remains. One of the most
important functions of literature is to achieve this empathy,
communion and understanding.

But, once again, a difficulty remains. For although the foot
fetishist felt what he felt, and saw what he saw, he did not
therefore understand why he felt as he did. Similarly, I knew
what and how I felt about Margaret but did not understand
why I felt as I did or how I could. I might have been able to tell
others how I felt about her, though of course I could not and
would not have tried to do so. And they might have recognised the feelings, because they had had such feelings
themselves, and yet still have felt that they did not understand. What I am suggesting is that a causal account of what
produces the feelings, a description of how they feel which
conveys or appears to convey how they feel, even experiencing

the feelings themselves, need not stop our being puzzled and worried by them. We may continue to be hunted by the questions 'Why do I feel like this? And how can I feel like this?'

So we may continue to look for a reason for certain feelings and a justification for them, but we may be forced to the view that they simply have no reason or justification. Of course we may continue to be puzzled. This is especially likely to be true if, or so long as we believe that, our feelings are unique or rare. But then perhaps we are back to a causal question, namely: what is it about me and my history that could have produced such feelings? If we learn that they are commonplace, we may not know the answer to the causal question but it may not exercise us. But if our feelings, whether rare or not, strike us as improper, a problem still remains. That will be solved when we are able to see them as not being improper.

In the case of my feelings about Margaret, what happened was that over the years I came to realise, with great relief, that such feelings as mine were not even unusual. I also came to see, or believe, that there was no incongruity between having those feelings and loving her tenderly. (I never wanted to hurt her, at least as part of my sexual desire for her. Of course I sometimes wanted to hurt her in anger, and so on.) I grew to be able to see them indeed as an expression of my intense and tender delight in her; and so did she. So the moral problem they presented disappeared, I found their reason in finding their justification.

But a problem could have remained. For having discovered that my feelings and desires were not rare, having satisfied myself that they were not terrible, not improper, but part of my intense but tender love, they could still have struck me as bizarre, strange, unlikely. Sometimes they do! And then I wonder why my love involves such feelings and desires rather than not, or rather than others that would seem unlikely to puzzle anyone.

The day at the primary schools I attended shared a routine which seldom varied. We started with prayers, either in the classroom or, on Monday mornings, in the Hall where we were also addressed by the head. Up to morning break we did what we called 'sums', until we reached the top class, when we had to learn to call the more demanding and varied activities with numbers 'arithmetic'. After morning break we did 'English', what I have since learned to call 'English language'. Once we had learned to print, and spell, then write, which we accomplished in the lower forms, we embarked on 'comprehension', which involved reading and then writing a précis of a passage, and in the top two classes we learned grammar. After our dinner hour, we returned to the classroom to do some history, or geography, and we often ended with a story. I vividly remembered when I 'jumped' a class into the top class, listening to what seemed an unending series of instalments of the Norse sagas. I would look forward to this pleasure all day.

This regime, which must have varied more than I remember, because some days we did 'PT' and on others played games, reflected, I suppose, a view about the relative difficulty and importance of these different subjects – religion being most important, though not academically difficult. I certainly thought so at the time, thinking that arithmetic was more difficult and more important than English, and English more important and difficult than anything we did in the afternoon, and of course, listening to stories wasn't difficult or important at all. That was just a rest. So that when I went to the grammar school, I was shocked by the way in which each day was different and by the order of subjects in any one day. It seemed almost indecent to have a reading class in the morning, and unreasonably demanding to end a day with a double period of mathematics.

My feelings about the various subjects were also affected by another change: at primary school the form teacher taught all the serious subjects, only art was left to a specialist. At grammar school, every subject had its own teacher. So progress, pleasure and interest in a subject depended very much on who taught it, and explains why I did geography in the sixth form. But more of that later.

I want to return to English and the primary school. When I first started to learn to print, I produced 'mirror' writing. It took me several years, and many tears, to learn to get 's's, 'd's, 'b's, 'p's and other letters, the right (I wrote then 'write'!) way round. Nor could I learn to spell – in fact I still can't spell well. I suppose I would have been diagnosed today as dyslexic, as have two of my children. And when later I did intelligence tests, which involved verbal reasoning, I found it impossible to rearrange jumbled letters into words, or jumbled words into sentences. The result of this incapacity was that although I was near the top of the class in the scholarship year, I was bottom in the intelligence tests, and was lucky that this test was not used until the following year when the eleven-plus was introduced, for selection for grammar school. I affected to think the intelligence tests were silly, though I did not really think so, and my poor performances worried me then and for many years after, so that I had to be persuaded by a psychologists when I was at Oxford that I was sufficiently intelligent to be a successful postgraduate student.

One incident from that earlier period bolstered my pretended view. We did a test which involved translating a coded question and then answering it in the code. The question turned out to be 'Are mice fierce?' All of us who had managed to decode the question wrote, of course, 'No' – except a boy called George. He wrote 'Yes' in code, and when our papers were marked and returned to us, Miss Powell 'went mad' at George. She called him all sorts of names. George defended himself doggedly, bravely, with sweet reasonableness and special knowledge, which drove Miss Powell madder. He told her that he kept mice and they were very fierce, they would attack and sometimes kill and eat each other! They *were* fierce. Miss Powell's reaction was to twist his ear and give him one hundred lines, 'I must not be silly when answering questions.' But as I enjoyed their encounter, George's eloquence gave me pause. Wasn't George right, perhaps? After all, if tigers were as small as mice, would they attack us? But that wouldn't mean that their *temperament* had changed. Conversely, if we were as small as mice, might they not attack us? Miss Powell was not interested in these philosophical speculations and told me and various other young philosophers to be quiet. But

I think George raised a question which the test presumed did not exist, namely just what does it mean to say of a creature that it is fierce?

However, once I had learned to print and spell, I was good at English. I could usually manage the comprehensions, and enjoyed writing stories which the teachers also seemed to enjoy. Difficulties started once again when I encountered grammar. We would be given a passage and told to make lists of the nouns, adjectives and verbs in the passage. We were told that a noun was a word that 'stood for' something, an adjective was a 'describing word' and a verb was a 'doing' word, and so on. The first passage on which I attempted this sorting procedure began, I remember, 'Down the dell marched little men.'[8] What sort of word was 'down'? What about 'marched', and so on? Although I managed to identify most of the verbs, I categorised almost all the words, including the verbs, as both 'nouns' and 'adjectives'. Every word seemed to stand for something! Every word seemed to describe! I simply could not do what almost all the other children could do, and many with great ease. I was mortified, and Miss Powell was again puzzled and worried.

In time, though not in time for the scholarship examination, I learned to do what others had found relatively easy. But again my lack of grip was not just, I think, a manifestation of stupidity. For, given the standard, simple accounts of nouns and adjectives and so on, why were my answers wrong? They undoubtedly were wrong, and since others learned to do what I found so difficult, there undoubtedly are differences between these sorts of words which most learn to recognise. But what exactly are these differences? I was delighted when I started to do philosophy to discover that philosophers were critical of the grammarian's distinctions. Russell wrote that it was a great mistake to think that the noun 'nothing' stood for something, and one which could have disastrous consequences for ontology. (Russell is right here, of course, though not always. If the sentence 'Nothing bothers George' means that George is never bothered, 'nothing' doesn't stand for anything. But if it means, as it may, that the slightest thing bothers George, 'nothing' hyperbolically 'stands for' these irritating trivia. Russell's enquiries led him at one stage to the conclusion that, with the possible exception of 'logically proper names', there are no names in language, despite appearances. But by a name he meant a word whose meaning is what it stands for.)

By now of course I was reading for pleasure, at first mainly 'comics' which were mainly pre-war copies of the *Hotspur, Rover, Adventure* and *Wizard,* or US imports, all of which I 'swapped' with my friends. The English comics then contained minutely-printed serialised yarns, including the marvellous Wilson stories, and very few pictures. The US 'wonder' comics were mainly pictures, and I found them bizarre. There were few books at home but I managed to borrow from a cousin one of the William books and having read it avidly, sought for more. There was no public library in Filton, so, using my paternal grandmother's address, I illegally joined Horfield public library. I entered it with trepidation, found some William books, presented them tentatively at the issue desk and was told to come back in a week when my tickets would be ready. My books would be held for me.

After a week of anticipation, I collected two William books, read them that evening, and returned the next day for more. I had soon read the library's stock of Richmal Crompton's books about William.

That I enjoyed these stories is obvious and of little interest. What is of more significance is that they also made me feel guilty. William was physically brave and effective. He was always ready to fight, and always won his fights. I was terrified of having to fight and invariably lost. The philosophical point of interest is that though I understood very well that these books were fiction, I saw them as both realistic and moral tales. I assumed that some boys were like William, and that in many respects, they should be. I had never believed, as some young children believe, and some philosophers, including Plato, have believed, that literary artists are liars, nor did I believe as some later philosophers believed, that the writer of fiction 'affirmeth not'. I knew the stories were works of the imagination, and that the characters were imaginary, but I believed none the less that the author was writing about real boys, and what she wrote bothered me. I may have been naive about the books in question, but I believe my view about how fiction often does relate to reality is correct and is, of course, general in our culture. Somehow I had absorbed it, and was never led to question it until I became a philosopher, when I came to realise how complex, elusive and varied it is and how difficult it is to give anything like a perspicuous account of its nature.

Writers of fiction can tell the truth – and so of course they can and sometimes do lie – but they can do so in a fuller sense than merely presenting us with a truth which we may or may not recognise. They can tell us truths in the sense of informing us of a truth that is new to us. This may seem unsurprising and unproblematic, if only because it is a common occurrence. The problem is that the work itself not only presents us with a truth, but seems to provide the evidence of the truth *immediately*. By that I mean that we feel it unnecessary or even inappropriate to range beyond and outside the work to check if what the writer is informing us about the real world beyond the book is indeed correct. But surely this is impossible? Surely the kind of learning from fiction must be illusory?

There is much to be said on this issue, but my reading of William books provided me with the problem and one of its solutions. At the time I was reading them, my best friend, Peter, caused me great unhappiness and sorrow. The reason was simply that he was, as we all are, a mixture of good traits and bad. But being young and naive, and so fond of him, I assumed that he was all good, and could not understand why, for example, he was prone to let me down. William gave the answer. For William was, realistically, a mixture of good and bad, though his faults were few and sentimentalised. Reading about him sensitised me to this fact about people, it helped me to think about Peter and understand how he was, and this brought me great relief.

But while I remained a devotee of the William books, I

could never be sophisticated about his sex life, which was so pure! (Though neither was I so intellectually and culturally naive as to imagine, as some philosophers have done, that there was no problem here.) I knew of my own experience that boys, some boys, most of the boys I knew, were not so pure. But I drew the inference here that we must be most unusual and most unusually wicked! In this case what I learned later, from other literature and life, had to undo the lesson learnt from the fiction. But that her young readers might draw such inferences and be thus caused so much unhappiness is scarcely likely to have been a thought that would have occurred to Richmal Crompton – especially as she first wrote for an adult audience. Even if she had known about the sex lives of small boys, which I doubt, the mores of the times in which she wrote would have prevented her writing about them realistic-ally. Today things are a little different, but not so different, I suspect, that stories for children do not still worry them about what life is, or ought to be, like. When we are grown up, we fondly recall the pleasure and instruction we got from reading when we were young. We tend to forget the puzzles, problems, unease and terrors caused by our early reading. Is this because while we may continue to devour reading matter, it can no longer produce such profound, naive responses?

It was – unfortunately – not life but reading more widely that first helped to palliate the sexual guilt induced by reading William. Having grown bored with the children's section of the library I forced myself to cross the invisible barrier to the adult section. Having juvenile tickets I thought I should not be there or that the librarians would think that I should not and I should not be allowed to borrow adult fiction. I was, I read and read, and what I read! A lot of what I searched for and read still filled me with guilt: guilt that I should be so minded, guilt that I aspired to the pleasures hinted at and vaguely depicted in the decorous, second-rate fiction that I read. But now at least I knew that I was not alone, that I and my friends were not unusual. And once I got close to that realisation it struck me suddenly as blindingly obvious, in just the same way as the facts of life had done. Up to a certain point in time it seems impossible that any of the adults you know, and least of all your parents, could do what gleeful, leering friends tell you they do do. Then suddenly you realise that what they say must be and is true.

My interests were not purely sexual, as it were. I read anything that took my fancy, and much did. I ranged over the shelves at random, peering into books, and never bothering with authors. It never struck me that authorship might be a useful guide to further pleasures like those I had previously enjoyed. (I identified the William books by their characteristic appearance and his name, not Crompton's.) So when I was interviewed for a scholarship to a boarding school and was asked, as someone who professed to enjoy reading, which authors I preferred, I could not say, I could not name a single one! Didn't I think authorship important? Surely I thought it important to know if, say, a bike was manufactured by Raleigh rather than some other firm? No, I said stoutly, I judged books by glancing through them. It was an imperfect guide but the best I knew. (I got the scholarship – and spent one unhappy week at the school before running away.)

This burst of reading occurred as I made the move to grammar school. One of its effects was to make the first year of English there even more boring than it would otherwise have been. There must have been other classes that were simply unmemorable, but the one I shall never be able to forget had the boys sitting in class taking it in turns to read aloud paragraphs from *Jock of the Bushveld*. (During this period the girls had a PT lesson which, in fine weather, took place on the school field, just outside the classroom window.) When it was not your turn you were supposed to read silently along with the performers. Unless you were terrified by the prospect of reading aloud in class, and the prospect was growing nearer, this was something no one could do for long. We all looked out of the window some of the time, and were reprimanded for doing so; others often read ahead. In either case, the person often didn't know when it was his turn to start reading and having been reprimanded for that, often did not know where to start, whereupon he was reprimanded for that too. Though *Jock of the Bushveld* seemed poor stuff in comparison with the delights I was used to from Horfield library, I had finished it in a couple of weeks. And when I revealed this to explain my inattention and failures to start reading at the right place on cue, I was reprimanded yet again! The justice of this escaped me then, as did the justification for the class. Only later did I realise that this class was held because there was no specialist English teacher free to take us for this period. I mention these trivia because it was through and actually in this class that I learned the platitude for pedagogues that their first task is to try to capture the interest of their pupils. Only later did I learn how hard it can be to implement the platitude, and that trying to do so can make teachers feel like prostitutes. And given the nature of my present task, and remembering what I wrote earlier about metaphor, I will add that even if prostitutes don't feel as I imagine they do, or should feel, that does not, or need not, prevent my simile – or is it merely a comparison? – conveying how teachers can feel.

English at the grammar school could only improve and the next year it did. We the started to do poetry and drama and read novels with Miss Cook, the head of the English department. Until I was forced to drop English after O levels, these classes gave me more pleasure than all the others, and a different pleasure.

Given that Miss Cook was a sympathetic teacher, which she very much was, this may seem unsurprising and easily explained. For the authors of English literature, whatever other reasons they may have, write with the intention of giving their audiences pleasure, of diverting and delighting them, and we read the best. No wonder it could seem an indulgence to 'study' such works in a classroom. Of course one did not always understand, and one rarely fully understood the work at first, but she helped us to achieve understanding so that we came to enjoy even Shakespeare, and felt pleased and proud of this accomplishment. Moreover, if you did not enjoy what you were studying, Miss Cook was interested to know this and

to discuss with you why you felt as you did. She was also prepared to allow that you could disagree with her and be right.
But this was not the last of the unique pleasures provided by
our study of English literature. For besides all this, the works
themselves and our approach to them made us feel that these
works might not only divert and delight, but instruct. In this
way, it was like reading William – only more so. Among the
many truths we learned were, of course, moral truths, or at
least we learned to make moral judgements, so that the study
of English was not only an enjoyable activity but a serious
one, and we felt this.

Now it may be an illusion to think that one learns moral
lessons from a study of literature, though I do not think it always
is. It has been said that it can only communicate these truths
to those who already have them in their possession. To explain
this point with an example: Jane Austen begins one of her
novels, *Pride and Prejudice*: 'It is a truth universally acknowledged, that a single man in possession of a good fortune
must be in want of a wife.' But it would seem that only those
who already share Jane Austen's morality will appreciate the
irony and the joke. If we concede this point but object that our
moral judgements may undergo transformation while, and as
a result of, reading this or some other work, we may then be
exercised by the question of how it can *properly* do so. For
although life may teach us moral truths, works of the imagination, being that, can at best suggest them. To think they can
do more is like thinking that imaginary experiments are as
effective in teaching us about the world as real ones.

I was not struck by those problems while at school, but I
was excited by the fact that critics could and did disagree with
each other. Beyond literary history and scholarship were there
no more than personal, subjective, critical judgements? Was
the seeming objectivity of critical judgements an illusion created by agreement, which in any case was never complete
and which might dissipate, and often had in the past?

The teaching of English today in schools seems much
more draconian than the teaching I enjoyed, and a lot of the
latest criticism taught in universities eschews appreciation

and moral judgements, perhaps because these are felt to be unscientific and played out. Curiously, much of it is highly moralistic in its own style, and some of it accepts as scientific the writings of Marx and Freud, whose status as scientific writers has been challenged by many philosophers. At any rate, I hugely enjoyed English literature at school, the practice of the sort of criticism I then learned has provided me with many philosophical problems, and I was very sorry to have to give up English on entering the sixth form.

I could not do English in the sixth form because whoever had constructed the timetable had assumed that no pupil would want, or none should be allowed, to do both English and mathematics. The periods for these subjects exactly coincided, so it was impossible to do both. Had there been *one* period of English that I could have attended, Miss Cook would have taught me the rest of the syllabus by myself. It was a marvellously generous offer and not being able to take it up caused me anguish.

I felt that I had to do mathematics in the sixth not only because it had been one of my best subjects, but because of its intellectual appeal. It seemed to me to be absolutely pure, and quite certain. One began with truths that were, or seemed to me to be necessarily and, often, self-evidently true, and derived from them further truths of the same sorts by 'moves', that is, inferences, which shared the same qualities. Besides this, the truths that one could obtain seemed to me then potentially unlimited, and I harboured the thought that perhaps the whole of knowledge could be expressed, explored and discovered by means of mathematics. I had got over my difficulties with the way in which we had been introduced to the calculus, and it was most particularly this part of mathematics which excited my wild belief. I remember in particular the following example: starting with a definition of acceleration as $(d^2s/dt^2) = g$, one could derive, by successive integrations with respect to t, the formulae $(ds/dt) = u + gt$, which gives the distance travelled by a freely-falling body in a given time, t, starting with an initial distance of ut. So, it seemed to be then, that starting with a definition, and by purely formal moves, one could establish how freely-falling bodies *had* to behave. Experimental confirmation of these results were therefore quite superfluous. This was amazing!

I now believe that the whole of knowledge could not possibly be reduced to mathematics but the belief that it can, or that most of it can, has been held by such philosophers as Descartes and Leibniz. However, as I did then cherish the hope that mathematics might be a way of proving every truth, and as I was then good at maths, I could not but choose to continue with it.

Having made that choice, what else should I do in the sixth form? The 'natural', that is, the normal, usual, expected choices would be physics and chemistry, or, possibly, one of those with biology. Science teachers and pupils alike seem to share a view that these were the true, 'hard' subjects, with physics being 'harder' than chemistry and chemistry 'harder' than biology. Everything else was a 'soft' option. We never examined what we meant by 'hard' in this context, possibly because we concurred in our judgements and so felt we understood what we concurred in saying. I think we meant and believed that physics was more intellectually demanding than chemistry, or, at any rate, organic chemistry, and that it was more 'fundamental' than chemistry, that is, that really chemistry could and should be reduced to, and translated into, physics, and that one day this would happen. And of course we held a similar belief about the relation of chemistry to biology. Other subjects were just chat.

But I felt that I could not study any of the sciences in the sixth form, and the reason was that however loath I was to admit it, I found them boring; and finding them boring, I was not particularly good at them. I felt ashamed by my lack of interest and was reluctant to admit it to myself. For I also believed that until mathematics had absorbed and eliminated the other disciplines, physics was a source, along with mathematics, of the most profound and certain truths, and after that came chemistry, until it was eliminated, and then biology. (This sort of view is held by many highly regarded, scientifically –

or scientistically – minded contemporary philosophers, and is especially popular in the United States and Australia.)

Just as I no longer believe that all knowledge can, in principle, be reduced to mathematics, I no longer believe that all the sciences can, in principle, be reduced to physics. Neither do I believe or even half-believe or confusedly suspect that all knowledge, questions and explanations are scientific. For there are questions raised by science which cannot be answered by doing more science, and there are questions which are not raised by science at all.

But given the beliefs I held, or was attracted by, when I was deciding what to do in the sixth form, how *could* I have been bored by science? Doing science was hard work, and my laziness may have played an important role here. But I think another and more interesting factor was that science as we were then taught it did not raise philosophical questions.

This may seem an extraordinary claim to make, for science raises many philosophical questions. Indeed there are philosophers who believe that the central and most important questions in philosophy are raised by science, and if philosophy ceases to be centrally concerned with them, it becomes trivial and attenuated. But we were taught to think of the laws, theories and hypotheses of the sciences as truths to be mastered, and if any were dubious it was not for us tyros to call them in question. Indeed it was not; but it is quite wrong to deny to students of science the thought that even the best established laws could be false and may have to be revised. We were taught, of course, that science would continue to expand, but not that this expansion might undermine what were taught as laws in the classroom.

This attitude was most clearly manifested in the way in which we were taught to view the simple experiments we performed. We were taught to think that there was a 'right' result to be achieved, and we would try to find out what it was so that we could, if necessary, fudge our 'observations', or even our calculations, in order to achieve it. We sometimes joked that our results had 'disproved' some well attested finding, for example, concerning the percentage of weight in iodine crystals that is formed by water, but we thought our jokes feeble. Again, no doubt, they were, but had we been taught not merely to learn but to think and think critically, we should have been encouraged to think about the nature and role of experiments in science. We were not. We were encouraged to think that our experiments either confirmed pre-existing findings or were bad, and that 'real' experiments performed by 'real' scientists had proved the laws of science and disproved hypotheses that had been mistaken.

These views are at best simplistic and according to some philosophers of science are fundamentally wrong. They have argued, for example, that scientific 'laws' are false, or not yet disproved, and none can be shown to be true. Others have argued that even this view is, in a way, over optimistic, because it presupposes, wrongly, that the claims of science are 'objective'. Claims in science are not proved, but neither are they disproved, but abandoned.

Whatever the merits of those philosophical views of science, they have, I believe, helped to bring about a change in the teaching of science in schools. Now pupils are presented with the idea that what they are taught is tentative, is hypothesis, though whether this actually helps them to be critical, and whether criticism is encouraged I am not sure. Teachers feel there is too much to be learned to indulge in critical questioning. At university they have also felt this, and only when the numbers of science students dropped were many of them ready to allow their students to take courses in the philosophy of science.

So, as long as I did science at school, the only time we briefly engaged in philosophical criticism, aside from the episode involving colour, occurred in the fourth form when we were being taught about the relationship between the volume of a gas and its temperature. The experiment conducted by the teacher yielded findings which were plotted on a graph. There emerged a straight line, showing that the relation between the two was simple and linear. Then I noticed that if the line were extended by decreasing the temperature, then the gas would cease to exist! But this was impossible: matter could not be destroyed. (We did not then know that atomic scientists had succeeded in transforming it into energy.) Our teacher was embarrassed. He explained that the temperature was 'absolute zero', the lowest possible temperature at which all molecular movement ceased, it could not in fact be reached, and in any case the line we had drawn, when extended, was not linear. But he was anxious to get on. And when I listened to sixth-form science students discussing their studies, the only 'interesting' question they raised was 'What would happen if an irresistible force met an immovable object?' The solution to this jejune problem, namely, that there cannot be both, which is a simple, logical point, occurred to no one. As to whether either phrase made sense, and, if so, what sense, these questions never occurred to us either. We were naive, and the way in which science was taught encouraged this naivety and the feeling that there was no time for critical speculation, which in any case was trifling and silly.

So what to do? I decided that I would do geography, and that because the person who taught it, though a terrifying disciplinarian, was such a good teacher. He not only got good results, but attracted by fascinating very able pupils, all of whom feared and some of whom loathed him. He also made geography easy, and the only philosophical question its study raised was raised by him. Is geography a single discipline? He was inclined to think both that it was not, because climatology, physical geography, and economic geography were so different; and also that it was, because they were all related. However schematic this view, it seems essentially right.

What should I do for my third subject? It was the school timetable which dictated the answer. It had to be either French or history. I hated history and was no good at French, although its teacher was prepared to take me on. As I also hated French, it had to be history. Perhaps I should say that my philistine reason for not wishing to do French was that I was more interested in saying and understanding interesting things, and not in painfully learning to say and understand very uninteresting things in a difficult medium. My interest was the message. And though I dimly realised that sixth-form

French involved the study of literature, I could not have borne
to do that when I could not study English literature.

My reasons for disliking history are commonplace among
school children. All those facts and dates to be learned, and
our teacher did not succeed in bringing the unfolding narrative
of past events alive. I realised now that he was a very good
historian, who later left for an Oxford fellowship, and he could
not avoid being bored, pained and irritated by his bored, idle
and ignorant pupils.

The first year of sixth form: history was as I expected, but
once into the second, things changed. For having grimly
mastered some basic data, we then began to tackle questions
which encouraged speculation and criticism. Or rather, they did
so for me, but our teacher tended not to think so. He wanted
a clear presentation of the relevant facts, with speculation
relegated to a paragraph at the end of the essay. This clash of
views, and in part of wills, resulted in my getting ordinary
marks for my essays, but I enjoyed struggling with his criticisms. Matters reached a head over an essay entitled, 'Who
was chiefly responsible for the unification of Italy? Was it
Cavour, Garibaldi or Mazzini?' After a week, I approached the
teacher and told him that I could not do the question. 'Why
not?', he asked, 'haven't you read the books?' I had, that was
not my problem. What was? I said that although I felt that
Mazzini had done very little, I could not be sure that his contribution had not been vital. I was raising what might be called
the 'last straw' or the 'Cleopatra's nose' question, namely,
that very small things might be turning points in history, or I
think I was. He was irritated. He told me to go away and simply write down what had happened. After some days I went
back to him. What was my problem now?

What I said, or what I like to think I said, was that I could
not say what had happened unless I knew what would have
happened if what had happened had not happened! This
seems like gibberish and perhaps what I actually said to my
teacher was gibberish; in either case it is not surprising that
he roared at me to get out, and get on with the essay and not
come back until I had done so. Yet I was trying to raise what

is, I think, a valid though very difficult question. For if one
says of Mazzini that he helped to form opinions in London
concerning the unification of Italy, does this not imply that if
he had not spoken and written pamphlets, London opinion
would not have changed as much as it did? If it would have
changed as much as it did even if he had not campaigned,
then surely he did not help to bring that change about? (If I
would have decided to do something without your encouraging
me to make that decision, is it true to say that you helped me
to decide?) Perhaps his oratory and writings changed no one's
opinion? But how could we know? Only if, *per impossibile,*
we could rerun the period again but abstract Mazzini from it.
The fact that we cannot do this means that the techniques
historians use cannot determine the answers to the questions
they raise or determine the truth of the claims they make.

An historian might make two replies. Firstly, the fact, if it is
a fact, that opinion would have changed just as much as it did
even if Mazzini had not been active as he was, does not mean
that it would have changed in the way that it actually did, or,
therefore, that Mazzini did not help to effect this change. (A
decision that would have been made anyway might none the
less have been helped to be made by another's encouragement, and would not have been made *as it was made*
without that encouragement.) Secondly, historians might say
that there are many cases in which the claim that something
different would not have happened unless something else had
happened has so much evidence in its favour, that the belief
that the claim cannot be established without performing the
impossible experiment is absurdly sceptical. These are very
difficult thoughts, I think, and I am sure that I did not fully
have them until many years after the incident at school. But I
almost had them, and should not such thoughts be encouraged in young historians even when they are still at school? I
fear that some professional historians might say that they
should never be encouraged, perhaps because they are
confused, confusing and destructive. And yet when historians
also say that history is an art and final 'objective' history will
never be written, are they not saying that at least some of

history's questions transcend the historian's capacity to give them a definitive, provable answer?

History, geography and mathematics is an unusual combination of subjects to study in the sixth form; at least it was in the early 1950s. But by the beginning of my second year in the sixth, it seemed to me a suitable preparation for reading economics at university. (Economics was not taught at my school.) I had decided to study economics because I thought it a good preparation for a life in politics, and, for the same reason, I decided that I would try to go to the London School of Economics. I knew almost nothing about economics, but believed that it must be a science that could be used to solve social evils. I knew virtually nothing about the London School of Economics, but believed it to be a training ground for young socialists, and I knew very little about politics. I remembered the euphoria of the Labour victory in 1945 and wanted to play a part sustaining the progress to a just society that seemed so much less certain than when I had entered the grammar school. I was ignorant and naive, but I was young, and I still believe in those early ideals, though in the Britain of today I despair of their achievement.

So, largely on my own initiative, I arranged to take the entrance and scholarship examinations for the LSE. My geography master read through my papers and thought my 'personal' style was a great mistake and I would be unsuccessful. This enhanced my surprise and pleasure in being selected for an interview, which involved my travelling to London for the very first time, and added to my joy in being awarded an open scholarship. Having, at about this time, been stripped of my positions as school vice captain and house captain because of my 'going out with' the younger Margaret – such relationships were only tolerated between sixth formers – I felt I had nothing to thank the school for, and refused to do so when my achievement was announced in assembly.

All that I now had to do to embark on my career as a great reforming politician was to get my three A levels. Despite working hard I almost failed to do so. I got my predicted distinction in geography, and just managed to get through in mathematics. History almost proved my ondoing. I had hoped to do well, and believed that my history papers were good, but they were found to be unreadable. The speed at which I had written was my undoing. Ironically, my geography master was on the panel which reviewed such scripts and proved that my papers were not entirely illegible, by reading them! I was given the lowest pass at A level and so was free to go to university, for although I would not receive a county award, my open scholarship would be made up to a state scholarship.

Only on arriving at LSE did I read the economic syllabus – and immediately decided that I could not manage it! If memory serves me rightly, the course seemed to involve lots of subjects that seemed boring and irrelevant. I am amazed and embarrassed in retrospect that I could have been so careless in not checking well before what I would be letting myself in for. Still, I decided I could not do it, and hoped that I could still be a politician or that some other career would prove possible and desirable. But what to do?

Like many would-be philosophers who misunderstand the nature of their interests, I decided on psychology. To my dismay I learned that LSE did not offer a degree in psychology and my scholarship was not transferable to other London colleges that did. So back I went to the handbook, and after hours of desperate search decided that the social anthropology degree offered more interest than any other. The lives of savages would surely be more interesting than local government or social administration.

Again I was in for a surprise. Social anthropologists do not merely give accounts of the lives of primitive peoples. I do not mean that they sometimes study groups in western cultures, though they do, but that besides ethnographic detail they provide a great deal of theorising. I found it all very puzzling. By the time I started to read social anthropology, the once-popular diffusionist theories were regarded as having only historical interest. A diffusionist theory postulates that elements of one culture have spread to it from another, and the most frequently postulated source was Ancient Egypt. The patronising view of such theories was that they were usually faintly dotty but that, in any case, since the cultures involved tended to be pre-literate, there could never be evidence which would decisively confirm or refute a diffusionist hypothesis, which would therefore remain an empty speculation. Hence such theories might have some faint romantic interest but were inherently untestable and therefore unscientific. I thought such theories could be interesting and that evidence for some could be quite impressive and exciting, as Thor Heyerdahl's work illustrated. The main objection seemed to me to be that since there are so many cultures in so many different places which differ enormously, the probability of any theory which claimed that all cultures had disseminated from one place is inherently low. And in any case, even if correct, unless the theory explained every feature of the culture under investigation, it would leave much unexplained.

This point immediately raises the question 'What is it that is to be explained by the social anthropologist, and what form should his or her explanation take?' According to Malinowski's functional theory, the social anthropologist explains institutions in a culture and does so by showing what ends and needs are subserved by the institution. For example, *rites de passage* and marriage ceremonies signal, display and so reinforce the changes that have taken place in their participants' social roles and status. Or again, the institution of 'bride price' is seen as marking, exhibiting and reinforcing the changed social role and the social worth of the bride, and also serves to legitimise and stabilise the marriage. If cows have been given, the bride cannot so easily go home to mother, or her husband so readily leave her or throw her out.

Again, this theory was regarded as somewhat outmoded, though the reasons given seemed elusive. But what they amounted to was roughly this: that the function assigned to an institution is often tautological. *Of course* a marriage ceremony signals that two persons have changed their social status and roles. Alternatively, where the function is not tautologically obvious it is inherently mysterious. If we cannot see, and see pretty immediately, why persons do something in a particular culture, we cannot uncover and demonstrate why they do so. So Malinowski's functionalism is either vapid or untestable.

Once again I found myself demurring. It seemed to me that there were cases in which a functional explanation of Malinowski's sort was both plausible and informative and answered the question which the institution presented. This is true regarding, for example, Cargo cults, and such cases tend to occur whenever a culture is changing in response to outside influences. Moreover it seemed to me that teleological considerations, that is, interest in the end subserved by an institution, had not been eliminated from the theory which was most widely accepted then, namely, Radcliffe-Browne's functionalism.

Radcliffe-Browne's functionalism seemed to me – though I was hazy about it then and still am – a sort of structuralism and cultural holism. Institutions are explained in this theory by showing, not what ends they subserve, but how they hang together to form the web of social relations that constitute a society.

Again, I was dissatisfied. It seemed to me that the claim that institutions interrelate and hang together to form a whole was at one level trivial. Of course this is true at the level of what obtains in a culture. But if there is an implication that the whole culture is an organic whole, namely, one that cannot be changed in one part without changing every part, it is simply false. For example, pre-marital sexual relationships and trial marriages are far more widespread in our culture than they were when I was a student at LSE. But the institution of marriage is as strong and popular as it was then. And if we ask why *that* is so, a non-teleological functionalism will give no answer.

It seemed to me then that ethnographic detail was both interesting and unproblematic. The social anthropologist studies and lives in a society until he or she has established an inwardness with it, a knowledge and understanding akin to that of the native. This he or she writes up in an ethnographic monograph. But beyond that he or she invariably attempts some large, general theory, and I couldn't see what questions were left to be answered by any such theory.

In my confusion and dissatisfaction I did a spoof anthropological 'study' of social anthropology. The problem was: why do social anthropologists produce bizarre theories about the behaviour of their chosen people? The answer I came up with was this: if highly intelligent, educated persons are incarcerated for some four to six of the best years of their lives with a bunch of savages, they are not going to be content with merely giving a descriptive account of the lives of their subjects. They need to invent or discover some large theory that will make their name or justify their sacrifice, and during these years of field work, they have ample opportunity for doing so!

So social anthropology confused and dissatisfied me as did all the other courses I studied, such as criminology, until in my second year I took my first philosophy course. This was a course on ethics given by the young Ernest Gellner. He would not have minded my saying that within a few weeks he had emptied the lecture theatre. (Ernest Gellner died in November 1995.) Apart from myself, the only students who continued to attend his lectures were a pair of twins who were suffering from clinical depression and a girl who was in love with the beautiful young man who talked to us, or more accurately, who discussed with himself, problems in moral philosophy for an hour per week.

I have to confess that I can remember almost nothing of what he actually said, except for some remarks about conscience in the works of Bishop Butler, and the rationale for joining up the dots on a graph with the smoothest curve. But what I do remember is the overwhelming and exhilarating sense of relief and joy with which I listened. Here was a man interested in questions which interested me, and who regarded my questions with respect and interest rather than puzzlement and dismay. So – I was a philosopher!

Now I am tempted to say that once I started to study philosophy and started to become a philosopher, I gradually ceased to be one. What I mean is that once I came to see that certain questions which obsessed me were philosophical, and what this meant, they lost their character of being enigmatic and profound. I do not mean that they struck me as facile or that they ceased to fascinate me; they did not. But I had learned how to tackle them and I ceased to be almost frightened of, paralysed and haunted by them.

Let me see if I can illustrate this claim with an example. When I was at the grammar school, in the sixth form, I was obsessed by the question, 'Who am I?' I knew very well who I was in the ordinary sense, namely, Colin Radford, born on the 27 February 1935, to Boyd Radford and Gladys Radford, née Ford, and so on. And I was not worried that I might have been adopted. So what was my problem? Well, it seemed to me to make perfectly good sense to say that I, like anyone else, might have been born in a different place at a much earlier time, for example, in fifth-century BC Athens. But how could this be possible if I was Colin Radford, born in 1935, and so on? For *had* I been born 2,500 year earlier than I was, all the facts about me which identified me as a certain person would no longer characterise or identify me. In which case, who and what was the I, the real me, that could survive unchanged in such a total change? Who was I and what was I, then? And *did* it make sense to suppose that I could have been born so much earlier? One Margaret listened to my wrestling politely but she was mystified by my questions and my interest in them.

What should I say now? I will say, first, that the way I have characterised the problem is much clearer than the way I could formulate it when it so exercised me. Secondly, what struck me then as an unfathomable mystery, now seems a problem which I should be able to sort out with imagination, critical thought, and if I do not forget that some – pretty basic – scientific facts may need to be invoked and added to the procedures and criteria we usually adopt to establish who a person is. (After all, I had been trying to envisage a sort of science-fiction phantasy.)

So: while it is true in fact of me that I was born at a certain time and place to certain parents, it is clear that these truths are only contingently, accidentally true. For, as is easy to imagine, I might have been born on some other near date, in a different place, or even to a different woman from the one who brought me up, fathered by some man other than her husband. After all, my mother *could* have been given the wrong baby at the maternity hospital! In which case, I, the person writing this, would still be Colin Radford; and what identifies me as Colin Radford is that I am the person known by that name who was brought up by Mr and Mrs Radford in Filton, Bristol, in the 1940s and 1950s, who went to university, and so on, and so on, and who is now engaged in this philosophical speculation. Still, if that mix-up of two infants, which did not take place, *had* taken place and I were now to discover this, I think – if I could believe it – that part of my reaction would be 'I am not the person I thought I was!'

Now suppose, again, that I was not my parents' son, was *not* given to Mrs Radford, by mistake. Then I should have had a different name, home, parents and history. I probably would not now be engaged in philosophical speculation but, perhaps, selling insurance. All would have been different. But then what would have made that person *me*? Well, the baby that grew up to be me would have still grown up to be me, but I should have had a different name, and so on. Indeed, the person who would (probably) have been known as 'Colin Radford', and who would have been brought up by Mr and Mrs Radford, would have been someone else! Fascinating; but these were not the speculations which baffled me.

So, could I have lived 2,500 years ago, in Ancient Greece? Had I lived then, I should certainly have had a different name, different parents, different language, a totally different history, and I should now be dead! In this case surely everything about me *is* different, or would have been different, so how could that person have been me? Surely he could not, and so the supposition that I might have lived in Ancient Greece makes no sense. And yet it *seemed* to make sense! I remind myself that stories can seem to make perfectly good sense, and be highly enjoyable, and yet do not. H. G. Wells's *The*

Time Machine springs to mind and, more pertinently, P. G. Wodehouse's *Laughing Gas.*

But wait! Perhaps my early speculations did make sense. Perhaps when I imagined or speculated that I might have lived in Ancient Greece I imagined a person with a body like mine, with my interests, or some of them, my attitudes, hopes, fears, and so on. And if I now object that this person is not me but simply someone like me in certain respects, the answer is that the imagined person would not in fact be me – for, if he existed, and if he were me, he would have to have survived down to this day – but only someone like me; *that* is enough for the supposition that I might have lived long ago to make sense. I imagine that someone like me lived long ago, and if I imagine that it is me, then to say that it is not me is like saying that when I occur in one of my dreams, it cannot be me because at the time I dreamt that I was riding a horse I was asleep in bed. (What makes the person in my dreams me is that I dream of him as me.) And in the early musings I thought of the imagined person who is like me in certain ways as being me. I did not, or should not, think of some real person who existed long ago and who was like me in certain ways as being me, and if I did, I should be confused.

The need for some medium that will connect me with that ancient person – who never existed – is therefore both impossible and unnecessary. (On completing this I feel a certain professional satisfaction, pleasure, a little excitement – and a tinge of anxiety. Perhaps I haven't got it quite right? I feel that if I were to do it again I should do it somewhat differently and I have to fight the urge to rewrite. But I don't feel as I did at 17, that I was struggling with huge and deep issues and that my thoughts would change my world, if not the world.)

Suddenly, many months later, when I start thinking about this problem yet again, yet a new thought strikes me. Suppose that I had been *conceived* 2,500 years ago in Ancient Greece. Suppose, that is, that the zygote that developed into a foetus and was borne by, and born to, Mrs Radford, had been plucked from the womb of my Ancient Grecian, biological mother, was frozen and thus preserved – we shall have to

imagine creatures with an advanced technology and inscru-
table motives, doing this – which was then implanted in the
womb of the poor, unsuspecting lady who brought me up,
some time in 1934. Then I could have been born, and lived,
in Ancient Greece – and not just someone like me in various
ways, but *me*!

So that early speculation of mind *did* make sense? Yes,
after all, it did. But if that described in the above paragraph
had happened, then though I should have been conceived in
Ancient Greece, I would not have been born and lived there,
and had I been, I should have been dead long before 1953
when I first engaged in this speculation! But couldn't one make
up a coherent story involving death, burial, being revived,
amnesia, regression, and so on, and so on? Maybe, but I shall
desist! (Well, suppose – however unlikely it may be statistically – that a child with exactly my genetic endowment had
been born in Ancient Greece? Then he would have been like
an identical twin, but from different parents. OK – suppose he
were my twin, and I was plucked, and so on? Well, he would
have been my twin, not the person now thinking about this
problem, Colin Radford, and so on.)

Instead, and finally – I hope – I will pursue another matter.
It now seems that I could have been born and lived in Ancient
Greece. But I wasn't. Now given that I was born (just the
once) in 1935, I could not have been born 2,500 years ago, in
Ancient Greece – or anywhere else. We can now see that the
impossibility is not that I couldn't have been born 2,500 years
ago, but that I could not have been born 2,500 years ago *and*
been born when I *was* born. Still, it is also and equally true
that I would not have been born just when I was born and, say,
ten minutes before that! Yet, in the case I tried to envisage it
was the 2,500 years ago that seemed to be the impossibility.
Was that just confusion? Obviously not, but having done some
philosophy in front of you, as it were – actually, of course,
what I have tried to do is to recapture and, as it were, try to
recreate the philosophical thinking I was doing before I typed
this (I cannot 'think' while typing, and you are reading this a

while after I typed it), I will leave further work to you. I play with some of these ideas in Part Three.

Having reached the point in my life in which I embarked on the study of philosophy and becoming a professional philosopher, I can end this autobiography. Because after this point the evidence of what I have thought and felt philosophically is best provided by various things I have written, such as the above, together with a few comments. So in the next part of this book, I have included some articles together with a few explanatory comments, and in the third and final part I have placed other writings.

Notes

1. It was reported in the *Times Higher* (20 September 1995) that Professor Stuart Antiss of the University of San Diego has claimed to have disproved experimentally the explanation of the elongation of El Greco's figures in terms of his suffering from astigmatism. For although experimental subjects fitted out with distorting eyepieces did initially distort their drawings, they rapidly accommodated. This exactly confirms my argument! He is now pursuing the theory that El Greco suffered from a distorted perception of ideal body shapes. Anorexics were equipped with a device whose distorting powers they could alter by pressing a button. They stood in front of a mirror and, when asked to alter their reflection until it represented their true shape, they made the reflection much *fatter* than they really were. (Not an altogether surprising result, one may feel.) So he now wonders if Holbein, whom he says painted shorter, stockier figures – Rubens would surely have been a much better example – and El Greco were suffering from eating disorders. Opposite ones, presumably?

   Martin Kemp, professor in the art history department at St Andrews, said that El Greco's figures could easily be explained in the context of sixteenth-century Spanish art, and that not to contextualise artists is 'deeply problematic'. Very deeply problematic; but this confusion will no doubt continue to run and run.

Like housework, the work of the philosopher is never done.

2. I had exactly this experience, after the removal of a cataract from one eye.

3. '"Beauty is truth, truth beauty", – that is all / Ye know on earth, and all ye need to know' ('Ode on a Grecian Urn')

4. Keats's lines invite construal as metaphorical, and are often thought puzzling and perhaps not the best examples of his art. Their punctuation is a critical crux. I am suggesting that he was making a statement about metaphor, and one which is literally true. More pedantically, he was making four statements in the two lines, and all four are true. Perhaps the implied heaven is fanciful, but this is poetry.

5. It might be pointed out that scientists have introduced a new and better scientific definition of 'blue'. The reply is that in so doing they have also introduced a new concept, i.e. attached a new criterion for applying 'blue', and so attached a new meaning to the word. And even if that could be queried, it remains the case that scientists – like me, but unlike the insects – rely on an exemplar to determine the meaning of 'blue'. So their knowledge of the meaning of their scientific language is as wedded to a knowledge of the world, and hence a knowledge of the truths of certain propositions, as is the layperson's.

6. For a discussion of particularity see the collection compiled by F. R. Leavis (who knew Wittgenstein) entitled *Selections from Scrutiny* (Cambridge University Press, 1968), vol. 1, p. 215.

7. See Part Two: 'Work(s)'.

8. This must be a slightly inaccurate memory of line 55 of Christina Rossetti's poem, 'Goblin Market': 'Down the glen tramp little men'. Either Miss Powell didn't know this or she hadn't read or understood the poem!

PART TWO

WORK(S)

KNOWLEDGE – BY EXAMPLES

INTRODUCTION

'What is knowledge? What is it for someone to have knowledge, to know that something or other is the case?'

This is an ancient philosophical problem, but anyone who finds it rather curious and unclear is right to feel uneasy – and is himself or herself a philosopher. After all, the philosopher who poses these questions must know what 'knowledge', or a foreign-language synonym, means. So he or she will be able to understand statements about whether a person knows something or not. So he has the concept – what then does he lack and want?

What we are seeking, with Socrates, is a true account of this knowledge and understanding. We want – or think that we want – what philosophers have sometimes called 'an analysis of the concept of knowledge', which is just a fancy way of saying that we have asked in a quite general way 'When would it be true to say of someone that that person knew, and why?'

Until quite recently, philosophers simply assumed that a generalised answer could be given to those questions and, since the time of Socrates, they have said 'Knowledge is justified, true belief.' Their somewhat gnomic answers can quickly be explained and defended. Suppose that someone has very good reason – all the reason he might need – for believing something, for example, suppose he has received in his pay packet a month's notice of redundancy with his name on it. Then, unless there are very unusual circumstances, he would be fully justified in believing that he will lose his job in a month's time. Suppose further that he accepts, he believes, that he will lose his job in a month's time? Does he know that he will? Not if he was sent the notice by mistake, that is, not if his belief is false. You can't know, if you are wrong.

Now take a different case. Suppose someone is absolutely certain about something – for example, that the second favourite is going to come second in the second race at the second flat meeting of the season which is taking place at Kempton Park, say, that afternoon. Why is he or she certain? Perhaps he has no reason or evidence for this belief yet is suddenly seized by an overwhelming conviction. Suppose further that the second favourite comes second? Did he know that it would when he backed it for a place to the tune of £150 – all the money he could get his hands on between receiving the intuition and the off? If, despite his intuition, he was just guessing, he didn't know that the second favourite would come second. (But perhaps he wasn't guessing? Possibly not – but how would we establish that he somehow *knew*?) If you believe but are guessing, that is, if your belief is not justified, you don't know. Knowledge is a rational state or condition.

Finally, suppose someone has all the evidence he or she might need to support some view, and that view is correct, for example, that the roses he cultivates in his garden will not bloom where they are in deep, continuous shade. He ought to realise this, because year after year, the roses fail to produce blossoms and gardening manuals warn that roses need sunshine. But somehow, some why, our man does not realise. Perhaps he is stupid? Perhaps he is very cautious and thinks that he has not exhausted all other possible explanations of their failure to bloom? At any rate, he doesn't know that the roses in his garden will not bloom where they are in deep, continuous shade, although he should know this; and he doesn't know this because he doesn't believe it. (Either he believes that his roses will bloom in deep shade, or he has no beliefs on the matter.) Knowledge requires belief and, therefore, guides and informs action.

We can now see why philosophers are not lovers only of wisdom but also of knowledge, and believe it worthy of love. For they have shown it to be a rational, action-guiding state which cannot mislead those who possess it. And this is just because knowledge is justified, true belief – or so most philosophers believed, until 1965 when Edmund Gettier published a short, beautiful article (in the journal, *Analysis*) in which he argued that this traditional analysis of knowledge was too weak, that is, that there could be – and indeed are – cases in which someone has justified, true belief but lacks knowledge. Roughly speaking, these are cases in which the believer's justification is actually irrelevant in bringing about the state of affairs which makes his belief true, so that he is right fortuitously. For example, I might be certain that I shall die of lung cancer because I have smoked eighty Capstan Full Strength every day for the last forty years and am unable to cut down. But unbeknownst to me, my lungs, though impervious to the carcinogenic effect of cigarette smoke, are so constituted that whatever I do or don't do, they will develop carcinomas when I reach 60. At age 50 I hold the justified true belief that I shall develop lung cancer. But unless I know about the curious nature of my lungs, I don't know this, though my justified belief is true.

Gettier's hypothesis was generally accepted and many philosophers embarked on the task of devising a new analysis of knowledge more stringent than the old, which would eliminate Gettier's counter-examples but allow in all true cases of knowledge. They mostly began to search for what are now called 'causal' analyses, that is, accounts in which the source of the true belief is traced causally to the state of affairs which makes the belief true.

In 1966, I published the article below, which does not threaten causal analyses but which appears to be quite the contrary of Gettier's position, though it is not. In this article I argue that neither belief nor justification for belief are necessary for knowledge. That is, I argue that there could be, and there are in fact, cases in which people do not believe something or other, and would not be justified in believing it if they did believe it, and yet they know – even despite the fact that they may believe to be false what they know to be true!

If I and Gettier are both right, what implications does this have for knowledge? It means that it lacks an 'essence', that is, that there is no unique set of features which are possessed by all cases of knowledge and which, if possessed, ensure that the case is one of knowledge.

This is both contrary to the assumption that there is a general answer to the philosophical question 'What is knowledge?' and is counterintuitive. We are disposed to think that wherever we correctly characterise something by means of a general term we are talking about something which possesses some one or more features common and peculiar to all cases to which the term applies in virtue of which it applies. However, Wittgenstein showed, I believe, in his *Philosophical Investigations* (published in 1953, but written many years earlier) that this demand of reason is false, that is, that for many – indeed most – general terms this is not true. Indeed he may have shown that it is never true. It is tempting to think that if language were precise, logical, scientific, it *would* be true. Again Wittgenstein showed that it is not true even in mathematics, and that this ubiquitous feature is not a defect.

But, vulgarly, you may ask 'So what?' What Wittgenstein's discovery means is that if we assume that the essentialist doctrine is true, we may therefore and thereby misunderstand the force, the implications of statements we make, and we may as a result treat as valid or invalid arguments which are invalid or valid.

Not all philosophers have accepted Wittgenstein's view about the meanings of general terms, which forms part of his so-called doctrine of 'family resemblances'. Quite a number of them seemed almost *upset* by 'Knowledge – by examples'. I think this was because they saw it as impugning and demeaning knowledge. One said that if in the unlikely and unwelcome event that my account of knowledge were correct, such a concept should be consigned to the intellectual junkyard and the concept as identified and refined by philosophers should be adopted instead! The article is still attacked.[1]

Example 1

MAN: Look, I *know* I locked the car. Still – I'll go back and make absolutely sure.

WOMAN [*irritated*]: Aren't you sure?

MAN: Well – yes, I *am* sure. I'd bet money on it. Still, I could be mistaken. It's possible, isn't it darling? And this is a tough neighbourhood.

WOMAN: [*surprised*]: Oh!

MAN: Yes. And since it would be disastrous if I hadn't locked it, I might as well go and check. I won't be long . . .

We may safely assume that, providing he has locked his car, the man knows that he has done so, namely, that p. Even so, it is not absolutely clear whether he is sure that he has or has not. (We should need to know more about him and his relationship with the woman to say.)

So what this example suggests is that a person could know that p and yet not be sure that p.[2]

The next example is less equivocal.

Example 2

MR REA [the new librarian]: What did we do with our copies of W. J. Locke's novels, Miss Tercy?

MISS TERCY: Oh! – I'm not absolutely sure. I *think* we may have sold them for pulp.

MR REA: But you're not sure?

MISS TERCY: Well, no, not really, Mr Rea. I *think* we did. It was several years ago – well, I think it was. Shall I just go and . . .

[*She leaves*]

MR REA: ?

MR GEE: Oh, that's what'll have happened. She's got a memory like an elephant.

MR REA: Well, why is she so . . . so . . .?

MR GEE: Anxious? Uncertain? I don't know. Perhaps it's her age

– she isn't sure about anything. But she knows everything about this library. What did she say – they may have been pulped? Well, you may be certain that's what'll have happened to them.

This conversation piece shows that a person may be judged both to know something to be the case, namely, that *p*, and yet not be sure that *p*. For although Miss Tercy's lack of certainty is, perhaps, neurotic and treated as such, it is also treated as real. She really isn't sure. It isn't that she is simply prone to hedge.

 The next example is more ambitious.

Example 3

TOM: Right. You won the noughts and crosses. Now we'll have a quiz: English history.
JEAN: Oh! No! I don't *know* any English history.
TOM: Don't be silly, everyone does. You must have done some at school?
JEAN: They don't teach English history at French Canadian schools.
TOM: Really? Well, this will be educational for you. And it's time I won something. Ready?
JEAN: OK. I'll just guess. Then I'll ask you some questions on French Canadian history!
TOM: Yes. Well: sixpence on the first question, shilling on the second, one and six on the third and so on up to five bob?
JEAN: Why not?
TOM: Right. First question, for sixpence: when did William the Conqueror land in England?
JEAN: [*hesitantly*]: Ten sixty-six.
TOM: There you are!
JEAN: Well, well! Ten sixty-six and all that?
TOM: Yes! Yes – for a shilling: whom did he defeat and kill when he landed?
JEAN: Oh! Oh. [*Pause*] Oh – I don't know.
TOM: It's easy, kids' stuff.
JEAN: I *told* you.

TOM: Harold! Whom had Harold himself defeated just before the battle of Hastings?

JEAN: I'm glad this isn't for real money. [*Pause*] Frederick?

TOM: Frederick? No. Harald Hadraga. That's – ah? – two bob. For another two bob – um? – um? Well – moving on a bit then: when did Henry the Eighth die?

JEAN [*pause*]: He had six wives?

TOM: Yes.

JEAN: Oh, I don't know. [*Pause.*] Fifteen seventy-seven?

TOM: Bad luck! Fifteen *forty*-seven. What about Elizabeth?

JEAN: Oh! Ah . . . Elizabeth. Elizabeth. Tsst! Ooh . . . Mmm . . . Sixteen-oh-three?

TOM: Yes! Now tell me you haven't done any history!

JEAN: No, really.

TOM [*sarcastically*]: That was just a guess, was it?

JEAN: Well, I don't know. Perhaps I picked that up on a Shakespeare course or somewhere. We didn't do all these kings and queens. Anyway – you owe me . . .

TOM: You owe *me* – four bob take away two and six – one and six. For *three* bob, when did James the First die?

JEAN: James the First?

TOM: James Stuart, the Sixth of Scotland and the First of England. The first Stuart. He came after Elizabeth.

JEAN: Oh . . . Ah . . . James the First. So he's sixteen-oh-three to . . . to . . . sixteen-oh-three. Sixteen twenty-five?

TOM: Yes! Look here, you must have done these people!

JEAN: Well, I certainly don't remember. As far as I can tell, I'm just guessing. And don't think you're going to get me to double up or anything like that!

TOM: I wouldn't dream of it; I owe you one and six. Well – this is giving you a chance: Charles the First?

JEAN: When did he get on and off this English throne?

TOM: Yep. He's the next. This is for three and six.

JEAN: Ah . . . the *next*? Charles the First? So that's sixteen . . . What was it, sixteen twenty-five? to . . . [*Pause.*] Sixteen-oh-three, sixteen twenty-five – sixteen forty-nine?

TOM: Well, I –

JEAN: Is that right?

TOM: You wouldn't like to double your stake on that?

JEAN: *Oh* no! Is it right, though?

TOM: Yes. No more clues. Um? [*Thinks.*] Oh! Easy: Victoria. When did she ascend the throne?

JEAN: Ah . . . Victoria? Victoria. Victoria. About eighteen twenty?

TOM: What date?

JEAN: Eighteen twenty.

TOM: Hmm. When did she die?

JEAN: Ah! Ah . . . the Victorian Age. Um . . . Eighteen ninety-eight?

TOM: No. She's eighteen thirty-seven to nineteen-oh-one. You're slipping. All right then. Last question. For five shillings: Edward the Seventh come to the throne in nineteen-oh-one. When did he die?

JEAN [*thinking*]: Nineteen nineteen?

TOM: No. Nineteen ten. That's the last three wrong. Let's see, that's four bob, four and six, five bob, take away five bob - nine and six.

JEAN: Well, there you are. Now do you believe me?

TOM: Well, no. You don't know much, that's true. But besides ten sixty-six, you got all the questions right about the Tudor and Stuart kings - apart from Henry the Eighth.

JEAN [*reflectively*]: Yes.

TOM: And even there you got a kind of near mnemonic miss. You know you must have done them at some time. You couldn't just have been guessing, Jean, could you?

JEAN: No, I don't suppose . . . Yes, you know - come to think of it - I think I remember I *did* once have to learn some dates . . . .

TOM: Ah, yes!

JEAN: Some kings and queens. Perhaps it *was* these. As a punishment I think it was. But I'd quite forgotten about it, really.

TOM: Oh -

JEAN: Yes, I think it *was* these - but *really* -

TOM: No, no, no - I believe you. Freudian forgetting, I expect.

Like the others this is not of course a real-life example, and this time we should consider whether it is possible one, that is, whether it is a conversation that could take place, and, if it could and did, whether its participants would be right in concluding, as they do, that the Jean-figure did know some English history.

Clearly such a conversation might take place, and I shall temporarily assume that the participants' conclusion would be correct if it did. I shall also assume for the sake of simplicity that Jean was sincere in everything he said and that the questions about the Tudor and Stuart monarchs that he got right he would have got right without any prompting, cues, or clues at all. For if we allow this as a possibility, then we should have to say about our hypothetical example that prior to the quiz, or at very least during the quiz but before hearing Tom's comments on each correct answer, Jean *did* know some English history, namely that William landed in 1066, Elizabeth died in 1603, and so on. In particular he knew, for example, the date of James I's death, namely 1625; that is to say; he knew that James I died in 1625, that *p*.

And yet of course, although in this situation Jean knew that *p,* he was not certain, or sure, or confident that *p*. Indeed he was fairly certain that his answer to the question was wrong, that is, that not-*p*, since he believed it to be a pure guess in a situation where only one of many such guesses could be correct.

Moreover, though he was not sure that *p*, Jean would not have had any grounds for being sure – or, at least, as he was not aware of them, that is, of having learned that *p*, and so on – he would not have been justified in being sure, and so on, that this answer was right, namely that *p*, had he been sure. For although he had at some stage learned that *p*, he had quite forgotten that he had done so, and was, indeed, quite sure that he had not. (Of course, when we *are* quite sure about such matters, but cannot remember learning about them, we characteristically infer that, since we are sure, we *must* have learned though we have forgotten doing so. But if Jean were both sure, for example, that James I had died in

1625, and yet sure that he had never learned or heard of or read the date, he would have no right to be sure, no good or adequate reason or justification for being sure that it was 1625 or whatever – unless, for whatever reason, his 'intuitions' about such matters invariably turned out to be right, and he knew this.)

So if example (3) is a possible one it shows that neither being sure that p nor having the right to be sure that p, can be necessary conditions of knowing that p.[3] Indeed, it shows that someone may know that p even though he is *neither* sure that p, and indeed fairly sure that not-p, *nor* justified in being sure, and so on, that p!

This perhaps is surprising. Certainly it contradicts most of what philosophers have had to say about knowledge. Moreover it raises further problems. So, before concluding by discussing a couple of these problems, I want to consider whether and, if so, why, the conclusion that Jean did know some English history is correct.

Since the example is a fabricated one, we may properly assume that the participants are right as to the facts, that is, that they are right in thinking that, for example, James died in 1625, that Jean had learned this at some time, and so on. Given this, then, if the conclusion that Jean knew is one that English speakers who shared this information would generally tend to come to, Jean did indeed know and this conclusion is correct. For, ultimately, whether he 'knows' is a question of what 'know' means, which in turn is very much a matter of when, in what situations, English speakers say or would say that someone knows or does know. Tom's conclusion, which Jean himself finally accepts, namely that Jean did know some English history, did know, for example, the date of James's death, is one, I think, that similarly placed English speakers would make, and is therefore correct.

However, whether we say Jean does or does not know is not simply a matter of appealing to one's intuition and then checking this against the result of some linguistic survey. We can provide reasons for our judgement that he knows – and weigh considerations which seem to tell against it – and this is what Tom and Jean do. After some discussion they agree that:

a.   Jean's answers show that he has – he *must* have – *learned* some English history, namely that which constitutes or, more probably, includes the answers to those questions he got right, which seems to be, almost exclusively, the dates of the Tudor and Stuart monarchs. That is, at some stage he must have learned that James I died in 1625, and so on. He did not get these answers right by sheer fluke or chance (or – a possibility they did not even bother to rule out – as a result of some mysterious intuition).

b.   His answers also show that he has *not forgotten* all the history, all the dates, that he must have learned – even though he *has* forgotten that he has learned it (them). For he produces various correct dates when asked, and does so in such a way and sufficiently often to preclude the possibility that he might simply be guessing and not remembering – even though he is inclined to think that he *is* guessing.

c.   Therefore he *remembers* some history, and hence he knows some history, including, for example, that *p*.

Of course, Jean's knowledge of English history is a poor thing, sparse, uncertain, unwitting, and therefore unimpressive and of little use. But that is not to say that, at the time of the quiz, it is wholly gone, totally forgotten, that is, that it does not exist.

Although the quiz reveals that Jean does know some English history, he does not know any until after Tom has told him that certain of his answers are correct.[4] For example, when asked, Jean knew the date of James I's death, namely that *p*, but he did not know that he knew this. For he did not think that he knew the date of James's death and was indeed quite sure that he did not and that he would therefore have to make a guess at it. Moreover, had he been sure that he knew the date, and yet still sure, as he was, that he had never learned it (and sure that if he *had* ever seen or heard or read it, it had left no 'impression', had not 'registered', and so on), he would certainly have had no right to be sure that he knew the date. But this last point is a complication. Jean was not sure that he knew the date of James's death for he was sure that he did not know it, and, having forgotten that he had learned it, and indeed being quite sure that he had never learned it, he did not have the right to be sure that he knew this date.

But although this conclusion is correct, the account above of why Jean did not know that he knew, for example, that *p*, is incomplete and in such a way as to seem paradoxical. For it appears to reintroduce at the second level (knowing that one knows that *p*) precisely those conditions for knowing which, I have argued, are not necessary conditions for knowing at the first level (knowing that *p*) or at any level at all.

In fact, of course, no paradox is involved here. For to say that being sure and having the right to be sure are not necessary conditions of knowing that . . . is not to say that it is possible to know that ø without satisfying these conditions for any value of 'ø', but only that one can know that ø without satisfying these conditions for at least one value of 'ø' (see note 3).

Even so, the account of why Jean does not know that he knows any English history, including, for example, that *p*, is incomplete, and we can remove the air of paradox by seeing both why we want to say that Jean knows at the first level – even though he is not sure and does not have the right to be sure (that *p*) and that these considerations do not exist or operate at the second level in this particular case.

We conclude that Jean knows some English history, for example, the dates of some of the Tudor and Stuart monarchs, because his answers, though diffident, are *right* sufficiently often and in such a way as to persuade us that he has learned these dates and not simply guessed them, that is, they persuade us that he has learned some history and has remembered some. And, since he remembers some, he knows some, even though he is not sure, and so on. In contrast, had the questions in the quiz been framed slightly differently, 'Do you *know* when . . . (or are you going to have a guess)?', Jean would have consistently and no doubt wearily replied 'No, I don't know. I'll guess. Was it . . . ', *even when he did know the date.*

Of course Jean would talk in this way precisely because he is sure that he has never come into contact with any English history and is, therefore, quite sure that he does not know any. But this does not mean that a man could not know that he knew that . . . unless he was sure that he knew and he had the right to be sure. For let us consider a slightly different case in which a man is not sure that he knows any English history and does not have the right to be sure that he knows any as it is years since he did any history. Despite this, he says at the beginning of a history quiz, quite modestly but firmly, that he *does* know a little history. He is then asked ten questions, and on the four occasions that he does know the date he says, sometimes after a little hesitation, that he does know it and gives the correct date, and when he does not know he says that he does not. I think we should have to say of such a man that he did know a little history, and that he knew that he knew a little history. (We could hardly say of him that he *didn't* know that he knew any history.)

So it is perhaps not merely Jean's not being sure, or his not having the right to be sure, or even his not believing that he has the right to be sure, that he knows the answers to any of the questions that Tom asks him, that debars him from knowing that he knows any English history, or knowing that he knows, for example, that *p*. It is rather that (being quite sure he does *not* know any) he says at the beginning of the quiz that he does not, and would say that he did not know the answer to any particular question in the quiz even when he did. It is because he gets or would get the answers to the 'Do you know . . . ?' questions wrong (and certain of the dates right) that we say that he is not *aware*, does not realise, that is, he does not know, that he knows any history.[5]

Secondly, although at the time of the quiz Jean knew some English history, namely a few dates, before he realised – before he knew – that he knew some, he had no *right* to say that he knew. It would, in some way, have been improper for him to say, for example, that he knew that James I died in 1625, prior to his learning that this was indeed the case, that is, that he knew. That is not to say that different circumstances could not excuse, justify, or even make praiseworthy Jean's saying this, but only that, whatever the circumstances, a prima facie objection remains, that is, to claiming that one knows that *p* when one is not sure that *p* or does not believe that one knows that *p*.

Cohen,[6] who distinguishes statements as acts, statements as the contents of a sub-class of such acts, and propositions (I am unable to make the latter distinction), argues that a man's lack of confidence that *p* does not *eo ipso* render his act of 'making the statement' that he knows that *p* unjustifiable, that is, *morally* unjustifiable (p. 39), which of course is correct. And for him the only question of justifiability that can arise is whether the proposition that is 'uttered' when the statement is made is true or not. But although special circumstances could, for example, make Jean's claiming that he knew that *p* morally justifiable, that is not to say that the prima facie objection would not remain to his doing so or that it would not have to be met and overcome if his action were to be morally justified. It is this prima facie impropriety, which Cohen misses or dismisses and which remains even when what Jean says happens to be true, that I want to explain.

Those who claim that being sure and having the right to be sure are necessary conditions of knowledge can give a clear explanation though, I have argued, an incorrect one. They can say that had Jean claimed that he knew that *p*, what he said would have been improper in that it would have been false. But, on my thesis, had he said this, it would have been true; Jean did not know the date of James I's death, and yet it would none the less have been improper for him to say this. Why?

The answer is of course simply that, although Jean did not know that *p* he did not know that he knew that *p* nor did he believe that he knew. In exactly the same way, Jean would have had no right prima facie to state, assert, claim – or, for that matter, agree, admit, concede, and so on – that p either, since although he did know that p he did not know that he knew nor did he believe that he knew that p (for he was neither sure that p, nor did he have the right, or believe that he had the right, to be sure that p).

This account presupposes that it is prima facie improper for someone to state, and so on, that he knows that p, or that p, or whatever, unless he believes that he does know that what he says is true, and his belief that he knows this is confident, sure, certain, and so on, and, he believes, well grounded or reasonable, and so on. This may be true, but how so? Well:

a. If someone states, and so on, that p, or that he or she knows that p, or whatever, that is, states or concedes, and so on, whatever he does state or concede (without qualification, 'as if it were a fact'), his doing this implies in some way that he believes that what he says is true, that he is confident that this is so, and that he believes that he has the right to be confident that this is so. (For if he is not sure, and so on, he should qualify what he says.) That is, it implies that he at least *believes* that he knows that what he says is true. But Jean did not believe that he knew that p, and so his stating, and so on, that p would have implied something false, and hence would have been prima facie improper in this sense.[7]

b. If someone does not believe that he or she knows that p, this may be because he is not sure that p, or not sure that he has the right to be sure that p, or sure that he does not know that p, or sure that he knows that not-p, and so on. So if a person does not believe that he knows that p, then, *ceteris paribus*, it is not likely that he *does* know that p and entirely problematic (for most values of p) that p. So if he says that he knows that p, what he says is likely to be false either because it is not the case that p or because he does not know that p. Hence, what he says is likely to be improper in this sense. Moreover, and as we have already seen, if a person states, and so on, that he knows that p, or p, or whatever, his doing this implies that he at least believes that he knows that what he says is true. So not only does he say something that may very well be false, his doing this implies that he at least thinks he knows that what he says is true, and this is certainly false. But not only is what is implied by his stating that he knows that *p*, or *p*, or whatever, false, it is something which, more than anything else he could imply by what he does, would tend to suggest to others that what he says is true. (Compare what he does, which is to *state*, and so on, that he knows that *p*, with someone's *guessing* that he, the guesser, knows that *p*. His doing this, namely guessing that he knows that *p*, does not imply that he, the guesser, knows or thinks he knows that what he guesses is true. *Au contraire.* So his guessing would not tend to persuade or suggest instead that the guesser was not at all sure that he knew that *p*.) Thus a person's stating, and so on, that he knows that *p* when he does not believe that he knows this has implications that are themselves false and which suggest to the naive hearer that he may accept as true what may very well be false, namely that the speaker knows that *p*. Such behaviour is intentionally misleading, and, of course, remains so even if, like Jean, the speaker does know that *p*.

I think this does explain how Jean's stating, and so on, that he knew that *p*, when he did not believe this, would have been prima facie improper even though he did know that *p*. The explanation, which has the advantage of allowing that Jean could know without believing that he knew, also has the advantage of offering an account, and precisely the same account, of the precisely similar impropriety of a person's stating, and so on, that *p*, when he or she does not believe that he knows this. Now as in this case the person does not state or claim or assert, and so on, that he *knows* that *p*, the rival explanation has no application here and so cannot possibly explain the impropriety.

'But' it may now be asked 'even if it is true that a person's stating, and so on, that *p* somehow implies that he or she is confident that he knows, and, he believes, properly confident that he knows that p, how does it do this?'

This is not perhaps a question that I ought to try to answer within the confines of this paper, but since it is interesting and difficult, and a problem that the paper leaves me with, I shall very briefly try to say something about it.

It is tempting to say that there is a convention, a linguistic convention, in English and perhaps in other languages too, that one does not state, and so on, that p unless one is confident and, one feels, properly confident that one knows that p. So anyone who breaks this convention says something or, perhaps, does something, that is misleading, and if he breaks it deliberately, then he is being deliberately misleading.

But this sketch of an account, though attractive, is not just inadequate but, I suspect, fundamentally incorrect. For it entails that there could be a language with a convention which allowed one to state, and so on, that p, even though one did not believe that one knew that p, that is, a language in which someone's stating that p did not imply that the speaker at least thought he knew that what he said was true, and hence a language in which, if someone did state that p without believing that he knew that p, his doing so would not be regarded as misleading or prima facie improper.

The difficulty here is that if there were such a language, we could not understand its users' 'stating', 'asserting', 'claiming', 'conceding', and so on, that p, that is, their saying that p without qualification and as if it were a fact, as *that*. We should rather understand it, if we could understand it at all, as their analogue of our saying 'I don't know whether p or not', but this of course is not a way of saying that p.

The reason for this is that stating and so on, that p, that is, saying that something is the case, is essentially something that we do to inform. But we cannot hope or try to intend to inform unless we at least believe that we are ourselves informed, that is, have knowledge. Thus we cannot construe something that a person does as his stating, asserting, and so on, that is, as his saying that something or other is the case, without thinking that either he at least believes he knows what he is talking about and so knows that p, if that is what he says, or he is misleading us and, therefore, his saying that p is at least prima facie improper.

To briefly summarise my negative conclusions: neither believing that p nor, *a fortiori*, being confident, sure, quite sure, or certain that p is a necessary condition of knowing that p.[8] Nor is it a necessary condition of knowing that p that one should have the right to be, or be justified in being, or have adequate grounds for being sure that p. Nor is it necessary condition that one should *believe* that one has the right to be, and so on, sure that p. It is, perhaps, rather that being sure that p, and believing that one has the right to be sure that p, are necessary conditions of *believing* that one knows, and hence of having the prima facie right to say that one knows that p.

Notes

1. This chapter was first published in *Analysis*, 27, 1 (1966).
2. It also suggests that checking up on something does not invariably require or imply doubt on the part of the checker with regard to what he checks up on, nor does it imply or require this to make his action rational. Security procedures at banks, routine daily inspections on aircraft, and so on, show that this is so.
3. That is not to say that one is not characteristically or paradigmatically sure of what one knows. But if being sure is a necessary condition, one cannot know unless one is sure. But see L. J. Cohen's remark, 'Claims to knowledge', *Proceedings of the Aristotelian Society*, Supp. vol. XXXVI (1962), 'if . . . confidence that p is *never* a necessary condition of knowledge that p . . . (p. 46, my italics).
4. Hence a gap can appear between knowing that p and knowing that one knows that p. That it does sometimes appear is suggested by remarks made when the gap closes, cf. 'I didn't know I knew that – you know, that the molecular weight of oxygen was sixteen.' But that it can has been denied for example, by Richard Taylor, 'Knowing what one knows', *Analysis*, 16, 2 (1955), p. 65, and queried for example, by Michael Clark (ibid., *Analysis* (1963), p. 48).

5. But could a person know that he or she knew some history if he were not merely unsure that he did, but pretty sure that he did not? Apparently not. But why not?

6. Cohen, 'Claims to Knowledge'.

7. Of course, what is implied in this kind of way is not always believed by a hearer, nor is it always morally wrong to mislead or to intend to mislead that person. But it is prima facie wrong.

8. The argument of Cohen's book, *An Essay on Belief and Acceptance* (1992) suggests that he would – or should – now say that although Jean knows that, for example, James I died in 1625, Jean does not believe this but *accepts* that this is so. (The book develops this notion of 'acceptance'.) I don't agree with – accept or believe – this latest position either, but Cohen has at last abandoned his earlier view that knowledge entails belief.

At one time belief in 'family resemblances' was held to be obscurantist and unscientific. Ordinary language concepts were not like that or, if they were, ordinary language was defective. These days, scientifically minded philosophers believe that (most) scientific concepts are not definable in terms of necessary and sufficient conditions. They speak instead of 'prototypes' without acknowledging that this notion derives from Wittgenstein's notion of 'family resemblances'. (See above.)

2

LIFE, FLESH AND ANIMATE BEHAVIOUR
A Reappraisal of the Argument
from Analogy

INTRODUCTION

Do robots have thoughts, sensations, feelings, emotions? *Could* they do so if they were made increasingly to look like, feel like and behave like human beings, or if they were constructed in some way or with some material, more like that of human beings?

These have become familiar questions. But since at least the time of Descartes, philosophers have been asking a much stranger question: do *human beings* (other than oneself) have thoughts, sensations, feelings, emotions? (This is the famous problem of 'other minds' referred to in the article which follows.) And *if* they do, or if those who do not suffer from some massive defect of, or trauma to, the brain do, *how do we know this*?

Descartes's answer was that they do (though no animal does) because men have souls. And we know that because God is good and because, in any case, only a creature with a soul can speak intelligently. No mere mechanism could do that.

Other philosophers have been dissatisfied with this answer. Some have sought to show that our knowledge of other minds depends on 'the argument from analogy' (also referred to in the article). The argument is simply that each of us knows that he or she has thoughts, sensations, feelings and emotions and notices how he or she behaves when he or she has them. The individual then notices that others behave very like he or she behaves in similar situations and so infers, by analogy, that others must have thoughts, feelings, and so on, which closely resemble his own or her own.

Many other philosophers, including Descartes himself, found the argument from analogy wanting. Perhaps their main objection is that, being an argument by analogy, it could not really prove anything. Indeed, it assumes the very point in question, namely that when others behave as I do, they have thoughts and feelings, and so on, like mine.

In this chapter I attack more recent philosophers, such as Stephen Prior, who argue that the problem can easily and obviously be solved, and others, like Wittgenstein, who say it does not arise, and yet others who say that the problem is incoherent and so, therefore, are attempts to solve it. (The philosopher's task is to show how it is incoherent and why it therefore cannot arise.) I argue that we do rely on the argument from analogy but try to show that the fact that other human beings are constructed from living flesh and blood – *like ourselves* – plays a crucial role. As for the point that the argument cannot be conclusive – I accept that, and the obvious corollary that no argument could be conclusive.[1]

LIFE, FLESH AND ANIMATE BEHAVIOUR: A REAPPRAISAL OF THE ARGUMENT FROM ANALOGY

The concern of this paper is twofold. I wish to challenge a now widely accepted account of the relationship between behaviour and being sentient. One example of such an account, on which I concentrate, is that of Stephen Prior.[2] The account claims that certain sorts of behaviour are constitutive of sentience, and so, of course, their manifestations are unproblematically indicative of sentience. I argue that unless we believe that a creature manifesting such behaviour is a living creature of flesh and blood, we do not see the behaviour in that way. Why then do we see such behaviour as constitutive and, thus, indicative of sentience when the actor is (we believe) a living creature of flesh and blood? The answer seems to be that, in such cases, we see an analogy between it and ourselves, who are living creatures of flesh and blood, which is missing when the thing manifesting the behaviour is (we believe) made from wire, plastic, silicon chips, and so on. It would seem than that the so-called 'argument from analogy' does play a role in our view of 'other minds'. But this is denied by those who hold that view of the relationship between behaviour and sentience which I examine and find wanting.

Stephen Prior seeks to dispel the problem of 'other minds' and to refute various connected claims and assumptions made by analogists, behaviourists and sceptics. He asserts that we are able to observe 'animate behaviour' in others, giving as examples their pointing, waiting, smiling, frowning, crying, grieving, hoping, intending, jumping for joy, being depressed, writhing in pain, and so on; and so we know that they 'have minds'.[3] He argues that although much animate behaviour, and its description, is 'mentalistic' and not reducible to (descriptions of) physical movements,[4] to think, therefore, that we are unable to literally see and hear it is like thinking that we cannot literally see a glass because we cannot literally see that it will probably shatter under certain typical conditions.[5]

I agree with Prior that we do see others pointing, smiling, and so on, yet I do not think that the problem of 'other minds' is thereby dispelled, or that analogist, behaviourist, or sceptical theses are seriously threatened. Why not?

Prior describes his position as Strawsonian and this is correct, though it derives, of course, from Wittgenstein, especially from §§281-4 of the *Philosophical Investigations*,[6] which I shall examine later. But it is, no doubt inevitably, not only cruder than the original (though, being simpler, it is in some ways clearer), it is also *stronger*, that is, more extreme. For, according to Wittgenstein, seeing that another is in pain, seeing his or her suffering, perhaps seeing him or her *as* suffering, though it does not depend on having an opinion, does involve having an *attitude* towards him or her. 'My attitude towards him is an attitude towards a soul.'[7] He raises the question 'Does this involve a tacit presupposition?' and replies that, if it does, our language game always rests on a tacit presupposition (*PI* p. 178). There is none of this in Prior or Strawson.

Yet in his attempt to dispel the classical problem, Prior, but Wittgenstein too on occasion, conflates matters which can be separated, and when this is done, the problem re-emerges.

Looking first at Prior and his examples of 'animate behaviour'; with the exception of writhing and, possibly, waiting, this is a large but biased sample and so somewhat oddly described. 'Animate behaviour' means the behaviour of a living (sentient) thing. It will include not only 'high-level' behaviour but also a snail's withdrawing its eye-stalk when it is touched.

Do, then, snails have 'minds'? Prior may appropriately say that they do, though of a very different sort from human beings. (They have only feelings, that is, sensations, and of a restricted, esoteric sort, but scarcely thoughts!) This shows that the classical problem can be raised not only in connection with other human beings, but all other putatively sentient creatures. If we tend to exclude other sentient creatures, it is because we wonder about our fellows: are they perhaps *automata*? This was Descartes's question, and possibly this was his question because Descartes believed that animals were automata (because they lacked souls) and so had neither thoughts nor feelings. However, we surely reject Descartes's view of animals.

So a better way of formulating the 'other minds' problem is: what other things besides ourselves do we regard as sentient, and how do we know that they are sentient? Does one indeed *know* this? (Or does this give 'know' a 'metaphysical emphasis' which Wittgenstein came to think it could not bear? (*PI* p. 179). Is it rather that we have that *attitude*, namely, that they are sentient, towards certain other things? Then the question becomes, does this attitude derive solely from how they behave, and is it warranted?

Compare a lower animal, say a snail, and its behaviour with that of one of the 'tortoises' invented and manufactured by W. Grey Walter of the Burden Neurological Institute. (These simple machines had a battery, a motor, a photoelectric cell, so that the machine was 'attracted' to light, and a strong light was placed in its 'nest box'. It also had a 'sensitive' shell so that when it bumped into an obstacle, it would back away.) Anyone who has seen one of these machines will remember how almost irresistible it was to see its movements as a frantic scuttle to the safety of its box. We also regard that feeling as anthropomorphic and vulgar. Yet we see the primitive behaviour of the snail, its shrinking from a probe, quite differently, as sensate. Why?

Compare, in contrast to the snail's behaviour, highly complex 'behaviour' which could be performed – or should we say simulated – by *machines*. Domestic appliances could be constructed that would 'point', 'smile', and 'wait' at a word of command. As it would help to protect their increasingly delicate and expensive machinery, they could easily be made to utter a shriek when struck a firm blow, or even to utter the sound 'It's too hot' when, say, the washing-up water was near boiling. Would we regard this 'behaviour' as 'animate' or sentient? Surely not. But why not? What they actually do is beyond not only that of the snail but higher animals. Perhaps only when General Motors or IBM constructed a machine that behaved – and so, looked and felt (to the touch) – very like a human being, would our attitude start to become uncertain. Or rather, only at that point would a feeling that perhaps these things do have thoughts, feelings, moods, needs, and so on, not be dismissed by philosophers, behavioural psychologists, electronic engineers, and so on, as vulgar. Why is this? Well, haven't we imagined that these machines were constructed from metal, wire, silicon chips and plastic? Now suppose instead that they were, at least in part, the work of biochemists, that is, that they are constructed from flesh, or something closely related, such as a living tissue.

I am, of course, suggesting that our perceiving 'behaviour' as animate, sensate, depends not only – perhaps not even *primarily* – on the physical movements we perceive, which can be duplicated by machines (and some of which are far beyond many animals). It depends rather on our belief that whatever it is that appears to be pointing, shrinking, waiting, smiling, depressed, and so on, is alive, a creature of flesh and blood. *Like ourselves.*

Turning now to Wittgenstein: In *PI* §281 he writes, 'only of a living human being and what resembles (behaves like) a living human being can one say: it has sensations; it sees, is blind; hears; is deaf; is conscious or unconscious.' Presumably, then, a mouse behaves like a living human being; but it is not that failure to make a distinction which presently concerns me. It is rather this: what could we properly say of a *machine* that resembled (behaved like) a human being? Of course, there is at present no machine that does behave very like a human being, and though I can see no reason a priori why such machines could not be constructed, there are philosophical problems here. But I do not need to tackle them (yet, or here). For what could one say of a machine that resembled (behaved like) a mouse?

In *PI* §282, Wittgenstein considers what can be said of inanimate things. After a brief mention of a fairy-tale pot, he considers dolls, and says that the child's use of the concept of pain when playing with dolls is a 'secondary one'. But what exercises us is not a doll, which is inanimate and *does nothing*, but the 'doll' which does something, the robot. 'Inanimate' means lifeless, and if something is lifeless it is, usually, inert. It does nothing. But machines can do things. Some can at least *simulate* low- and high-level animal behaviour. Are they then 'inanimate' or not?

In *PI* §283, Wittgenstein considers the argument from analogy. Does this explain why we have the 'idea' that living things can feel? He does not answer this question, but it is difficult to read §283 without feeling that he is rejecting the argument. Other passages reinforce the view that Wittgenstein is saying that we do not reason or argue here.

He then asks if a stone or plant could feel. But again, these are not the cases which exercise us. Stones are inanimate in all ways. Plants, though living, are apparently not sensate. But suppose they shrieked and writhed? And suppose a machine did? He reiterates the earlier point, 'Only of what behaves like a human being can one say that it has *pains*.'

Again we wish to ask: so what can we say of machines which behave like mice? Surely Wittgenstein is not saying that no machine could behave like an animal? And if he were saying that, could he also be saying that we could *see* this, that is, rather than infer this (despite how it carries on) from our knowledge of its material structure?

In *PI* §§359-60, Wittgenstein addresses himself to a restricted form of the question we wish to ask him, namely 'Could a machine think?' (He does then ask 'Could it be in pain?', but doesn't pursue it.) His answer is: 'No. We only say of a human being and what is like one that it thinks.'

But what does 'what is like one' mean? Does it mean, what behaves like one, or what looks and feels like one, or what is composed of living tissue? Or what? The remarks with which he continues 'We also say it of dolls and no doubt of spirits too', scarcely helps us.

On *PI* p. 178, he finally mentions automata, saying '"I believe that he is not an automaton," just like that, so far makes no sense.' Presumably Wittgenstein means that, in ordinary circumstances, we may believe that someone is in pain, or not be sure *for some specific reason*, but the question whether he is an automaton does not arise. So it is not an opinion, or a conjecture, or a belief that he is not. It is then an *unquestioning attitude*, presumably.

But now we want to ask two further questions. *Why* doesn't the question arise? Is it solely because of the way he behaves? Is Wittgenstein saying that if he were an automaton, this would show itself in its behaviour? (He does say, 'this man always behaves like a human being, and not occcasionally like a machine' (*PI* p. 178.)

But how can Wittgenstein be so sure? In any case, since human behaviour is so rich and complex, it would be the most difficult behaviour to duplicate, but, as we have already seen, the behaviour of lower animals could be much more easily duplicated, and that raises the problem which exercises us (namely, is this sentient?).

Secondly, suppose IBM were to construct robots that stimulated human behaviour. (Let us merely imagine that their machines are sufficiently complex and realistic for us to be unsure sometimes whether the thing in the kitchen or on the other end of the telephone is a fellow human or a machine.) Wouldn't the question which Wittgenstein says does not arise, then arise?

It would seem, then, that a machine's duplicating the behaviour of a sentient creature is not enough to lead us to say that it is sentient. It may duplicate behaviour which is, *qua physical movements*, indistinguishable from 'animate' behaviour, but we do not see it as animate.

If this is right, then the ascription of sentience to something is not solely dependent on its observable behaviour, even when that looks very like, or even just the same as, the behaviour of a living thing. So what is observably (indistinguishable from) animate behaviour is (almost) never regarded as even *indicative* of sentience in machines, even in those capable of high-order or symbolic behaviour. But it is Prior, Strawson and (sometimes) Wittgenstein's view that animate behaviour is *constitutive* of sentience – and of course it is, or, as Wittgenstein puts it, this is our attitude in the case of living creatures.

Can we explain and justify this difference in attitude or, as Wittgenstein seems to think, is raising the question some sort of mistake, and the enterprise doomed to failure?

Now of course, it is almost a tautology that when we do not raise these questions we do not argue here. No doubt we simply take over the prevailing attitude of our fellow human beings. (And that there is a prevailing, unquestioning attitude is not a tautology, but one of those pervasive features of our natural history that tend to go unnoticed. But this feature could change, disappear, and I am convinced it will as robot technology develops. Indeed it is already disappearing, not because of articles like this, but because of the work of computer engineers and such writers as Isaac Asimov.) What seems to inform the attitude, namely, that this is sentient, is the knowledge that this is a living creatures of flesh and blood, *like ourselves*. But this consideration when articulated, as I have now done, is the 'argument' from analogy. And now we can raise the questions that Prior, Strawson and Wittgenstein (in his own way) would try to stop us asking. Is the argument from analogy really superfluous? Is it a good one, or is it parochial? Is it testable? If it is not testable, what then?

At this point Prior might say:

> Look: you may have shown that there is or could be an 'other minds' problem in connection with machines, but I wasn't talking about machines. The question concerns other human beings and, perhaps, other animals. And you haven't shown that there is a problem here. Indeed you concede that in these cases what I called 'animate behaviour' *is* constitutive of having a mind, that is, having feelings, thoughts, moods, intentions, sensations, *et al.*

What I have 'conceded' is that we have that attitude, as Wittgenstein says, but I am asking what can justify it. And Prior does talk about machines; or rather he mentions them, albeit dismissively. In any case, Descartes's question was exactly 'How do I know that others are not automata?', and this is precisely the question that Mill raises in the passage Prior quotes, and which Mill attempts to answer with the argument from analogy.

If someone now says 'But we *know* that other human beings and animals are not automata, but living creatures of flesh and blood, like ourselves!', we can now ask 'But why do we think (*do* we think, *should* we think) that *only* creatures of flesh and blood can think, feel, and so on?' Conversely, we may ask with Wittgenstein (who paradoxically doesn't want us to ask this question) 'What gives us *so much as the idea* that living beings, things, can feel?' (*PI* §283).

What our questions reveal is that the notion of being an automaton is ambiguous; or, rather, it yokes together two ideas, namely, that of being a mechanical and perhaps an electrical construction (at any rate, not being composed of living flesh and blood) and being insensate. And the question is: how do we know that these do go together? (In fact, the notion of a zombie suggests that there are three ideas going together in this area, because the zombie is a creature of flesh and blood; it sees, hears, acts, and so on, and yet it is *dead*!

But let us just assume that this widespread notion of the 'living dead' doesn't make sense.) Similarly, our questions show that the notions of animate behaviour and sentient behaviour are also ambiguous; or better, they yoke together two ideas, namely, that of behaviour which can be observed, that is, physical movements, sounds, and so on; and the thoughts, feelings, sensations, moods, and so on, which they embody or express in living things but not in machines. But how do we *know* when they do go together, apart from in our own *individual* case?

How then *do* we know that machines, that is, constructions of metal, wood, wire, plastic, silicon chips, and so on, are insensate? I imagine that Prior and Strawson would allow that we do know this. So they must allow this question as legitimate, though Wittgenstein might reject it.

It is tempting to think that the answer – and so the question – is an empirical, scientific one. We know that lumps of metal, wire, and so on, are insensate. We can see this. (The sceptic should remain quiet at this point.) When they are arranged into a machine that will perform various operations, nothing has really changed. So when the machine is constructed so that it will simulate, duplicate bits of animal or even human behaviour, still nothing has really changed.

But now suppose IBM constructs that machine that looks, feels and acts very like a human being. Let us suppose that it can 'point', 'wait', 'smile', 'writhe in pain' and 'get depressed'. Now we wouldn't be quite so sure, perhaps. Some would say 'But it is not a creature of flesh and blood!' True, but why is that a *sine qua non* of being sensate? How do we know that? Others would say 'But it is not alive!' Perhaps that is true, but what does it mean, and whatever it means, how do we know that a thing must be 'alive' to feel and have feelings? Perhaps that is parochial. Or it might be said 'It doesn't have a nervous system, and we know that possession of a nervous system is necessary for having thoughts, feelings, and sensations.' But the presence of a nervous system explains *how* something is sensate. And, of course, this machine would presumably have something structurally and functionally analogous to a nervous system, but which is materially different from that of animals and human beings. Why should that make all the difference?

Someone might say 'But although this thing is sensitive, it is sensitive in the way in which a jeweller's floor is sensitive. It doesn't really feel anything, even if it responds to a touch that a human being could not feel!' Perhaps so, but how do we know this? And remember, we are imagining a machine that shrieks, writhes, and so on, when it has inadvertently plunged its hands into the near-boiling washing-up water!

Now someone might produce a version of the 'argument' Wittgenstein considers – and *rejects* in *PI* §284 (and which in fact was mentioned first in a crude form in this section). He or she might say 'This robot is simply more complex than a writhing machine or a jeweller's electrified floor. Feelings, thoughts, sensations cannot come about as a result of a mere increase in complexity!' But, as Wittgenstein replies, could this not be a transition from quantity to quality?

What I am trying to imagine is a machine that massively duplicates, simulates, 'apes', imitates, matches, the most complex sentient behaviour, namely, human behaviour. And what I am suggesting is that even here our 'picture' of the 'inside' of the robot may be a 'blank'. Less metaphysically, I am trying to imagine a machine that behaves very like our-selves, so like that we cannot tell that it is not human without opening it up, and yet which we may still regard as not really having sensations, or feelings, and which, I suspect, we should regard *therefore* as not really having intentions, aspirations, beliefs or thoughts.

If these imaginings make sense, 'physical movements' which are observably indistinguishable from sensate, sentient, intelligent, emotional behaviour are not of and in and by them-selves sufficient for, or constitutive of, sentience, thought and feeling. And if they don't make sense, that doesn't threaten the self-same point when it is made in connection with the 'tortoise,' or the machine mouse or snail. In the absence of flesh and life, we see it all as a sham.

But now someone might say:

Suppose we lived in the twenty-first century, and those robots you tried to envisage were commonplace, as common as, perhaps even more common than, human beings. Imagine they had unions, civil-rights movements, had been received into the Catholic Church. Imagine extraterrestrial beings had turned up, whose basic material was silicon or cellulose! What would – what should – our attitude be then?

Well, our attitude would no doubt be different. Perhaps there wouldn't be one attitude but fierce disagreement. And no matter which attitude we held, or which prevailed, it wouldn't be an unthinking, unphilosophical one. Perhaps moral considerations would weigh heavily with us. We might say 'We have all the *reason* we could have for treating them like ourselves, so let our attitude be that they *are* sentient, and so on.' But it would be an *attitude*.

And now to the other question: how do we know that other creatures like ourselves, that is, human beings and animals, *are* sensate? How do we know this? Why do we think like that? The answer is: because they *are* like ourselves, that is, they not only behave like us – indeed, they may not do so; the paralysed human being does not – but they are living creatures of flesh and blood like us.

I have been arguing, then, that if we see behaviour as sentient, or what Prior calls 'animate', then *eo ipso* we see the actor as sentient, animate; but *that* we see the actor, *or* its 'behaviour' thus is not simply a function of (our observation of) how it behaves, but also of its material composition. And the sceptic asks 'Why should this be so?' The fact that perhaps his or her question cannot be answered does not mean that it is senseless. (Here I may part company from Wittgenstein.) This non-philosophical, unquestioning view of other human beings and animals is not so much a product or expression of knowledge, but an attitude. Here, as so often elsewhere, Wittgenstein's gnomic thought turns out to be largely right, and not what many Wittgensteinians attribute to him, or get from him.

Finally, and in summary: according to Prior, Strawson and countless others, we can observe 'animate' behaviour and animate behaviour is constitutive of animacy or sentience. So the argument from analogy is superfluous, for we have just as much evidence or reason for thinking that other human beings and animals are sentient as we have in our own individual case. Or, better: we don't exactly have *evidence* in our case, but in the case of others we do and it is logically sufficient. The argument from analogy, therefore, is not merely superfluous, having at best an otiose psychological force. It is potentially misleading. This is because if it were not superfluous, this could only be because it treats animate behaviour as merely indicative of sentience. But this is an incorrect, reductive view of animate behaviour which leaves a gap between evidence, that is, itself, and conclusion, that is, that the actor is sensate. So if the argument is not merely a sort of decorative, useless and misleading appendage in philosophy, it must employ a view of behaviour which seeks improperly – and hopelessly, according to Prior[9] – to drive a wedge between the physical movements which (in part) comprise it and what Prior calls its 'mentalistic' character. This cannot be achieved, but if *per impossibile* it could, it would not answer the question it is designed to answer, but leave us in a state of chronic doubt, which is scepticism. Moreover, since behaviourism tries to adopt this view of behaviour, it too is mistaken.

In reply: I agreed that we do treat 'sentient behaviour' as constitutive of sentience in other human beings and animals; in those cases we see it as sentient. However, we treat the physically similar or indistinguishable 'behaviour' of machines as, at most, suggestive or indicative of sentience, and in fact we do not see it as sentient, for we reject the view – if it ever occurs to us – that machines are sentient. And even if a machine massively, virtually totally, duplicated the behaviour of a mouse or a higher animal, even that of a human being, we should at least be *in doubt*. Hence, that something is a living creature of flesh and blood plays a crucial role in determining our view in this matter. So, however difficult it may be to drive a wedge between the physical-movement component of sentient behaviour and its being sentient, this is something we can do, because it is something we do do. Hence, the argument from analogy is not superfluous, or incoherent, and though it is not conclusive, it is what seems to explain that attitudes we have. As for behaviourism, whatever its demerits, its view of behaviour is not incoherent.

As for sceptics, I want to say that they have seen and understood something Wittgenstein saw and many of his followers have blinded themselves to: we are dealing here with *attitudes*, 'seeing as', rather than knowledge. The worst we can say of the sceptic is that his or her questions are *idle*.

But to say this is to say that they cannot be answered; it is not to say that they should not be asked or should be dismissed as empty nonsense. Indeed as – or if – robots develop and proliferate, or if alien beings appear, the question of their sentience may become pressing.[10]

Notes

1. This chapter first appeared in *Philosophical Investigations*, 4, 4 (1981).
2. Stephen Prior, 'Other minds and the argument from analogy', *Philosophical Investigations*, 2, 4 (1979).
3. Ibid., pp. 30–1.
4. Ibid., pp. 26, 28.
5. Ibid., p. 20.
6. Ibid., p. 24.
7. Ludwig Wittgenstein, *Philosophical Investigations*, Blackwell, 1953. References to this work in the text give the section or page number, preceded by the letters *PI*.
8. Ludwig Wittgenstein, *On Certainty*, Blackwell, 1969, §482; see also §§423, 553.
9. Prior, 'Other minds', p. 30.
10. In preparing this chapter I was helped by discussions with my friends Tony Skillen and Chris Boyne.

3

DRIVING TO CALIFORNIA

INTRODUCTION

When philosophers were Ancient Greeks, indeed until towards the end of the nineteenth century, when philosophy became an academic discipline and teaching it a profession, their interest in moral problems was similar to that of any other person's, namely what should I do? Being philosophers, however, they tended to ask this question, not in particular situations, where a practical answer was required, but in a quite general way. Instead of asking whether they should compel their 9-year-old daughter to continue with her piano lessons, or give up, as she wishes to do, or put their aged parent in a nursing home, or allow her to live with them, they were inclined to ask 'What should one do *in general*, that is whenever one is faced with a decision?' And, not surprisingly, they were inclined to assume that there were reasons or considerations which, in all and every situation, ought to determine one's decision. (Aristotle is sometimes an exception to this generalisation, but, perhaps in part for this very reason, some philosophers think that he had no conception and, hence, gave no account of what it is to be *moral*.) Thus Kant thought that, whenever one was confronted with a moral decision – and it is an interesting question if and when one is, one ought always to make a decision in those terms[1] – one should be guided by a single second order principle: so act, that the principle on which you act could be adopted by anyone and everyone.

Kant's moral doctrine, as with so much else of his philosophy, does not carry its meaning on its face. It seems to exclude special pleading, that is, we cannot, or should not, think or act as if we were special, privileged, different from others and merited different treatment; but what else does it exclude? Indeed, would it not allow that each of us could always act on the maxim: put your own interests first, the interests of those you happen to care about next, in an order that corresponds to how much you care about them, and let the rest go hang? It is true that if all of us adopted this as the principle by which we acted, life would be as harsh and selfish as it threatened to become under Mrs Thatcher's aegis. But Kant was adamant, as Adam Smith and Mandeville were not, that human happiness had absolutely nothing to do with morality. Kant was satisfied that he could prove that we should not adopt the maxim, 'Tell lies when it suits you', on the grounds that if we all tried to do this, none of us could succeed. (Because we should *know* that the other was, or could be, trying to misinform us, so he or she could not do so.)

Both before the time of Kant, and after, other philosophers argued that the only consideration which was morally relevant in trying to decide what to do was human happiness. And, of course, because always and only, or, indeed, ever taking into consideration no one's happiness but your own when trying to make a moral decision is clearly wrong, they tended to argue that what mattered was everyone's happiness, and everyone counted as much as, though not more than, everyone else. The best known of these philosophers were the utilitarians, Bentham and John Stuart Mill. Hume, who antedates both them and Kant, had propounded something not dissimilar and it was as much this as the rest of his empirical scepticism which aroused Kant from what he was pleased to call his 'dogmatic slumbers'.

Comment on all or any of this seems almost superfluous. Anyone who is not a philosopher knows, as the philosopher himself must know in his heart, that life ain't that simple. To take the most banal type of example: if I have promised to do something, I have an obligation to do it. But if other conditions supervene, for example, my child is suddenly taken ill, I have other matters to take into consideration which, in this sort of case, would – or should – lead me, however regretfully, to break my promise. But that doesn't mean that the considerations which bear on my decision are all of one sort, or that the correct answer can always be worked out by attending to, and applying, the principles laid down by anyone, not even Jesus Christ himself – who, in any case, thought that there were claims on man which transcended mere moral considerations. Indeed, pondering the reality of actual human dilemmas and choices may lead one, as it does me in the following piece, to query the philosopher's assumption that, in theory anyway, there is always a correct answer to the moral question 'What should I do?', even if we mortals cannot always know what it is.

Once philosophy became a profession, philosophers, not surprisingly, became much shyer about telling the rest of us what we should do. But this shyness has another source, which is an argument of the aforementioned Hume, and which I allude to in 'Driving to California', but which, assuming when I wrote it that I was writing for fellow professionals, I felt no need to spell out. This is the famous is–ought gap. Hume was a convivial, genial, benevolent man who enjoyed himself and his life and who was sufficiently independent, tough-minded and intelligent to think that he should not allow the mores of his day, including those with a religious backing, to dictate his behaviour. We know that this fine scholar, better known in his day as an historian than as a philosopher, loved his study, but also loved backgammon, company and, especially, the company of actresses. This, together with his rumoured religious scepticism, scandalised Johnson and, especially, Boswell.

Hume's philosophical, logical, problem was this: he had his views about how one ought to live, and was sufficiently aware of the differing views of persons who were more powerful than himself, and dictatorial, to keep some of them to himself. He thought he was right, of course. Indeed, if some such concept of being right is abandoned entirely, the whole concept of morality seems to buckle and collapse. But how to *prove* it? Let us assume that we can establish what the facts of some particular situation are. When doing moral philosophy, Hume did make this assumption, though he found it undermined when he was doing epistemology, theory of knowledge, that is, a general account of what we know and how we know it. How now, on that basis, do we establish what we ought to do?

Hume's problem was simple, but devastating. Suppose someone, having made a promise, believes that, no matter what, he or she therefore ought to carry out that promise. In certain, indeed many, circumstances, most of us will disagree. But how to demonstrate this? Our benighted friend and we do not disagree about the facts, for example, he knows that, as a result of going to give the paper he promised to give, he will not be able to be at the bedside of a parent stricken by a heart attack, who would be unable to understand or accept his absence. We do not disagree about what *is* the case but only and rather about what ought to be the case, namely what he should do. How do we get from the facts to the moral conclusion? Since his position is coherent, and it must be because we understand it, an appeal to logic won't help us. Neither, as we have seen, will an appeal to the facts. The only way, it seems, that we can show that he is wrong and we are right is by assuming the very matter which is at issue, namely what he should do and why, given the facts of the case, he should do it.

The result of Hume's celebrated is–ought gap, together with the professionalisation of philosophy, led twentieth-century philosophers to give up telling the rest of us what we should do. They sought instead to give us an account of the *meaning* of moral remarks, which, in the case of the radical empiricists who called themselves 'logical positivists', led them to say that moral utterances were meaningless – because there was no way in which their truth could be established or denied.

Subsequent philosophers, such as the so-called 'prescriptivists', unable to accept this affront to common usage and moral sensibilities, tried to preserve and give an account of moral utterances which allowed them to be meaningful but which ruled out their being true or false, right or wrong.

This, of course, and in its turn, led to a reaction among younger philosophers. They could not believe or accept that philosophy could have nothing to say about what is right and wrong, and why, or accept that such claims could only be made but not argued for, if not actually proved.

'Driving to California' is a reaction to, and a rejection of, what is common to this whole tradition. Read in this light it will not, I hope, seem merely domestic and inconclusive. The considerations which inform, or should inform, our actions are not all of one sort. Many of them are not contested, and, if they were seriously contested, the participants in our real, domestic dramas would lose their grip, not simply on what they should do, but on what they are actually doing, and on what is going on. (For example, kindness is a desirable human trait. Suppose someone, Nietzsche perhaps, were to claim that kindness was not a virtue, but, perhaps, a weakness, and the very best persons were free of it. He or she might be able to explain what he meant in saying this, but I do not think that we would or could see his position as a moral one – rather, if anything, as one denying the claims of morality.) None the less, in those situations, our knowledge of what is going on, why people are acting as they do, whether they could really act differently, and what the outcomes of the various things they might do, is often denied us. We do not need Hume's is–ought gap to show us why we so often are uncertain about what we should do, and yet its existence cannot deny the reality of our certainties and the defining, constitutive role they play in our moral discussions and decisions.[2]

DRIVING TO CALIFORNIA

As in other areas of philosophy, so in moral philosophy, what may be seen as domestic, even trivial, examples can serve to remind us of the actual nature of that aspect of our lives which worries or puzzles us. Unless we have the misfortune to live in interesting times, or have decided to dedicate ourselves to politics or public causes, such problems form the moral stuff of most readers' lives.[3] Now just because they are embedded in our lives, and are familiar, they have – or in the case of philosophical examples, they can be given – great detail, density; and we are able to see how, without that ramifying detail, we do not – cannot – know what we should say about them, or what we should do if we were placed in such a situation. They also serve to remind us that we often lack that necessary information – and may suspect that we could not have it. The small beer that is the staple of our moral lives is cloudy, and perhaps necessarily so. Perhaps then examples which may strike us as picayune can be philosophically valuable? Finally, by way of introduction and apology, domestic moral problems are unheroic and, in consequence, exercising and illuminating in yet another way. If I am mean, and you care about me, my meanness raises moral problems for you, and for others who have to do with me. Indeed, I create a problem for you, even if you do not care for or about me. Your problem is not mine. You (probably) are not at fault. You are not responsible for me or my acts of meanness. Yet I and my behaviour saddle you with problems. An attempt to give an account of such problems is, therefore, a description, however hazy and incomplete, of the web of our relations with others, and hence a portrait of ourselves. What could be more interesting, instructive – and, frequently, humiliating!

Consider, then, the following situation: before arriving in the USA, a family plan a car trip across the Rockies to California, and back. However, after being there a while, and a few day trips by car, the man suddenly realises that the distances are so vast in the USA as compared with England that his 8-year-old daughter would find the projected car journey exhausting rather than enjoyable, and her mother finds the mountain passes terrifying rather than exciting and beautiful. He himself realises that he is somewhat intimidated by the sheer amount of driving the trip would entail, and by the prospect of a breakdown – and their car is not new. He is deeply disappointed because he had so wanted to go. Indeed, he still wants to go, but realising what it would mean for the others, decides that the family car trip to California will have to be abandoned. He realises this, and announces it, during a day trip by car. He feels, and clearly sounds, bitter.

After a silence, he then announces that there is a solution. The child and her mother were hoping to enjoy a ride in an

American railway train. They could go by train! He adds that he, however, feels that he cannot go by train. He had so much wanted to do a drive that he had done some twenty years before, so much wanted to revisit the little towns where he had stopped before, find those seedy motels, etc. And the tedium of being on a train all that time . . . He cannot go by train.

The woman says that, in that case, she and the child will not go, either. But the man's immediate, and vehement, response is to insist that they must! It would be selfish of him to ask them not to go, selfish of him to allow them to not go because he has chosen not to go. So they must go. The woman agrees; and the man goes into a sulk! At least, he seems preoccupied, cool and very distant. The child becomes anxious and confused, the woman unhappy and increasingly desperate. She wonders what she should do. He insists that she and their daughter should go. She has made arrangements with friends at the other end. She had very much wanted to go. Indeed, she and the child would like to go to California and see the woman's friends. But anxious about the man, she delays booking the train tickets and confirming the trip and dates with her friends until she can delay no longer.

So she books the tickets and phones her friends, and when the man learns of this, his sulks, gloom and bitterness get worse! He says that she must make arrangements to get to the railway station, he could not bear to take her and the child. She does so. He says, bitterly, 'You are doing what you want to do. I am not. However badly I am behaving, that, as they say over here, is the bottom line.' The facts that he is paying for the trip, that he has been working while she has done very little paid work while in the USA, that he will continue to work, and be lonely, while she and the child are in California, where he had once briefly lived and worked, and so wanted to revisit, and now may never do so – hang in the air between them. She says, 'This is not what I wanted to do. I wanted us all to go.' The man shrugs and say nothing.

Of course this is an absurd situation, and compared to so many moral problems, it is trivial. But isn't it a not untypical situation, and of a sort which makes people unhappy, and which can lead to greater unhappiness? And is it not, and clearly, very complex?[4] What should we say about it? And what can such a situation teach us, morally and philosophically?

Well, it is clear, even to the two adults involved, that the man is behaving badly. But although, by comparison with most examples discussed in moral philosophy, this one has been described in profuse, embarrassing detail, do we know enough to be able to say more than this? How much more do the participants know? What would they need to know in order to make correct judgements? How could they learn this?

Where to begin? Well, what *did* the man want? Originally, of course, he wanted to go, by car, with his family to California. But perhaps he was more uncertain than he knew about going, because of the age of the car, and the possible consequence of that, and about being away from work so long, and what it would be like in California, staying with her friends? Do we know? Does he? At any rate, when he realised that the journey would terrify the woman and bore and exhaust their daughter, he decided that they should not go. But was he right in thinking that the woman would not have overcome her fears, or have been desensitised to her fear of heights by the journey? Or perhaps he thought only that this was less rather than more likely? Would she have enjoyed the trip? Can we say? Could she say? Perhaps part of her anxiety about the trip was an anxiety about the child – who, at the time that the trip was announced, the woman thought – wrongly as it turned out – was going down with a bout of tonsilitis, to which she was prone. But perhaps the child would have enjoyed the trip, or parts of it? Perhaps she would have enjoyed it, in retrospect? Perhaps she would have learned various things worth learning from the trip, which it would have been good to learn at that time? Who can say? At any rate, the woman and the child endorsed his view that they wouldn't enjoy the trip and agreed that they would not go by car. But, of course, the woman agreed to that decision before she had to deal with, and no doubt before she could guess what would happen as a consequence of that decision. But how well does she know the man? And if she knows him well, what does she know? Does she know what he is like when he is disappointed, or why?

Having ruled out the car trip, what did he want? It is not clear to us or, perhaps, to him. Given his childish and impossible behaviour after the woman had agreed to go without him but with the child to California by train, perhaps what he really wanted was for the woman to say, 'We will not go' or 'We will not go without you.' Of course she did say that and he vehemently insisted that they must. But, without benefit of psychoanalytic theory, we know, and so perhaps did the man, that perhaps he was vehement that they should go by train (without him) precisely because that was *not* what he wanted, but thought that he should not selfishly want them not to go, or, even if he did, his selfish wish should not determine what should happen.

If those were his reasons or motives for insisting on what happened, it is at least ironic that the woman and child could scarcely enjoy the prospect of the train trip, or enjoy its reality, as much as they could – and should – have done. For his unselfish decision, if that is what it was, was self-defeating. If he really were concerned that the woman and child should not be disappointed over the trip, and that they should enjoy it, he should have controlled his disappointment at not doing what he had so looked forward to doing. (Which he *had*, even though we are not sure how great his reservations were about going.) Indeed, we might want to go further and say that if his concern was for them, and it should have been, he should have gone with them by train to California, and done so with good grace. He should have done his best to enjoy it, and if, none the less, he had still felt disappointed, bored, even resentful, he should have controlled the expression of those feelings and behaved as if he were enjoying it.

Perhaps, ideally, this is what the man would have done. And, perhaps, that remains true even if he could not have made himself go by train or, having done so, could not have controlled (the expression of) his boredom and disappointment. In which case – in this case, anyway – 'ought' does not imply 'can'. But before looking at the question of what he could have done, we need first to consider the possible consequences and implications of his doing these things (assuming that he could have done so).

It does not appear to be an illusion that sometimes individuals do succeed in doing, unselfishly, what they very much do not want to do. Suppose, however unlikely it is, that our man had succeeded in doing so. A few months later when he is free of work, the woman plans another long trip by train! Believing, rightly, that each of us has his or her own interests, wishes, and so on, which if not inherently improper, we have some right to pursue, the man . . . does what? (The mere fact that we each do have our own interests, wishes, and so on means that, even if we were perfect, we should still make others less happy, sometimes, than they would be if we were – not better, but – different.) Does he say he doesn't want to go, and manufacture reasons? Does he tell the truth, and risk spoiling the woman's fond memories of the family trip by train to California? Unless he does so, won't his life, increasingly, become a guilty secret which separates them? (Perhaps it is not, then, so surprising that very quiet people, who are said by their friends and families to have had, apparently, no reason for doing so, sometimes just walk out of their lives?) So even when we do succeed in making ourselves do what we believe to be the right thing, and which – in that context – may very well be the right thing, our act of domestic heroism may set up moral problems which we would have avoided if we had not behaved so well! Surely, this *is* true, even if our recognising it adds to our uncertainties about what we should do, and invites abuse.

The above is just a specimen of the possible implications of acting very well; how about the possible consequences, which in the paragraph above, I relegated to a bracketed parenthesis? However reluctant, cautious and uncertain we may and should be in allowing this, is it not true that sometimes we just cannot go on behaving well, and that our having acted well, and our attempts to go on doing so, can suddenly break down, with consequences which vary from the amusing to the appalling? In at least some such cases, then, perhaps it would have been better if a person had not struggled with a difficult situation, or against a weakness of character, or not struggled for so long? But in how many situations is it clear that the person would have done better to have given up the struggle earlier? Still, just because it is not clear, and because it may be both tempting and self-serving for an individual to declare that it would be – or would have been – better to give up the struggle sooner, does not mean that that judgement is not correct. Perhaps we are only confident when the struggler's final collapse issues in something dreadful?

But notice the ambiguity of talking at one time of 'giving up the struggle' and at others of 'breaking down'. In any particular situation, which is correct? And how do we know? And *what is it* that we know – what is it that we could point to or describe – when we know that we literally could not, were 'physically unable to', as we sometimes graphically say, to – say – keep the feelings and thoughts that we cannot control unexpressed any longer?

So, could he have suppressed, if not his feelings of disappointment, their nasty expression? It is very tempting, and no doubt correct, to say that he could have done so. After all, he should have done. But does that imply or presuppose that he could? Logically – which is to say, vacuously – he could have done so. But if there is a question here, it is: could, in fact, this man in that situation have done so? Impatient with what may appear to be merely special pleading, or a typically misplaced philosophical ingenuity, we may say, 'Look! Controlling one's disappointment is something we learn to do while still children. If he hasn't learned to do so, he should have done!' Again, this may well be true, but it doesn't answer our question, exactly. However, it is a more interesting remark than may strike us, or the speaker. For it appears to suggest that even if the man could not control his pique, he should not have allowed himself to become, or go on being, that kind of person. But could he help *that*? Sometimes such a question is merely sceptical. The drunk could not help driving into your car, but he shouldn't have got drunk and driven. And if he cannot help getting drunk, or couldn't help getting drunk when he did, he shouldn't have driven then, or ever, and that is something which he *can* and should avoid doing. But (how) could we apply such homilies to this case?

I think – without special pleading, as it were – that we could add to our description of the man in such a way that we might then allow that, perhaps, he could not help his sulking, and so on, and not simply condemn him for being such a person. Some people, and perhaps he, remain childlike in the intensity of their desires. (Yeats observed and regretted that 'the heart grows old'. For some artists, Picasso, Thomas Hardy, Dumas *père*, and others, it does not.) Suppose we know of him that he does want the things he wants with not so much a childlike but adolescent passion and, we agree, that makes him a vivid, though stormy and exhausting companion? Then perhaps he cannot help those outbursts, which (later) we may forgive him. Of course, in any particular, and real, case, we may still not know if the person could help himself, or even be able to imagine in those cases what it would be like to know. And yet we may still feel in some such situations that perhaps the person could not help himself.

But his refusing to take them to the railway station! That was – spiteful. Yes – but only that? And are those who are spiteful, or those who occasionally act out of spite, always in control of the expression of their feelings? Are they always when the spiteful deed is a remark, followed by an immediate apology, and contrition? 'The words were out of . . . I could bite off my tongue. I didn't *mean* that! I mean, I don't really feel like that', and so on. Of course these defences are not available to our man, and it would seem that any that might be could not lead us to withdraw our saying, and roundly, that he acted spitefully. And more light might be harsher.

But among all these uncertainties, one thing appears clear. Even if an individual cannot help being, say self-centred, cannot help acting in that way on some occasion, he or she *is* none the less self-centred, *did* act in that way on that occasion. The platitude shows that (many of) our judgements of a person's character, and our characterisations of particular actions, do not wait upon our knowing if he could help it or them! So a great deal of our moral thought and talk simply *bypasses* questions about freedom of the will and (metaphysical) responsibility.

Of course, that is not to say that it should, or that if our knowledge of the determinants of human behaviour continues to grow, it will continue to be able to do so. Even as it is, the platitude leads to what at least sounds like a paradox, namely, that a person's fault may not be his or her fault. If we respond by saying that the paradox merely depends on the ellipsis – it says no more than that, for example, unreliable persons may be so constituted that they cannot help being unreliable – if their not being able to help it is irrelevant to that judgement as a moral judgement of their character, what differentiates it from verbally identical judgements made about, say, a dog, or, even, a clock? Intentions? But persons don't intend to be unreliable – and, if they do, they are not (just) unreliable. Knowledge, perhaps? – with the hasty proviso that if someone doesn't realise that he is unreliable, he or she should? No doubt – but if a person can't help being unreliable? Some of our talk suggests the following metaphor: we are dealt a hand of physical, intellectual, and emotional traits, and our life task is to play them as best we can, or as we choose. Leaving aside the difficulties that some of the cards are not (wholly) visible, and, even when they are, their value is uncertain or must be decided by the player, who – what – is the player? An impatience with this problem, however natural it is to us when we are engaged in the business of our lives, doesn't condemn it and won't make it go away. In some future, the problem may be the desperate wish to hang on to some aspect, shred or indeed, shard, of responsibility and individuality, or uniqueness.

Much of the preceding discussion is predicated on a view of what happened, which is in large part a view of why it happened, and which is the man's view. (Briefly: he wanted to go by car with his family, and would have done, had he not realised that they wouldn't be able to enjoy it. They would enjoy going by train, though he would not, indeed, perhaps, could not, or could not with grace. So he decided that he must insist that they go by themselves – and then spoilt this solution with disappointment and resentment.) This view is not necessarily correct, of course. But was it, in fact, correct – in particular, was it, in crucial matters, complete? We allow that people can be mistaken about their motives and intentions. Indeed, even philosophers who are, understandably, puzzled by the coherence of the notion of self-deception, often feel compelled to allow that the phenomenon may occur. Perhaps it did in this case? Could we say? How?

One silent evening, shortly before she left for California, the woman dropped a remark which suggested that she did not accept the view – or, even, perhaps, the kind of view – offered by the man. Apropos of nothing she said, 'I feel that I am being punished.' What did she mean? The man asked her, but she was unable, or unwilling to say. Anyway, she would not reply. During her absence, he pondered her gnomic remark. What had she meant? Among myriad possibilities, he decided that, whatever else, she must have meant that (she felt as if) he blamed her for giving up the car trip, resented that, and that she and the child were going by train, and so on, and that his subsequent behaviour was not merely an uncontrolled – much less, an uncontrollable – expression of disappointment and resentment, but was *meant* to make her unhappy? *Had* he intended to so upset her? He quickly, though reluctantly, came to the conclusion that he had. Did he *blame* her? He remembered one of his soliloquies in which he had said that *he* had once been scared of heights, still was, but after he had had to find several hundred pounds to have a roof mended, or do it himself, had learned to control his fear, and so on. Oh! God! She was right!

This chain of thought is persuasive, and (we shall assume) his remorse is genuine. But does that mean that the revised account is (more) correct? Does it *make* it right? But how could it? Couldn't plausibility and regret produce conviction and remorse, but inappropriately? Surely. Is there, then, a way – are there ways – of finding out what is the truth in situations like this, and how do we establish their provenance?

If we cannot answer these questions is truth a chimera here? Perhaps sometimes we just, say, behave badly, or even nastily, in a situation and, properly and naturally exercised by our having done so, we make up stories afterwards about our motives and reasons that are inappropriately detailed – and compelling!

Is this mere philosophical scepticism? If so, it is not uncommon among the laity, who will say to those engaged in such recrimination and speculation to forget it! It won't help! And not just because it won't change anything, and distracts us from our present concerns, but because it won't establish anything, either. And if, as I have been arguing, it is rather a matter of misplaced confidence, why is that confidence not uncommon?

First, as we *do* know as a result of recent scientific work, where there is a question, human beings will find, in that they will make up, an answer, and do so with great confidence.[5] Secondly, confidence in such matters has been offered by depth psychology and, not surprisingly, in the light of the previous observation, the devotees of its various forms have eagerly accepted their often competing assertions.[6] Thirdly, there is the unthinking use of literary examples in moral philosophy. Now part of what I have been trying to demonstrate in this chapter is that moral philosophy needs detailed examples and, of course, literature can provide us with wonderfully extended and detailed stories, presented with power, finesse and beauty. But when the writer presents us with his or her authoritative descriptions of why a fictional character did what he or she did, we cannot assume that our attempts to give such accounts of real individuals, even ourselves, can be so authoritative. Bethinking oneself is not purely, or even primarily, an imaginative exercise, even though its results may be. To my knowledge, this difficulty has not been noticed by those who deployed this technique.

But does this mean that philosophical examples must be real? Is ours real? That is not the point. The point is that most of our lives and, hence, much of our moral lives is composed of a series of interlocking, complex situations, which ramify.

And we stand to them as one of the participants, one of the spectators, indeed, as one of the historians of these events, concerned not only with what led up to this, and what happened, and what is going to happen as a result, but also with what would have happened if we, or someone else, had been or done differently. Only to a very little extent are we the sovereign – and, to an even lesser extent – omniscient authors of our lives.

Let us return, briefly, to our example, and this time try to concentrate on the – perhaps, understandably – more shadowy figure of the woman. We could ask if she could have been less panicked by the mountain passes she was driven over on those early day trips. Could she have done more to conceal her panic, when the other two were so clearly enjoying their excitement? Yet don't we now feel that these questions are pointless, theoretically and practically? The practical question is how she will behave in the future, and time will tell. Of course, if she goes on being as panic stricken as she was, we – and she – won't *know* if she could try, or could have tried, harder to master her fear. Those concerned with her would, therefore, do well to forget it, and concentrate on how to organise their lives, given that she is thus frightened.[7]

What did *she* want? After the incident was over she said, 'I wanted what I always want. I wanted us to be *happy*. That's why I wish we had gone as we arranged, or all stayed at home.' But she would have been terrified a lot of the time? 'Yes, and I would have preferred that. I would have been much happier than I was!' Why didn't she insist on that at the time? '*Insist*! Look, you were doing all the insisting. And you were so angry! In any case, I thought you *wanted* us to go by train!' But when she realised, as she must have, that that was not all that the man wanted – what then?

At this point, the woman became uncertain and impatient, and the man suggested that that, perhaps, was because he was (then) being impossible – insisting that she and their child go by train and yet not wanting them to go? Possibly. So she is a utilitarian, but not one who is distressed (sufficiently) by not insisting on her equal right to decide what should be done? Isn't that supine? Victorian? What would the feminists say?

'I am not a feminist,' said the woman. 'And I hate these discussions. They always end with me in the wrong!' 'That's not what I intend', said the man. The woman looked sceptical, and sighed. The man said, pleadingly, 'Look. Let's try to learn *something* from what has happened. Supposing something like this happens again?' 'I've already answered that one. Let's do what *you* want to do. What you *really* want to do. Not what you think you *ought* to want to do, or what *ought* to be done, or what *we* should do!' 'That's terrible!' 'Don't be so dramatic. It's not *terrible*. It's just the ways things are. It's only *terrible* when you start getting on your moral high horse. And start falling off.' 'But what you're saying is, there's one set of rules for me, and another for you!' 'Hadn't you noticed?' 'But –.' 'People *differ*. It's as if you think they should all be the same – or could be. But, really, you know they're not. And would you really want them to be?' They looked at each other.

There were many more questions that the man wanted to discuss, but he felt that he had pressed and pestered the woman enough. Instead, they went for a long walk and, feeling happier with each other, went to bed. Afterwards, the man thought that they had *solved* nothing, but now the problems seemed theoretical. Indeed, it seemed to him that philosophy seemed of less and less help in *solving* moral problems, the more one looked at the particular case, and the more one allowed that individuals are opaque, imperfect, different, and that we relish and value, and don't merely – and uselessly – regret some of those differences, even when they are imperfections. Platitudes all, of course. But had moral philosophy properly acknowledged them? He wondered if he should try to write something about all this.

When philosophers in our Graeco-Christian, analytic tradition think about morals, they think of morality as something which requires us to be perfect – while readily acknowledging that we are not. We are then left with the requirement that we should strive, however hopelessly, for perfection. But even when we think we know what that means, is that always good advice? This morality supposes that we are omniscient, or merely that we have knowledge, when, so often, we do not. Indeed, parts of our lives seem impenetrable, at least when looked at in the terms we presently look at them. (And if we had such knowledge, whatever it could be, might the very thing which now puzzles us not disappear?) The difficulty of achieving moral knowledge does not merely depend on the putative 'is–ought' gap. Philosophical morality also presupposes, requires, that, as subjects of moral judgements, we be free, and perhaps it should. Yet when we make such judgements, we are often not concerned with this metaphysical question, and if we were, we should be at even greater loss than we are. It tends to look at large, and rather simple – though often terrible – moral dilemmas and at isolated individuals as they are confronted by them. But most of our problems are not like that. It speaks of the universality of moral judgements, but which of the differences between us are relevant and allowable?

Our lives are seldom heroic, though we are flawed. Our domestic tragedies rarely depend on our having to choose one right rather than another. More often we are trying to choose between lesser evils, while not knowing which is less than the others. But small, cloudy beer? More, perhaps, a wine-dark, stormy, unfathomable and largely uncharted sea?

Notes

1. Apparently, Churchill knew in advance exactly when Coventry was to be bombed during World War II. He decided not to warn the citizens of Coventry because doing so would reveal that the British had cracked the 'Enigma' codes. Presented with a moral dilemma, he resolved it in political strategic terms.
2. This chapter was first published in *Philosophical Investigations*, 12, 4 (1989).
3. Perhaps they should not? J. S. Mill tells, us, in chapter 2 of *Utilitarianism* that for most of us, and for all of us in most situations, 'the interest or happiness of some few persons, is all

he has to attend to'. But should we not take a larger view, some-times? And should we not take up larger issues, sometimes? When politicians talk of the obligation to serve, an affirmative to the second question is their rationale.

4. In comparison, Antigone's problem, though terrible and insol-uble, seems simple!

5. See James L. Gould, *Ethology*, Norton, 1982, pp. 492–6.

6. Such confidence, often combined with a similar confidence in Marxist thought, is conspicious in much recent, theoretical, lit-erary criticism.

7. Isn't the woman's fear of heights pathological, and irrational? Possibly so. It's not normal, common. But even if it is irrational, given that pathology, she is not irrational in trying to avoid sit-uations which will terrify her.

4

ON THE POSITIVE DESIRABILITY OF EVIL

INTRODUCTION

In 'Driving to California' I was primarily, though obliquely, attacking what (many) other philosophers have said about morality. In this short piece, I am primarily concerned to examine a question which rarely occurs to them or, indeed, to any individual who is involved in some particular situation, trying to decide what he or she should do and then trying to do it. How would it be if we all always knew what morally we should do, and always did it?

Have you ever wondered what heaven, if there is or were a heaven, would be like? If you have, as I'm sure you have, did you think, guiltily no doubt, and like Huck Finn, that from what little you had heard or read, it all sounded a bit, well, uninviting, *samey*?[1] Did you learn to dismiss this thought by saying to yourself or being told very firmly, that heaven was not some ideal or idealised version of life on earth, but the bliss, ecstasy, perfection of being at one with God? – And of course this is not something that we can comprehend.

If you found this unsatisfying, did Marx's material account of heaven, that is, socialism, seem more satisfying? Socialism, you will remember, is achieved when all socio-economic injustices have been eliminated and when, therefore, the state, with all its power to coerce, penalise or even organise the lives of human beings, has withered away.

But what would it be like to live in such a world? Marx disappointingly, but not surprisingly, has little to say. Certainly he promises us activity and diversity of activity, but his vision, in which we shall all be able to go hunting, shooting or fishing most afternoons, will strike many of us as risible, others as offensive.

This problem is closely related to the one discussed in the short piece that follows. Can we imagine living in a morally perfect world, and, in so far as we can do this, would we – should we – desire to live in one? Would it indeed be a *moral* world? Without being able to give a definite answer to the last question, I agree that in so far as we can imagine a morally perfect world, we wouldn't want to live in one, and – in some sense of 'shouldn't' – we shouldn't want to do so either.

Some decent souls may be shocked by what appears to be a plea for, and defence of, evil. It is; and I am not so much shocked as puzzled by this. Others will say that since I am not arguing for more wickedness or evil in the world, since I clearly think it would be entirely comprehensible and desirable that there should be a lot less of it, and since there is no conceivable or at any rate foreseeable time in which a future human world is even going to approximate to being morally perfect, my problem is totally unrealistic, and, in that way, quite uninteresting – and typically philosophical.

But this robust view doesn't deal with the real problem which is revealed by considering the unreal possibility. For this seems to show, or at any rate suggest, that we *need* the wrongdoer. Without him or her our lives would be much less, perhaps not even moral, and much less worth living. And this remains true even in our world with its excess of evil.

This seems to give a new and unwelcome slant on Christ's teaching that we should love the sinner. What has struck some as a piety now looks like an impropriety, yet an unavoidable one. If the wrongdoer ever were to become an endangered species – which of course I agree won't happen – the rest of us would and should cherish its members. Not because we loved them, though I think we sometimes genuinely do love the rogue, and not despite, but because of his or her naughtiness (naughtiness used to be a much more serious thing than it has become, and, needing this word, I hark back to that sense), but because the existence of wrongdoing not only guarantees that both we and the wrongdoer can act well but ensures that our lives are rich, diverse, challenging, puzzling, anguished, worth living.

Heaven would be hell.

ON THE POSITIVE DESIRABILITY OF EVIL

Motor racing of whatever sort is a dangerous sport. So those responsible for administering it try, if they are acting responsibly, to reduce its risks to participants (and spectators, though their needs can clash). But do they try to eliminate every danger, all accidents and hence all risk of pain, disfigurement, death, and what stems from them?

Surely they and we do not. First, because we cannot imagine how we could completely eliminate risks. Secondly, because when we do try to imagine a version of motor racing that more and more approximates to being risk free, it becomes increasingly unlike the activity which attracts its supporters. Thirdly, most importantly and also most problematically, those who love this sport – and indeed, any lover of any sport which involves risks – would feel that without danger the sport would be a mere game, a charade, meaningless. Without the possibility of crashes, drivers would be under no constraint – except perhaps to decide tactical matters such as when to change tyres, refuel, nurse the engine, and so on. (And since these decisions could be made more scientifically by the pits, allowing drivers to make them would seem to be artificial, 'unreal'.) They might as well play at motor racing on video machines or in virtual reality. That, of course, might appeal to some but not to those who love motor racing.

Real motor racing cannot be risk free. It is pious to think that it should be or, if it cannot be, it should be banned. We should rather strive to reduce its risks when they are deemed to be too great by the drivers, or merely gratuitous. We should strive to do this while recognising that we cannot eliminate all of these risks and should not want to get rid of all of those that are consequent on the drivers' lack of skill, judgement, fitness, concentration, speed of reaction, and so on.[2] I intend this as an illuminating, though of course not perfect, analogy for what follows.

Moral philosophers tend to take one of two lines about such things as lying, killing others, hurting them, going back on one's word, and so on. They have either said, with Kant, that lying can never be right and so should never be practised, or, more frequently, and intelligibly, said that it can, unhappily, be right, and so sometimes obligatory, to lie, but only to avoid a greater evil, such as great suffering.

I shall attack the second, more intelligible view in this brief chapter with the intention of thereby showing that both views are wrong, and that only the confused, the insincere or the crazy could support them.

It is difficult to imagine a world in which no one ever lied for his or her own ends, or was jealous, or vindictive, or selfish, or cruel. But if we make any serious attempt to imagine such a world – and what is really required is a novel – I think that we end up describing something that is not recognisably human and is not obviously a moral world at all and something dreadfully inferior to the world we know.

Suppose, for example, that on one ever told a lie for his or her own ends, that is, that lies were told only in the belief that some greater evil would be avoided and that that belief was characteristically correct and that it was never incorrect because of anything but miscalculation. Clearly the opportunities to tell self-interested lies are so myriad that if no one ever accepted one it would be a matter, not of great debate whether anyone could do such a thing, but of certainty that he or she could not. At any rate, such lying could not be a *moral* issue; if persons 'struggled' with themselves to avoid telling such lies in any such world it could not but strike them as a sham battle, for the outcome would always be known, if only on inductive, third-partyish grounds. (It might be thought that the very stupid could avoid such knowledge, but even if their presence was possible in such a world, the very concept of such a lie might be difficult for them, and indeed for any-one in that world, to comprehend.)

But in such worlds it is not only wicked lying that would not exist. Most of its rationale would be lacking too. People tell such lies out of, say, vanity; but that, if not an evil, is a bad thing and hence something that has no place in a possibility imperfect but perfectly moral world. Or they lie out of greed, or cowardice. But these too are evils or the products of moral evils and have no place in a perfectly moral world.

A detailed description of a perfectly moral world is, to put it at its weakest, very difficult, and the above description is very thin. But surely it is substantial enough to reveal at least some of its bland, blameless, boring horror. For example, in any situation whatsoever in a perfectly moral world, no one could have any reason for thinking that anyone, including himself, was acting for base reasons, and every reason for thinking, and for thinking correctly, that everyone was acting with pure motives – though possibly cloudy minds. The only 'evils' would be natural ones; the things closest to moral evils in such a world would be man's physical imperfections, and perhaps especially his mental ones.

Some may still feel I have described nothing that is not wholly desirable and even patently so! But the sketch above shows that life, though less painful than it is here, would be almost infinitely less complex, and hence less interesting, much less challenging, and so less worthwhile. Of course, these facts, if they are such, raise paradoxical questions about our describing the world as a morally perfect one – but, though these questions are real, they tell against traditional views of morality, not my objections to them, since the world in ques-tion is one in which there is no selfish lying, vindictiveness, gratuitous cruelty, and so on. *Some* virtues, such as those of forbearance and forgiveness, would indeed be absent – but again that is no objection to my description of a world in which they are lacking as 'morally perfect', since they would be missing not through moral lack on man's part, rather the contrary, and hence through sheer lack of opportunity to exercise them.[3]

If my arguments are correct, a morally perfect world would be either unintelligible, or its description would be inconsistent, or it would be undesirable, and I am inclined to the last view.

The way or sense in which a morally perfect world would be undesirable depends on whether it would indeed be a moral world at all. If it is not a *moral* world because, say, it lacks the reality and substance of acting on a moral decision, and the remorse, guilt, feelings of inadequacy and weakness which are attendant on failing to act as one should, and so on, then it is morally desirable that our world should not be 'morally perfect'.[4] And this is a paradox. If, however, the morally perfect world is indeed a moral world, and, as such, a perfect one, then what I called the positive desirability of not living in such a world is a desirability which is and – in some sense of 'ought' – ought to be one which is more important than, and hence transcends, the demands of morality. And this too will strike us as paradoxical. How could it be the case that there is something which morally we ought to want, and yet which we ought not to want? In either case, a morally imperfect world, in which people do, at least sometimes, act badly, is the only sort of world in which we should choose to live. The question of how much evil there should be in the most desirable world is an intriguing one, but even if there were a right answer and one acceptable to us all, I cannot begin to imagine how, as a philosopher, one might proceed in trying to answer it.

Why then do moral philosophers tend to subscribe to the views I attack? Perhaps because we are impressed by the amount of evil in the world and by the fact that such evil will always exist? But these facts (and I shall probably be misunderstood as advocating evil in the sense of arguing for more of it) cannot make either of the views attacked correct, but only explain why we hold them. Of course, my own view is not free of paradox, for it requires thinking of certain sorts of behaviour as both evil and yet desirable. But this paradox is softened by two considerations: the first is that the view does not entail thinking of any particular sort or piece of evil as desirable; and the second is that evil can, without confusion, be thought of as something we should hate and strive to

reduce, believing as we do that it can never be wholly eliminated (see the first section).

Objection: I began with talk of motor racing. Consider instead
rail journeys, or, better still, going up and down buildings in
lifts. Don't we or shouldn't we try to eliminate all risks from
travelling in lifts? Would it not be possible to envisage a fail-
safe lift, travellers in which could only be hurt if the larger
structure of which it is a part failed? And wouldn't be a bless-
ing to have such lifts? In which case, if we draw the analogy
between living a worthwhile life with travelling in a lift rather
than with engaging in a dangerous sport, we reach a different
conclusion.

Reversing the direction of illumination, I suggest that the
second section itself shows which is the better, closer analogy.
But I will end with one further point in favour of that claim. For
most of us on most occasions, going up and down in lifts is a
purely instrumental activity which we do, not for itself or the
pleasures and satisfactions it brings, but in pursuit of something further. Motor racing, for those for whom it is a sport, is
done for itself, done because people like doing it and think it
worthy of their liking. We don't feel this about travelling in lifts
and we should be lesser creatures if we did. On the other hand,
if we preferred an inherently worthless existence or construed
our lives as inherently worthless, merely a journey to somewhere else, then we might desire a morally perfect world. But
if we see our lives as inherently worth living and not simply as
a vehicle to something we really desire or value more than our
human life, we may only imagine that we desire the morally
perfect world.

Notes

1. In the first chapter of Mark Twain's *Huckleberry Finn*, the
   Widow Douglas's sister tells Huck about 'the good place'. 'She
   said all a body would have to do there was to go around all day
   long with a harp and sing for ever and ever.' Huck doesn't think

much of that, and when Miss Watson says that Tom Sawyer will definitely be going to 'the bad place' which she had told him about earlier, he is glad that he and Tom will be there together.

2. The real problems are many. For example, how much would improving safety standards cost and could the sport afford them without making watching it too costly and, at the same time, insufficiently exciting? In the early 1990s those governing Formula One decided that technical improvements had made racing boring and reduced the role of the drivers, so they introduced regulations to recapture some of the excitement of Formula One racing of the 1950s. After a spate of accidents (May 1994) the drivers insisted on technical changes to improve safety. Driving had become for them too much of a lottery, and a lethal one.

3. Compare this with Blake's 'The Human Abstract' from the *Songs of Experience*, especially the second stanza of the first verse, 'And Mercy no more could be / If all were as happy as we.' For a professional philosopher's views, see J. L. Mackie's discussion of 'second-order goods' and 'absorbed evil', *The Problem of Evil*, Clarendon Press, 1982, pp. 153–5.

4. At least this follows if it is morally desirable that our world should be a moral one rather than a non-moral one.

5

MORALITY, UTILITARIANISM AND THE
NOBLE ART

INTRODUCTION

The two previous chapters contained discussions of particular moral issues, but were primarily concerned to raise general and fundamental questions about the nature and claims of morality. They are, therefore, primarily meta-ethical. The following begins in similar fashion with an examination of utilitarianism, a global doctrine about the nature of morality, which is also a substantive morality. I use this by way of introducing an examination of the rights and wrongs of a particular issue, one which exercises many people and has led to attempts to bring in legislation to ban it. I could be talking about one of a variety of issues, for example, euthanasia, abortion, fox-hunting, positive discrimination, factory farming, and so on, but I chose to discuss one where my thoughts and feelings are, if not confused, at odds. The topic is boxing, whether it is ignoble and improper, and whether it should be banned. The issues involved are many, and some complex, and they arouse strong feelings.

Partly for these reasons, and also because of the efflorescence in philosophy I mentioned earlier, this article too has been recently attacked. More interesting, perhaps, is that when the article was first published (in the journal *Philosophy*, in 1988) the editor got mail in which he was attacked for publishing the piece, not – or not just – because it was seen to defend boxing but because it contains a section in which I sing a paean of praise to one of my sporting heroes, Muhammad Ali. This, the writer complained, is not philosophy; and a person who published a reply to the article seemed to agree because he ignored the tribute to Ali, presumably because he too thought it was irrelevant to an argument about whether boxing could be defended.

But my feelings are scarcely idiosyncratic; after all, as Ali himself said, when he was at the height of his powers he was better known and more widely loved and admired than Charlie Chaplin; and even the grudging *aficionados* also rated Ali as among the very best; so not only supreme achievement in a sport but the love and admiration of millions of people are considered as irrelevant by these critics to what is at issue.

Yet a case can easily be made for this view: we should not be impressed by the adulation of the Roman world of a glad-iator, or the Hispanic world of a toreador, however enraptured it was by him and his performances in his particular ring, and however elegantly, passionately, even movingly, the adulation was expressed – though Roman, gladiatorial combat is, mor-ally, barbaric, and so are bullfighting and boxing. Coming to see and, indeed, understand why their spectators loved these sports and adored some of their exponents doesn't address the issue.

But now suppose that the defender of boxing has pointed to differences between what he loves, though still exercised by it, and those other activities, such as, for example, that gladi-ators were not free men, and were forced to try to kill each other, or that bullfighting involves participants who have even less choice in and understanding of their being slowly butchered to make an audience's holiday. As – or if – the inequities of the allegedly parallel activities are shown not to characterise the activity in question, do we not and should we not become increasingly interested in how those who know and love it think, feel, react to and talk about it? When moral – and, indeed, political – issues become fine, nice, minute, finely balanced, is it irrelevant, improper, question-begging, to look at those who are for and those who are against and ask oneself, 'Are these my people? Do I feel as they do? Do I want to be one of their company? Could I stand being thought of as one of them? Do I cringe when they say what they think and feel, or do I feel some sympathy, though perhaps I wouldn't have put it quite like that?'

Obviously, the answer to questions like this about the matter at issue need not all tend in the same direction. For myself, in many of them they do not. But the question is: are such considerations irrelevant – or, rather, should they be considered irrelevant – to our struggles to reach a view and a position? In this article, I assumed that they were not irrelevant, and could not be. My critics seemed to think the opposite. There is an issue here, difficult and important. It seems to me an issue that requires understanding and reflection, and its resolution agreement. I feel, therefore, no failure or lack of seriousness and effort if I now hand it on to you.

MORALITY, UTILITARIANISM AND THE NOBLE ART

Utilitarianism tells us that actions are morally right and good if, and to the extent that, they add to human happiness or diminish human unhappiness. And – or, perhaps, therefore – it also tells us that the best action open to a person is the one which makes the greatest positive difference to human happiness. Moreover, as everyone will also remember, utilitarianism further tries to tell us, perhaps intending it as a corollary of that first, main claim, that the motive for an action has nothing to do with its moral rightness or goodness. (This, of course, is just a philosopher's excessive and incorrect way of making the platitudinous point that one may do the wrong thing for the right reason and the right thing for the wrong reason.) But even if, as utilitarians, we accepted the dubious corollary, it would not follow, as many have thought, that utilitarians have no moral interest in motives. For unless, absurdly, a utilitarian believed either that there was never more than a fortuitous connection between, on the one hand, what we intended to do and, on the other, what we did and the consequences of what we did; or that, if there were such connections, we could not know of them, he or she must believe, as a moralist, that the best motive a person can have for performing an action is likely to be the desire to produce the happiest result. Indeed, utilitarians ought to be morally committed, it would seem, to trying to find out as much as they can about the consequences of human actions, for example, what connections exist, if any, between how we raise children and what sort of adults they grow up to be.

Now let us suppose that we are utilitarians who believe, as apparently Mill believed, that among the greatest of the removable bars to human happiness is not only ignorance, and, in particular, ignorance of the likely consequences of our actions, but selfishness, that is, behaviour motivated by a desire to please oneself coupled with an indifference to the happiness or wishes of others. (This is a reasonable belief and one held by persons who are not utilitarians.) Such utilitarians might then arrive at the conclusion that the best motive from which we can act is the desire to make *others* happy, or to give them what they desire (if they are 'preference' utilitarians). Such utilitarians might think of Utopia as being inhabited solely by angels, that is, creatures whose sole motive is always and only that best one.

My first claim is that this Utopia, like any other perhaps, is unobtainable – not because we are weak and selfish; it is unobtainable by angels too – because it is not, as it is fashionable to say, a 'possible world'. For consider, how would the angelic inhabitants proceed? Either they know what would make others happy or what they desire, or they have to phone them up. In either case the result is the same: each angel's only and hence self-stultifying desire is to do what the other angels would like him (or it?) to do to make them happy or give them their desire.

If the incoherence of this fanciful situation is not manifest perhaps the following will make it so.

ANGEL A: Hello B! What should I do to make you happy, give you your desire?

ANGEL B: My desire is that you make other angels happy, try to satisfy their preferences, including yours. But actually I was about to call you – what would you like me to do? What would make you happy, satisfy your desire?

ANGEL A: I don't think you are at your brightest and at your best B! I of course want that you . . . .

The conclusion I draw from the above is that neither men nor angels can always and only be motivated by the desire to make others happy or give them what they want. Unless at least some of us have first-order, self-directed desires and preferences, that is, desires, preferences and satisfactions which don't primarily involve or consist in pleasing others, motivated action is impossible, and so *a fortiori* is that form of moral action which all utilitarians see, when it is successful, as the highest form of moral action. Indeed, if the very notion of a moral action involves *disinterest*, that is, if, in order to act morally, the agent's primary concern is not primarily with himself, the conclusion follows more generally, and not just with regard to utilitarian theory about what constitutes what is morally best to do.

So if only disinterested actions can be moral, we cannot always and only act morally. We must have 'selfish' desires and preferences and act on them sometimes if moral action is to be possible. (Others cannot always execute them for us, given the nature of some of them.)

To call every action that is not directed at pleasing or helping others 'selfish' would be, therefore, not just priggish but nonsense. We are then – happily – free from the universal tyranny of moral obligation and could make a start on solving a problem which neither Bentham nor Mill do more than glance at and hurry on by, namely, that since I may – indeed some of us must sometimes – act 'selfishly', when is it proper to do so? Both tell us that everyone, including oneself, is to 'count as one', which means that we may – perhaps must – consider our own preferences and happiness when deciding what to do; which of course does not solve the problem. Still, in raising it we must not forget that, given the desire to add to the sum of human happiness, the problem of what we should do will in large part be an empirical question whose answer will vary as the situation varies – so utilitarianism cannot provide a general, a priori answer here. None the less the question as to when we may act selfishly is especially pressing in the modern world, when we are in increasingly close contact with others and in which in any foreseeable future there will continue to be others who are desperately in want, in dreadful need, at least some of whom we could help to try to help. And yet if no one could properly pursue his or her own interests until everyone was freed not merely of unsatisfied desires but of real distress, we should always and only be frustrated, that is, never able to do what we 'selfishly' want to do!

Confronted by this dilemma, what should a utilitarian do? What indeed should anyone do, who wishes to act well? Some will devote their actions entirely to the service of others, though, as we have seen, not everyone could act in this way. Others, comforted by that thought, may decide that the best informed and most effective course of action, and at least in those ways the best one, will be to look out for number one and for those they know personally and care about. Others may find themselves seemingly thrashing about, sometimes acting 'selfishly', sometimes out of concern for others but in no principled or obviously consistent way. We may very well be led to wonder if there is always a generally valid answer to the question, even for anyone placed in a particular sort of situation, for perhaps if everyone similarly placed did arrive at and act on the same decision about what to do, that would not always produce the happiest result.

At any rate, sincere utilitarians would appear to be committed at very least not only to large-scale sociological enquiry but to everyone's practising social welfare. Yet this too sounds not only impractical but horrible; the programme sounds as if those who accept it would form a proselytising band of interfering, do-gooding, nosey parkers. It also looks as if it might be self-stultifying, because the resulting situation looks most unhappy and one in which many preferences – for example, for privacy, integrity, and independence – would not be satisfied. Paradoxically, the radical and selfless utilitarians' programme would seem to be the less threatening and unfortunate, the more a good proportion of persons do not accept and try to act on it! To argue this is not to endorse or justify

the cold-hearted, self-satisfied – or even anguished – acceptance of the doctrine propounded in the eighteenth century in
Mandeville's *Fable of the Bees* and by nineteenth-century
(and contemporary) *laissez-faire* thinkers that it is right only
to pursue one's own interests and doing so produces the best
result. But it does mean that thoughtful utilitarians would have
to abandon a programme of unremitting concern for others in
favour of something radical enough but much more modest
and practical, like a large expansion of foreign aid, Oxfam and
welfare programmes, and minimum wage legislation at home.
(Irrelevantly I will add that I would support such a modest,
radical programme.)

I have raised a lot of difficult questions, but I hope to have
established at least that, whether utilitarians or not, we could
not all be angels or wish that we all were – and, more interestingly, no doubt, that the world could not be a happy place
at all unless at least some of us had self-interested desires and
sometimes tried to satisfy them. Given my purposes in this
chapter I shall not pursue these problems further, but turn
now to my next reflection: if we could choose, what kind of
creature should we choose to be, as utilitarians?

The answers are sometimes surprising. Worry I think can
go; concern, of course, remains. Whether concern could retain
all its virtues if it were drained, as it were, of worry, I am not
sure. How about anger? One might, idealistically, regret a
world in which there were occasions for anger, though I suspect it would be unbearably anodyne without it – and I shall
return to this important point later – but, speaking personally,
though not I believe idiosyncratically, anger can be not only
justified and effective but enjoyable, and on that last score too
not to be eliminated by utilitarians from the human repertoire
of responses.

Given the existence of the appetite, the inclination, I cannot
see any utilitarian objection to necrophilia, and so, I think, a
utilitarian ought to feel that, other things being equal and
unchanged, if people could free themselves from their horror
at this practice they should. Here I think utilitarianism is right
since the horror is aesthetic and visceral, I feel. Anyway I

should be prepared to donate my body.[1] But what I want to look at in this context is pain: if we could choose, would we choose not to suffer physical pain? (Other pains are so by extension or even analogy, and are quite different and raise quite different problems.)

It is no utilitarian defence of pain to say, truly, that it is functional, serving to protect us from, by informing us of, damage. That end could, surely, be achieved painlessly and efficiently by other means. Think of the eye blink, which is automatic, defensive, marvellously efficient and quite painless. Nor could we say, here, that if individuals were anaesthetic, they would be cut off from their fellows, for *ex hypothesi,* all would be the same.

So should we choose to eliminate pain(s), and, if not, why not? Certainly we could do with a whole lot less than we now suffer; but *none*? Surely not, and I think we can say why, without being reduced to a defence of head-banging because it's so nice when you stop. It *is*, but what is nice here is simply that the pain has stopped. In other cases what is nice is something much more positive which could not be experienced without the antecedent pain. Water to the thirsty, warmth to the chilled, food to the hungry, are positive pleasures that could not be experienced by anyone who has not lacked drink, warmth or food.

Pains are also of course a price we often pay for betterment and achievement, and when they are, they are often suffused by our knowledge of what they mean, so that they become not just tolerable but marvellous. The weight-lifter, the runner who competes over distances of greater than 200 metres, the rower, the domestic digger, even the woman in childbirth would agree – though in the last case the pain is usually so great that few women will choose to experience all of it, though many want to feel some of it.

How about danger? I will look at what must be most difficult for anyone trying to justify its inclusion in a chosen world: gratuitous danger, danger that could be avoided, danger indeed that is sought. My line of thinking will be predictable; for many, and especially those who have most to lose – but, presumably because they are so far away from their expected, natural end that they fear death least – danger is a spice to life without which it lacks savour. Should we regret this, as utilitarians? Would we choose, if we could, that human beings did not need and did not seek danger? Surely, since dangerous activities must sometimes end in death, disablement, disfiguration and distress, we should want to eliminate this trait? Well, again, I can easily imagine that we might want to reduce this desire as we do indeed now when we see it as pathological and self-destructive. But remove it entirely?

Someone might try to defend the existence of the desire to experience danger by saying that without it we should not have explored the widths, heights and depths of our world, we should not have tried experiments, new techniques in many fields, and so much else that has yielded human benefit, and this is true. But we could imagine that substituted for a desire for danger was a sober but passionate desire for knowledge which drove men and women to risk their lives, but not gratuitously.

But would that – in some broad, vague, but important sense of 'happy' – be a happier situation than the one we are in? What would happen, for example, to rock-climbing? This world sounds too careful, too joyless to me. If it does to you, then the instrumental justification of taking risks might fail to preserve something we cherish and delight in.

Someone might say: 'But if the change were wrought, neither you nor anyone else would feel the change as a loss! You are arguing in a circle in assuming the present state and point of view.' No: I am pointing out the perhaps unforeseen consequences of a perhaps pious and too quick desire to improve man which on consideration doesn't seem an improvement at all. 'But your point of view is still *parti pris*?' Perhaps, but how can one avoid a point of view? Someone else might object: 'But you are no longer talking about morals!' But I have already tried to show that morality is parasitic on what is non-moral. Similarly an examination of what we should do, should want, should feel, cannot be separated from an examination of what we do do, do want, do feel.

My third reflection is connected with the second: according to the more primitive form of utilitarianism, we should seek to produce human happiness, and reduce unhappiness, and in deciding on the best course of action, we should strive to perform a hedonic subtraction sum in which we subtract the unhappiness that would be caused by our action from the happiness that it would cause. That action which we calculate will produce the largest positive balance is the one we should perform.

But this is nonsense, and not just because the talk of computing and subtracting pains and pleasures is nonsense. (In fact we do engage in estimations and comparisons of gains and losses of various courses of action, and where they are or involve economic matters, a calculus is possible.) It is nonsense because it would mean, for example, that if, on balance, a fellow human being's life were likely to be unhappy, we should terminate it. Or if that would introduce feelings of danger and suspicion on the part of human beings regarding the likely behaviour of their concerned fellows, the individual himself, if rational, would terminate it.

Reasoning of this sort, if one may call it reasoning, is what leads silly, hard-hearted people to say of lifers, 'Wouldn't capital punishment be kinder?' Few lifers think that it would. At the least, few lifers *would make that choice*. And only very few persons who are not lifers but are suffering and depressed would make that choice either. And unless their agony is intense or seemingly inexorable, do we not think such a choice rational?

Or again, life in a sterile padded cell, the inhabitants of which are drugged or lobotomised, may be less unhappy in all the obvious ways than a drug-free, whole-brain existence outside the cell, but who would choose it? Only those who are very unhappy indeed.

So utilitarianism has been revamped. What guides moral action is not the pursuit of others' happiness, but attempts to realise all preferences whose realisation would not improperly interfere with the happiness and the realisation of the preferences of others.

I draw two morals from this third reflection. First: sheer experience itself is a *desideratum* for us – life one might say, and a life that has *variety*, and so, as we have seen, a greater possibility of *intensity* of experience.[2] Such a life is likely to be a happier one than its deader alternatives, whatever the results of a subtraction sum of first-order pleasures and pains. Secondly: if the satisfaction of a person's preferences do not threaten the satisfactions of other persons' preferences, there seems to be no good reason, and, *a fortiori*, no good moral reason, why we should interfere with their being realised. Indeed, there is, in such circumstances, a very good reason, and a utilitarian one, for not interfering with their being realised, namely, that persons are not free to satisfy their desires. And even if, and when, doing so does not give them pleasure, or make them happy – indeed even when doing or getting what they want doesn't give them pleasure or happiness, or even makes them unhappy – *not* being able to do as they please will make them unhappy.

So although we might wish that others weren't so selfish or irresponsible as they are, we should none the less not – morally should not – stop them doing as they please, when this does not interfere with the freedom of others, or think that we could coherently wish their self-directed desires away. I have also tried not merely to leave room for the irresponsible, but show that we do, at least sometimes, though not always, welcome and value their lack of care, their gaiety, their craziness.

Turning now to what its precursor was called, 'the noble art of self-defence': this is a false description of boxing. So is any description in terms of 'scoring points' or 'winning rounds'. Because what each boxer is trying to do is not merely to score points or to win rounds by punching his opponent, and to avoid being hit himself, he is also trying to stop his opponent from scoring points, and the best way to do that is to *stop him* – as they say. If he is wise, he therefore tries to hurt the other man and hurt him so much that he will be unable to fight back for a minimum of ten seconds. And since the activity is either entertainment for paying spectators or a preparation

for that and perhaps for a professional career, the more spec-
tacularly a boxer can do this the better his prospects, reputation
and self-esteem. So let us be clear: the boxer's intention is to
win, and he can only do this by knocking his opponent out,
or by out-pointing him, and he can only do that by punching
his opponent more frequently, cleanly and effectively than he
is punched himself. And he tries to do that, in part – unless
he lacks a heavy punch – by hitting his opponent so hard that
the opponent's capacity to make effective punches in reply is
impaired. A boxer, therefore is hoping and trying to hurt his
man.

I am claiming that we cannot deploy the doctrine of double
effect in defence of boxing. For both the effect of boxing and
the boxer's professional intention is to hurt, to temporarily
incapacitate a fellow human being. The consequence of doing
so can be, and sometimes it is, permanent damage, often of
an especially unpleasant sort, namely, brain damage, which
may be gross and may result in death.

Given that this is so, I thought, when younger, that boxing
should be banned. Men are not allowed to kill each other;
surely they should not be allowed to try to damage each other
– especially for the pleasure of other men and women and the
profit of some? However I was troubled by the embarrassing
fact that I loved watching boxing. So, I loved the spectacle of
watching something evil take place – moreover, I enjoyed
watching something evil take place which I could try to help
prevent taking place. (Watching boxing is not like watching a
film of a past disaster: you are not conniving at that. I *was*.)
When I enjoyed boxing more than I do now, because Clay was
in his pomp, the most exquisite and trivial dilemma I could
imagine would be having to choose between watching Clay
box and Donald Jackson skate!

The next step in my odyssey was taken when I heard, on
TV, Bobby Neal, a boxer turned manager, who had been nearly
killed in the ring, defending boxing against moves to ban it,
then being made by Edith Summerskill. His argument was a
simple one: for most boxers, including himself, boxing was
their only escape from hard labour – or, as it is more likely to

be these days, unemployment. (Whether a country has a lot of good boxers, or few, is a pretty good indicator of the state of its economy, or of the economic opportunities available to some community within that country.)

Clearly, Neal's simple argument could not warrant the permitting of any activity that freed a man from unemployment, menial labour, manual labour, boredom, obscurity, and so on. Hit-men ought to be stopped from plying their trade. But Neal made me think again about the nature of the boxer's trade. Boxers, unlike hired assassins, are not, as boxers, trying to kill anyone – and it is bad news for them and boxing in general if that is what they do. (Admittedly, getting a permanent k.o. against one opponent may give a boxer notoriety, and may make him a big draw, and so jack up his next purse, and so on. But he had better not do it again. And there had better not be too many such deaths in the ring.) Remember the Emile Griffiths–Benny 'Kid' Parrett fight? It nearly brought about a ban on boxing, not only in the USA, where the fight took place, but here in the UK, where a film of the fight was shown on Panorama, not on Sportsnight, and was much discussed in both the press and in Parliament. Griffiths not only killed Parrett, it emerged that Parrett had goaded and poured scorn on the allegedly effeminate Griffiths before the fight and at the weigh-in, and Griffiths had gone into the ring intending to kill an opponent who had so persistently and grossly tormented and insulted him. This happens very rarely, and is not constitutive of the activity – and perhaps it is not irrelevant to add that even this tragedy could and should have been averted, if the referee had stopped the fight when he should have. Parrett did not throw a punch in the preceding round – the eighth – and took upwards of thirty punches to the head before the fight stopped. Admittedly, Griffiths fired off those thirty shots in nine seconds, and Parrett was trapped in a corner. But most ringside spectators seemed to be shouting to the referee to stop the fight for what seemed to be ages before he finally intervened. I too was uselessly shouting at the replay of the fight – and one wonders why the towel had not come in – a boxer's seconds know better than anyone, usually, when their man has had enough. Perhaps Parrett had told them – and the referee himself – that under no circumstances were they to pull him out? Perhaps they just did things differently in the USA.

Which brings me to a further difference, that is, a difference between boxing and assassination: a boxer's target is not an unsuspecting and unwilling victim. He is a fellow boxer, that is, another man who, and not only in theory, has *chosen* to pit his skill, strength, heart and luck against another's, who has also thus chosen. Moreover, unless the contest is what is called a mismatch, and boards of control have increasingly striven to avoid and prevent them, the *opponents* – for that is what they are – are not hunter and hunted, but – what past form suggests anyway – well matched. They are there to have a contest not to hunt or kill.

Of course there are grudge matches: the Kalor–Christis fight was a case in point. And the great boxing public loves them – for an obvious and not entirely sordid reason, namely, that they are more likely to see an all-action contest in which both men will really be trying. But, again, the boards of control don't like them, they are often synthetic, that is, there is no real grudge, and the clamour that there is, is often a promotional device. Boxers are in fact often quite friendly with, and respectful of, each other, like Mohammed Ali and Joe Frazier. In the Kalor–Christie case, the animus, partly racial, was produced by the weigh-in shots set up by shrewd and unprincipled press photographs. (Incidentally, there was one grudge fight which seemed to exercise and offend no one, with the possible exception of one of the participants, and this was the return Joe Louis–Max Schmelling fight. It was said of Louis that he fought with hate in his heart that night because of what the representative of the Third Reich had said – or was alleged to have said – about Negro auxiliaries before Schmelling had won the first fight. Louis's dignity as a fighter, a Negro, a citizen of the USA, and a man, had been impugned. In fact the truth seems less romantic. Louis was annoyed because Schmelling had struck him repeatedly after the bell in the first fight, in which of course Louis had lost his world championship. Anyway, few were disturbed when Louis destroyed Schmelling, broke a couple of his vertebrae, caused him to scream in pain, and knocked him out in round one. Pride and dignity restored, defeat avenged, honour satisfied, ascendancy and the world title restored, with the passing of the Third Reich, Louis and Schmelling became friends, and the successful German businessman made it his business to visit the ageing, ill, heroin-addicted Louis, then earning a crust as a handshaker at Caesar's Palace.

As David James[3] has pointed out to me, the kind of respect and affection which boxers can feel for their opponents is perhaps peculiar to the sport of boxing. Why? The hard match is produced by a close match of skills, strength and art; it presupposes a common basis of work; it may well constitute a crux in the life of both; it produces an intimacy – of an albeit peculiar sort – and it is thus not entirely surprising that at the end of such a bout, exhausted but jubilant at what they have achieved and survived, two boxers will fall into each other's arms. And, one shouldn't try telling them they are gullible, moronic sentimentalists in so doing, simply because that would be false; or if it is true, that doesn't follow from their embrace. And if one is tempted to think that, even so, this all sounds rather queer; as well as being cheap, trite and probably false – and, hence, rather enjoyable – if *true*, why should that demean and diminish the boxer?

So, in searching for a true account of boxing that will, *eo ipso*, not merely be a defence of not banning it, but an elucidation of something that can be not just justifiable but, indeed, noble, I am not committed to a parallel account of, say, duelling. Here there is animus, at least on one side, and there may properly, as it were, be the intent to kill. I am not committed to the defence of an activity like duelling but professionalised and so without animus – the gladiatorial combat. None the less, I am committed, I feel, to the defence of an activity which necessarily involves trying to punch another human being more often than he punches you, or with more effect, in which activity you may properly seek to achieve that end by hitting your opponent so frequently or so damagingly that he cannot go on trying to punch you or cannot succeed sufficiently often to outscore you. Must such an attempt yield, at best, specious bullshit?

Let us see: I shall now include a piece I was moved to write about my hero, Mohammed Ali, soon after he lost his world heavyweight crown to Larry Holmes. Some of its thoughts are now out of date and since I wrote it, we have discovered that something terrible, undoubtedly brought about or exacerbated by boxing, has happened to Ali. It looks like brain damage, it may also be Parkinson's. It is particularly terrible and distressful that it has happened to such a marvellous man and superb boxer as was Ali. (I shall say something about this in the last section.)

THE GREATEST

Those of us who had seen Zbigniew Pietrzykowski fight a few times on TV remember how good he was. A cagey, yet aggressive boxer, a destructive puncher, and an aura of Eastern European professionalism and strength, which made it seem unlikely that even if he got hit he would get hurt, made his opponents look the hopeless amateurs they almost all proved to be – except one. The odd glimpses we were allowed of his fight for the 1960 Olympic Light-heavyweight title, showed him outclassed, cut up, and reduced to desperation and indignity by a slim, black American.

That for most of us was our first glance at a phenomenon of which we have had our last, live glimpse. However long he lives, and let it be long, Mohammad Ali – 'Cassius Clay', as some of us secretly, guiltily, still think of him – has lost what was not exhaustive of but crucial to our attention. And he was pushed off his world stage by an ex-sparring partner, and went sitting down.

There is no contempt in that last remark, only

sadness. He cannot lose our respect, or what I have very seldom felt for anyone I never met, love. That should sound unlikely, mawkish, but only the Ali-haters will feel it so. Given what he was – a black, American prize fighter – it is a tribute to what else he was.

Perhaps Ali was the greatest heavyweight of all time. Since the only knockdown proof of that claim involves the impossibility of matching him, Rocky Marciano and Joe Louis in their primes over a series of matches, I won't argue it but just consider his merits as a boxer.

The most obvious was his speed, and not just of foot. In fact, he lost the ability to 'float', except for brief spells, quite early in his career. He also had quick hands, and could sway like a disco dancer. In most of his fights he made it look impossible that he would be caught by a solid punch, so that when it very occasionally happened, as it did in his fight with Henry Cooper, you felt as shocked as he looked (as shocked almost as one would have been by Donald Jackson's falling over, or Alain Calmat's staying on his feet).

He was, less obviously, very tough. Presumably punches hurt him, but he never showed it, and they never seemed to drain his strength or will. Only age did that. He not only fought seven rounds with a broken jaw – Bruce Woodcock fought more against Joe Baksi – but I don't think any spectator realised that at the time, nor did Ken Norton for that matter. And he didn't cut.

With the dubious exception of his k.o. of Liston in their second fight – and Clay didn't know if he had knocked him out with a left or right until he saw the replay – he was not a one-punch finisher of top-class opponents. Neither was Sugar Ray Robinson. He didn't set himself to throw bombs, and being the combination artist that he was, why should he? Had he ever done so, it would have seemed crude, unnecessary and hence cruel.

Clay was not a tentative finisher, but he never looked like Marciano when about it. His frenzies and hatreds he kept out of the ring; and even then they were often, though not always, stimulated.

He was uniquely imaginative and inventive, which is very difficult in any sport and especially boxing. I'm not thinking of the 'Ali shuffle'; that was never more than a gimmick which often left him so off-balance that he needed all his other boxing attributes to be able to risk it. He was the first successful heavyweight to avoid punches by swaying *away* from them since Jack Johnson. The wisdom of the gym had it that you moved inside punches, and Ali showed this was crap. He didn't get hit, and if he did he was going backwards anyway. This seems obvious now, but so does evolution. And what fighter has since showed the skill, nerve and individuality to do what untutored fighters naturally do, invariably with disastrous results?

Tactically he was totally unpredictable, and successful. To achieve the first isn't so difficult, it's combining it with the second that is. How could he have ever thought of lying on the ropes and letting his opponent exhaust himself, when you think who that opponent was – George Foreman – and remember what Foreman had done to Joe Frazier?

Remember his earlier practice of dancing for a round and not even trying to land a serious punch? The intention seemed to be to demonstrate that he could not be hit, though this may be a simplistic view of what was intended and achieved. Certainly it reduced Sonny Liston – who frightened Harry Carpenter just in talking to him – to anger, impotence and despair. And I haven't mentioned his predictions! These may have put pressure on him sometimes, but they seemed to put more on most of his opponents, as well as bums on seats.

All this, and yet the only other innovation in boxing arts and skills since the turn of the century is Bob Fitzsimmons's solar plexus punch. (Cerefino Garcia's bolo punch, at least as I saw it delivered by Kid Gavilan, looked no more than a flashy cross between an uppercut and a hook.)

Until the last, the Greatest never fought a bad fight. The closest he got to it was against Doug Jones, and he was a vastly underrated fighter who in that fight was concentrating on getting beyond the round of his predicted fall. (Jones's tragedy was that he was too small for the new breed of super-heavyweight, it was merely his misfortune that he was too big for a cruiserweight.)

Which reminds me of another of Clay's merits, his size. Great size often means lack of athleticism. When it does not, it is all crushing gain. Mohammad Ali was over twenty pounds heavier than Marciano when both were at their best weights. This is the only merit that one can see as wholly or even predominantly a gift of genes. The other qualities look like moral ones; at any rate we want to praise him for them while merely congratulating him on his height and weight.

Clay was not quite unflawed. This unique performer never overcame a common weakness in orthodox, that is, left-hand forward, fighters; he was vulnerable to a left hook. That's why he had so much trouble with Frazier, and why Henry dumped him. Of course he was messing about in that event, waiting for the next round, five, when, as he had predicted, he stopped Cooper, making him look, with the help of a split glove, like a Glasgow gang's victim. Still, having invited nemesis, he never moved to avoid it, and if luck had not timed Henry's opportunity less than ten seconds from the end of the round, Ali might have been a faint memory for a long time.

He so nearly became one on a much greater occasion. He wanted out in the first Liston fight when, it seems, lineament got in his eyes. If Angelo Dundee had let him, the effect would have been so enormous that it's difficult to believe now that this took place, especially as he never ever again showed less than total resolution. I think one can and should discount this incident in the final weighing of his talents as a fighter and his qualities as a man.

That unique, glittering array of golden talents must go a long way to explain why people, many of whom were not boxing fans, were excited by a Clay fight, both in its usually gripping reality and its always fascinating prospect. But it doesn't go all of the way, or even most of it. And unless we assume that they were all interested in the aesthetics of boxing, and only that, this doesn't explain at all why his loss against Frazier – who was, and could be seen to be, a thoroughly decent, brave man, and a smaller one than Clay – was felt by the great majority of that great public to be a tragedy. Outside the ring, Clay excited everyone and pleased most. Some, like me, reacted to him as American citizens were so perceptively shown as doing to Superman in the first film – any difference depending on the fact that we idolators knew that Clay, though unbelievable, really was real. What was it about him?

Well, he was outrageous. His boasts and threats before he fought Liston sounded hysterical and mad, and didn't they make you fear for him? There were the predictions of course, and the rhymes that sounded embarrassingly awful at first but, later, when we had become more relaxed with him, were hilarious – and delivered with such enjoyment and panache that, for a moment, they edged towards a weird, literary merit. Until we knew him, or he changed, his rantings sounded megalomaniac, yet terribly vulnerable, and later we could enjoy them as the marvellous, self-parodying promotional exercises that they were.

So he was a sharp, funny, and original seller of fights. But so was John Conteh, and there was much, much more to Ali. He not only fought managers, as Conteh had done, but refused to fight the Vietnamese. In doing so, he opened himself to the jibe of cowardice from those who hated him, and lost his crown and his income, doing all that for a new-found religious and political faith. And though some might think a black separatist movement impractical, or worse, Ali's radicalism demanded a true appreciation of the black man's problems in the USA and a proud response.

Could we say that any other successful, black fighter came near that? Jack Johnson's pride was for his prowess and himself. Louis was exploited, degraded, and conformed – or did so where it matters, in public. Robinson was a great fighter and a great showman outside the ring, but there he danced, crooned and straightened his hair.

Ali's attitude to the wretched Floyd Patterson is especially revealing; lots of us felt sorry for the glass-jawed, reformed delinquent, with an inferiority complex the size of Madison Square Garden. Ali was *angry* with him – and that is what you would feel, or should feel, if Patterson wasn't merely another boxer, but your brother. Ali loved the blacks, a number of whom he spent his career not only physically but verbally drubbing. (His pleading with referees to stop fights he was winning easily is only the most obvious indicator of this, and one which cynics can dismiss as his excuse for not being able to finish victims he could only exhaust.) But you feel his love for his fellow man; at any rate I felt I could feel it. He could not manage to be cold or even hot for long, even with the white devils he professed to hate. Ali was a warm man without coming in spitting distance of being a mild one.

As consequence and further proof of these large claims, remember how he interviewed on TV, for that is where we met him. George Best, another genius, was diminished in his TV chat with the wildly enthusiastic, self-indulgent and congratulatory Jonathan Miller. He could not there exercise the attribute being lauded, and so was shifty, deferential, bored, embarrassed and out of his shallow depth. The pseudo-articulate but undoubtedly shrewd Kevin Keegan comes across as the Cliff Richard of football. And who can forget that terrible, wonderful interview with a man who was no mere performer, but then a manager, Tommy Docherty, in which he declared himself in favour of capital punishment for soccer hooligans? Only the faintest, alarmed flicker of an eye suggested he didn't mean that, and one's suspicion that – terribly – he might, told you what you thought of him.

The mature Ali granted interviews, organised them, and ended them – sometimes by walking out. Whether in so doing he was selling tickets or making a moral point, the scandalised, panicked reaction of the interviewers made them, and their sense of values, look ridiculous. When he chose to stay, and without wanting or trying, he made them look parochial, not just because he was urbane, witty and famous, but because his interests – and I mean here the issues and areas that concerned him – were so much larger than theirs, as was his effective engagement with them. The Louisville Lip, the most uppity nigger of them all, the man who therefore was the most widely loathed and yet loved of his race, became a man whose presence and concerns a statesman might envy, and whose worldwide fame and adoration even Chaplin could not excel.

Now it's all over, and a distant fan waves good-
bye. Of course, had I been closer, I might have seen
him more clearly, but not much. Clay *was* larger
than life, and so full of life, and grace, and when I
saw him in the Holmes fight, and when a few years
ago I saw him weighing twenty stones, giving exhi-
bitions, and when then, as in the Holmes fight, he
could scarcely throw a punch, I turned away, in
tears and anger, not for him, but his passing.

Then I comforted myself with the thought that he
might resurrect himself, and later that he might do
so again – though surely this time in a less physical
mode? And if Ronnie Reagan – on any true reckon-
ing, a much lesser mortal – did it, and with so much
outside help and widespread indifference, so surely
can the Greatest?

Cassius Clay! The rest of life is more important
than boxing, so the rest of your life can be too. But
when you boxed, I didn't feel that.

I cannot anticipate how the above section will strike a reader,
but something like the following seems likely and most damaging to my defence of boxing.

'Yes, no doubt Mohammed Ali *was* outstanding as a boxer
and as a man. But what made him outstanding as a boxer
did not make him outstanding as a man. Boxing merely made
what he was and did outside the ring *possible*. The connection is merely genetic, not internal, so it proves *nothing* about
the morals of boxing, or about the moral nature of the boxer.
Moreover,' my critic might continue, 'even if some of the moral
traits which Ali displayed outside the ring were displayed inside
the ring, for example, courage, compassion, wit, originality,
foresight, dignity, and so on, and so on, their being displayed
in that purview has as little tendency to make boxing an
inherently noble or virtuous activity as it does war. In fact it
has less, because war, or an individual's becoming a soldier,
may be morally unavoidable. With the possible and fictional
exception of Rocky IV, no boxer may similarly feel that,

however terrible it is, he has to become a boxer. So this hurt, the damage he does to a fellow human being, the courage that they may both display, the indomitability of spirit, acceptance of defeat, and so on, and so on, do *not* have a terrible beauty; they are in fact gratuitous and hence misplaced, indeed obscene.' (Concerning dignity: remember Pedrosa, in the McGuigan fight, after he was knocked down? He rose, shrugged, and nodded to his corner, and fought back with such cool resolve that he was not knocked out though he must have known in his heart that he could not win this fight. I have seldom seen such resolution or pride, never seen such composure and dignity. 'Grace under pressure', as Hemingway said – though one might wish that it had not been the romantic, macho Hemingway.)

Now I could try to argue that it is not *only* an implacable enemy that provides a moral imperative for a course of action that would otherwise be inexcusable. That is, I could argue that for many men, such as Jack Johnson, to refuse to box, as it were, would have been to accept not merely a humble, obscure and penurious life but a degraded one, and that boxing has been their only way to protest and demonstrate their equality, their right not to be exploited, humiliated, and so on. But I shan't do that because I can't. And I can't because I do believe that even if a boxer's life were gratuitous, that is, even if he were so placed and gifted that he had no need to fight for his life, like Gene Tunney, perhaps, I could still find in his professional life everything – or at least much and enough – to stir my admiration, and lead me to feel that he had chosen well and not badly.

How? At the start of this chapter, I tried to show that we cannot all of us always and only, be acting 'morally', that is, trying to make others happy or trying to give them what they want. Such moral behaviour, moral attitudes, and beliefs can only exist, therefore, if they leave room for the non-normal, that is, for what individuals do for themselves, for what they want independently of, in addition to, what they benevolently want for others. So, I argued, just because an activity or desire is not a moral one, it does not follow that it is improper or regrettable. Indeed, it does not follow that such activities and desires are less important or worthwhile than the moral. Secondly, I also sought to show that variety, fullness and intensity of experience, and hence certain dangers, fears, even pains, are phenomena that we value, because without them life would be a lesser, duller matter. Hence I now claim, provided that these dangers, pains, even sufferings, are our own, are freely and wittingly chosen, and do not harm others, we should, morally, be permitted to take part in activities which court them. For to proscribe them would not only interfere with our liberty, and our happiness, it would diminish, by reducing the fullness and intensity of, human life.

So provided that boxing is freely chosen, harms no one but those who have chosen to engage in it, and they know its risks, boxing is not moral, but it is not immoral either, and should not be proscribed. And boxing *is* freely chosen, and so on, – or it may be – so it should not be proscribed.

Of course, I wish to make a stronger claim than that. Because – and no one would contest this – boxing *is* – or can be – painful and dangerous as well as demanding of skill, strength, wit, originality, invention, stamina, it provides many opportunities for many of those non-moral situations, achievements and experiences which we value, which some of us seek, and which, if denied to men and women, would diminish their freedom and their lives. But beyond and above all this – which, if correct, shows that boxing transcends morality – I want also to remind readers that boxing provides an opportunity – albeit in a situation that could have been avoided, and which is gratuitous – for the exercise of moral virtues, including courage, compassion, self-knowledge and determination. Given that this is so, and given that boxers can also deploy all those non-moral virtues I listed above, boxing has been and may truly be called 'the noble art', and in my view the noblest of all its artists was Ali.

But if I think boxing is so wonderful, my critics may appropriately wish to raise some *ad hominem* points. Would I allow a son of mine, or indeed a daughter, to box? Well, boxing can be wonderful – but it can also be horrible, and it is especially horrible when it is inflicted on unwilling children. Still, if a son of mine wanted to box, then provided he knew the dangers, I would fear for him – boxing is a hard sport – but I could not stand in his way. How about a daughter? She would be a remarkable and unusual female; moreover boxing associations, amateur and professional, do not permit women to box. But I might even try to help her to lift such a ban.

Why then am I not a boxer? I was not able to take up boxing as an asthmatic child and I was over 30 before medicine found treatment that would control exercise-induced bronchial spasm. At that age, to have attempted boxing would have been fatuous – it *is* a hard game and I was soft. None the less, I have played, taken part – if only sometimes token part – in many games and sports and have loved doing so, although I am not much good at any of them and hopeless at many. And why, of all of them, do I prefer association football, cricket and skiing? The answer is very complex but at least part of the answer is that they all involve not only beauty and skill, but danger. Batting against a quick bowler, fielding at silly mid-on or short square leg, especially if you are as ungifted as I am, are risky. Going up for a ball in a crowded penalty area, especially against a not uncommon sort of defender, and rushing down a snow-clad slope so fast that you are not in control, are risky. I, and many others, find that marvellously exhilarating: those moments when you are on one leg, trying to avoid a bouncer, catch a ball driven at your face, and so on, have a quality that swells and glows and lives in the memory, and makes other parts of life somewhat grey, however necessary and indeed enjoyable. It is ignorance, or sloppiness, that allows anyone to dismiss this as a macho, self-indulgent romanticism, or even – as I have been told – masochism!

But if I am allowed all this, how can I avoid not merely permitting but praising activities in which men agree to try to kill each other? And wouldn't we – wouldn't I – object to those other non-intentionally but none the less potentially lethal activities if they were more likely to end in death than they are? Taking the lesser problem first: if I assume that the participants know the risks involved, and that to incur them is not

mad or desperate, I can still deplore the selfishness and irre-
sponsibility of those involved and the terrible waste of their
usually young lives if it ends in disaster, and I can and would
remind would-be participants of the agony and useless regret
of the dying participant. (I remember a young racing-car driver
trapped in his burning car pleading with those attempting to
remove him, 'Don't let me die!') Yet I think I would not only
not stop them – even the most desperate – but, despite everything, I think I could find many of the less excessive wonderful,
just because (in part) of their gratuitous riskiness. I shall never
forget standing just below an 8,000-feet-high ridge in the
French Alps and suddenly seeing, rising like a lift over the
ridge, a hang glider, manned by two skiers. It wobbled as it
was buffeted by cross winds, and plunged in a down draught
past and below me. It staggered, recovered, and soared up
into the cerulean sky, wheeled and then swooped down the
valley, round and out of sight, behind a shoulder of the mountain. How wonderful and beautiful it was! How I envied those
flying skiers! How sharply I felt my cowardice – I could not
risk that! But if I could, oh how I would! Should I really not?
Why not?

Turning to the harder question: am I not committed, at very
least, to *permitting* – indeed, if there is a demand, to advocating – the legislation of such activities as gun fighting? Well,
I should of course be against gun fighting if and when it was
a product of despair, bravado, selfishness, boredom, cruelty,
financial strait, and so on. But it does not follow that I should
want to stop it – nor does it follow either that I am obliged to
argue for its introduction. However, I have to confess that I am
sufficiently a utilitarian – and therefore, with Mill in defending
all permissions that do not militate against the proper free-
doms of others – to find it hard to condemn such an activity,
harder to proscribe it, and hardest of all to say why I should
proscribe it; and no doubt I would find this much more difficult than most of my readers.

Back, once more, to Clay. He is a wreck, a shell. Boxing
surely has wrought this tragedy? Very probably, and it is
certain that it has contributed to it, and it is a tragedy. But it

was avoidable. But it was not avoided and often is not. (Boxers of all athletes and sportsmen find it so difficult to abandon their art.) But I could not choose, that to avoid this, Mohammed Ali should never have been a boxer. Or Tommy Farr, or Marcel Cerdan, or Jersey Joe Walcott, or the Sugar Rays, or Duran, or Terry Downs, even Willie Pep – surely one of the dirtiest boxers who ever boxed – or even Fainting Phil Scott or Jack Doyle, 'the Irish throstle', both of whom clearly abhorred violence, in the ring, anyway. Should McGuigan be singing like his father did, in the Eurovision Song Contest? Would it really be better if he stayed behind the counter of his shop? Even Pedrosa would not – or should not – think so. Would we be without Doug Jones – who went the distance with Ali? What an achievement! Or all the *domestiques*, the spear carriers, who never got in the ring with anyone of any distinction? And think of Marlon Brando, in the back of a taxi with Rod Steiger, in *On the Waterfront,* saying 'I could have been a contender.' And that is not a metaphor, not for the fighter; and it is not I think a metaphor for those of us who have never boxed. It is I think a condensed, and therefore, gnomic, literal truth.

Now I have not discussed closer and therefore harder cases, for example, bare-fist fighting, bar-room brawls, playground fights (but think of the fight in *Tom Brown's Schooldays*), and closest, worst and therefore hardest of all, unlicensed boxing. But it is no objection to theatre that some forms of theatre are improper, unsavoury and should be stopped, for example, cock-fighting. Similarly it is no objection to conventionalised physical contests that some forms are obscene and certain examples of legitimate forms are terrible in various ways. And for me boxing is a true theatre, it can provide true drama, indeed – terribly – real tragedy. If only Billy Conn, having thoroughly out-boxed Joe Louis for the first ten rounds of his heavyweight contest for the World Championship, had not decided to have a fight with Louis. If only Howard Winston or Joey Maxim had had a punch. If only that superb boxer, turned referee, Ruby Goldstein, had not had a glass jaw. If only poor Floyd Patterson had not had a glass jaw . . . These are tragedies in some informal, but none the less genuine way, and paradoxically I could not choose that life should be without them.

Where's my ticket? my TV ringside seat?

Notes

1. Coprophilia? Well, I wish that they preferred nut cutlets, but this condition is unhappy, I suspect, not morally wrong, and if that is what they want . . .?
2. See Mill's remarks on variety and excitement in chapter 2 of his *Utilitarianism*.
3. Formerly Sports Director, University of Kent at Canterbury.

6

FAKES

Pop art, op art, minimalist art, conceptual art, abstract art, Fauvism, cubism, impressionism – all these genres of painting, and no doubt many others, have produced incomprehension and fury in laypersons, critics and indeed in other artists who were not part of the movement whose works were in question. Are the problems which these works have created philosophical?

Many of them are, at least in part. Consider abstract art which I mention in discussing Plato in the Introduction to part Three of this book: abstract paintings are not representations, that is, they are not paintings *of* anything. But a painting which is not a painting of something isn't really a painting, is it? It's *paint*, a painted surface, it may be decorative – though many abstracts are not – it might be a pattern, but it's not *of* anything.

Abandoning the representational dimension of painting involved a shift in our concept of paintings, of what counts as a painting, and this shift was very large and disturbing. For when artists started to produce abstract art, many of the tests, criteria, of a painting's being good or even competent thereby disappeared. One test of a portrait's being competent is whether the artist got a likeness (though, interestingly, despite Reynolds not being able to do this very well, while his great rival Gainsborough could, Reynolds was still a most sought-after and highly esteemed portraitist). If an artist, like Cuyp, paints cows, his cows should look like cows, should they not, cows lying in what look like fields, and so on. And in order to

174

meet the demands of verisimilitude, an artist has to be able to draw, he needs to master perspective, he must be a good colourist. Of course he will need much more to be a good artist, for example, an eye for the various elements that go to make up good composition, and to be a great artist he will need – well, something peculiar to his work, original, which captures our feelings and commands our admiration.

With abstract art, however, there is virtually none of this, no demand on, or test of, draughtsmanship, verisimilitude, mastery of perspective, or many of the dimensions that contribute to the composition of representational painting – no wonder David Hockney gave up painting abstracts because he didn't find it interesting.

How then can we decide if an abstract is any good? What is it trying to do? Has it succeeded? Is the success of any interest? Or do all such considerations go out of the window? All that we seem to be left with of the traditional tests for good painting are originality and the ability to command our interest, respect, and so on. And, not surprisingly, to do something quite different has become the goal of many contemporary *serious* artists. After all, what other goal can there be? But doing something that hasn't been done before, though necessary for originality, doesn't guarantee anything other than novelty.

So in many cases, when viewers are confronted by an abstract, they feel at a loss, foolish, may suspect that they are being conned, and any respect they might feel may be more a matter of intimidation, induced by the hushed gallery, the hype, and an anxiety not to appear ignorant and insensitive.

These are philosophical considerations which not only explain, but go some way towards, justifying the unease that people very much used to feel and some still do feel about abstract art. But does this mean that philosophy is the enemy of abstract painting just as Plato made it of poetry? Must philosophers be philistines? They must not and should not, and for the following reasons: first, the attack above on abstraction confuses representation with verisimilitude, but these are not the same. A stylised representation of, say, a railway engine on a road sign is that, though it lacks verisimilitude. A child's crayon drawing of swans may not look much like swans, but is still a picture of swans and may be quite charming, colourful, innocent, very much her work, and so on; and the same, or more, may be said of folk art and primitive paintings. (Such cases are discussed in the ensuing article, though for a different purpose, to make a different point.) Secondly, a painting may be of or about something and hence in this sense not be abstract, and yet not be a representation in the sense of looking like what it is of or about. A painting might be titled *Happiness* and be nothing but a large canvas covered uniformly in buttercup yellow. A lot of twentieth-century painters exploit this possibility and do so in various ways (for example, Klee, Kandinsky and Mondrian).

Certainly these distinctions need to be made, but now let me try to defend art that is abstract in both ways, that is, which is neither a representation of, nor about, anything, and which, not surprisingly, is sometimes entitled *Untitled*. We don't have tests to determine if we like someone, find something interesting, are moved by something, awed by something else. We just are – or, of course, are not. In arguing about art, it has been said, we begin with our conclusions, that is, our reactions. Of course, we can and should – at least sometimes – examine those reactions, seek to explain, and indeed to justify them. We may find, for example, that on reflection it would seem that we like certain writers because their work is *relaxing, comforting*; it doesn't threaten or challenge us in any way, and we can enjoy the prospect of the surprise provided by the twist in the tail of the tale. Well – *fine* after a stressful day at work, but surely art has greater aspirations and achievements? Now returning to reactions to visual art: some completely abstract paintings do profoundly impress some of their viewers, some of whom indeed came to view them with a prejudice. I had seen some small reproductions of Rothko's paintings and did not find them very interesting, and then saw them hung, as Rothko intended they should hang, in a large, darkish room. I thought they were – well, it is difficult to say what I thought or felt but I certainly felt myself in the presence of great paintings: profound, sombre, mysterious paintings.

The philosopher and the philistine might retort: *you* respond in this way, no doubt. But suppose that I and others do not? Well, if there were no consensus about Rothko's paintings or any others, that's all we could say, namely, that people feel differently, they don't in that sense 'agree'. But many disinterested persons, who are interested in art and try not to be blinkered, do respond in this way. The philosopher who is also a sceptic will then say: is it then just a matter of consensus among the *cognoscenti*? Well: it's not *just* among the *cognoscenti* – but what more could there be than widespread agreement among those interested in painting? After all, what 'proof' could there be of Oliver Hardy's being funny other than his making people laugh with mirth? But we are here talking about something serious which, if only implicitly, claims to be an appropriate and *correct* response: we wouldn't say we were *correct* to laugh at Oliver Hardy and, moreover, we shouldn't forget that in his case there is an overwhelming 'consensus'.

Can we make any sense of the undeniable fact that those who are impressed by Rothko's paintings feel that they are right to be so impressed even though anything they might say by way of explanation or justification is, as they acknowledge, dismally inadequate, and their taking the sceptic back to view the paintings doesn't work?

I cannot here go on discussing this problem, which is just as well because I am afraid that I have little more to contribute. I will only add that a very similar problem comes up, or it can arise, in relation to moral judgements and disagreements.

I have been trying to show how philosophical problems arise in connection with painting. I shall now move towards that problem discussed in what I hope is professional detail, in 'Fakes'.

Rembrandt is generally held to be, and, I want to say, *is* a great painter. Those who share this view greatly admire his self-portraits, especially those done in his old age. Apart from responding to the wonderfully free technique, persons trying to express their feelings about these paintings will often say how 'unsentimental', 'straight', 'honest' and hence 'moving' they are. Now remarks like this don't appear to be problematic when made by those who know the subject, who know what he or she looks like and perhaps something of the person's character. Comparing the person and the portrait we can see if the artist has got a likeness, whether he or she has flattered the sitter, made that person look younger or more beautiful or nobler – though whether people who are noble or intelligent look noble or intelligent (and, when asked to make such judgements on the basis of looking at photographs, experimental subjects do poorly) is a further problem, and, if good portraits can succeed in doing this it would be an interesting exercise to find out how. But in the case of Rembrandt, since he died 300 years ago, none of us knows him, and – of course – there are no photographs of him. And even if there *were*, or if there were portraits of him by other artists, or detailed accounts of his looks in old age, those who respond in the ways described above don't feel any need to consult such evidence before expressing their feelings.

I do not wish to be misunderstood. I am not saying that the responses in question are meaningless or romantic, self-indulgent, inappropriate – though some professionally interested in art do say such things – I am raising a question about what they mean and the related question of how we could justify them. And the facts of the matter are, I think, that we should be embarrassed by the question but would strive to answer it by taking the questioner back to the paintings and saying, 'Look! Can't you *see* and so on, and so on.' But what is it that we should be trying to get the questioners to see, and how could one hope to do so by simply getting them to look again at the painting? I should mention at this point that when I learned how badly Rembrandt behaved towards at least one of the women in his life (he had her thrown into gaol) I was shocked and disappointed and looked again at the paintings I so admire. Yet I saw what I had seen before, that is, my reactions were virtually unchanged, there was no shift of aspect.

Here is a further, related problem. Rembrandt's genius was recognised in his lifetime. He ceased to be fashionable as a portraitist in middle life (which may explain why he then started to paint so many self-portraits) but, even within his lifetime, he was copied and forged by less successful and, one supposes, less honest fellow artists. Now at one time there were no less than ninety-odd self-portraits of Rembrandt in the canon, that is, accepted as such by art historians and critics. But in the last thirty or forty years, more and more of these have been rejected as forgeries. Imagine: someone like myself – I, in fact, am told that one of the two majestic self-portraits, done in old age by Rembrandt, which hang in the National Gallery, is not by Rembrandt. Imagine that I am told that *neither* is now authenticated! Well, I have looked at lesser pictures which, on stylistic grounds, critics and historians have judged to be doubtful and not been able to believe them. Now you might say, reasonably enough, that that's my problem. But my problem is different, though fortunately hypothetical. Suppose I cannot but accept that the historical evidence proves conclusively, that the painting of Rembrandt in old age, with a mysterious circular line in the background, is not by Rembrandt. How should I then feel? (And my grammar here conceals the descriptive and normative dimensions of the question.) In fact I don't entirely know what I would feel, and I am not even clear what I should feel. But I certainly would look at the painting differently, and however I reacted then, that is, whether I still felt the painting 'honest', my reactions would be something I would want to think about, scrutinise, examine, as I did not when the painting's authenticity was not in question.[1]

FAKES

Anyone interested in aesthetics should ponder the fascinating and perhaps disturbing story of how Van Meegeren painted

what was widely, though briefly, held to be one of the greatest
Vermeers of all, the *Meeting at Emmaus* – a painting thought
to be of such quality that it, together with Van Meegeren's
fake *Last Supper*, changed the master's *oeuvre*.[2]

Van Meegeren fooled not only the scientists, who routinely
carried out their tests on his 'finds', but, as he felt, the real test
of his pretensions to be a great artist, the art critics. Of
course the usual doubts were felt about the 'discoveries', but
the main grounds for these were not aesthetic but art historical,
namely that too many Vermeers were turning up for them all
to be authentic. It was Van Meegeren himself who finally
revealed the identity of these paintings to disbelieving critics,
by painting yet another 'Vermeer', though of understandably
inferior quality, while in prison. In so doing he avoided a charge
of collaboration with the Germans, but no doubt the sweeter
triumph was his victory over the critics who had been so
contemptuous of his earlier, attributed work.

This rich story grows richer still when we learn that the
critics were able to see the stylistic weaknesses of the
Meeting at Emmaus but only after they were persuaded it
was a fake; and richer again when we learn that those who
continued to insist on the merits of the forgeries also continued
to insist on their authenticity; and one, Van Beuningen, was a
collector who had purchased the *Last Supper*! It seemed to
Van Meegeren that the only thing which mattered to the critics
was, not the quality of a painting but, who painted it. Indeed,
without that knowledge (or belief) they could not see the
qualities of a painting.

We should, it seems, be grateful to Van Meegeren and his
colleagues:[3] their activities reveal as nothing else could the
self-deception, snobbery and, indeed, the cupidity which sur-
round works of art and our 'appreciation' of them.

Now I shall not deny the existence of self-deception, snobbery and cupidity in the world of art. But in this chapter I want
to try to answer the following questions: could critics be
justified in feeling differently about a painting after they have
learned – and particularly if they had to be told – that it was
not what they thought it was, a Vermeer, a fake, by a minor

artist, and so on? And what would a justification come to? Correct answers to these questions will throw light both on the ontological status of works of art and the nature of our aesthetic responses to them.

Let me begin by trying to spell out the rationale of the sceptic's reaction to such episodes as the Van Meegeren case. It runs, I think, thus: a painting is, essentially, a man-made object comprising some sort of surface with some sort of – usually coloured – shapes or marks on it. Hence, our response to a painting *as a painting* should be a response to that configuration of coloured shapes. But if a person's feelings about a painting are transformed by a discovery about its authorship, this shows that these were – and perhaps still are – bogus, For although no doubt they were directed at the painting, they crucially depended on and were generated by something else. They must have been, of course, because the painting *qua* configuration of marks is the same before and after the discovery.

In making this last claim the sceptic is not, of course, denying that as a result of a discovery which produces a change in attitude to a painting, the painting may not 'look different'. The point is that physically it is the same as it was, and so to the observer unaffected by other considerations it will look the same; and these other considerations are clearly, and must be, irrelevant and so improper.

Neither is he concerned to deny that as a result of such a discovery, a person might look more closely at a painting and see things that he had not noticed before – and these could justify a change in his appreciation. Perhaps there *is* weakness in the composition of the heads in the *Meeting*, and perhaps the critics only found it possible to see this when they no longer believed it to be by the master of composition, Vermeer.[4] But the sceptic maintains that such differences need not and do not in fact always exist between fakes and originals, so that the differing feelings which critics have about them are not always justified.

I mention the point that, if we look closely at paintings by different hands, we should be able to see differences between them because various aestheticians have proposed solutions to our problem which invoke and depend on the existence, indeed the necessary existence, of relevant, perceptible, physical differences between fakes and originals. Consider what Clive Bell has to say about copies:[5]

> A literal copy is seldom reckoned even by its owner a work of art. It leaves us cold; its forms are not significant. Yet if it were an absolutely exact copy, clearly it would be as moving as the original, and a photographic reproduction of a drawing often is – almost. Evidently, it is impossible to imitate a work of art exactly; and the differences between the copy and the original, minute though they may be, exist and are felt immediately.

Perhaps one should interject here that for people of true appreciation there can then be no problem in identifying, as such, copies passed off as originals, but of course the difficulty will reappear when we try to identify people of true appreciation; it will surely turn out that there are none. He continues:

> just what made the original moving is what does not appear in the copy, but why is it impossible to make an absolutely exact copy? The explanation seems to be that the actual lines and colours and spaces in a work of art are caused by something in the mind of the artist which is not present in the mind of the imitator.

Bell, then, does not deny that we do feel differently about fakes or copies and originals, and, unlike the person I labelled a sceptic, believes that we are justified in so doing. So, he concludes, there *must* be minute perceptible physical differences between them and originals, and it is these differences which *must* produce, explain and justify our differing responses.

Now there will be, no doubt *must* be, physical differences between any two objects, and when the two objects are paintings one of which is several hundred years old, the other quite recent, these differences will be important in establishing authenticity. No doubt there will in fact always be visual differences between fakes and originals. In fact one way of distinguishing originals from copies, whether they be paintings or signatures is to study the pen or brush strokes. Do they flow? Are they bold? Or are they drawn hesitantly, as if their perpetrator had one eye on something else? (Perhaps he or she had, but not another's picture.) But Bell's claim that there must be differences is clearly an inference transmitted into an a priori claim. And so is his claim that these differences must explain and justify the differing responses to fakes and originals.[6]

These claims stem from Bell's doctrine of 'significant form'. 'Significant form', it will be remembered, is that mysterious, perhaps unanalysable property possessed by certain combinations of shapes and colours, which enables them to generate aesthetic emotion. It is, Bell argues, or perhaps asserts, a property possessed by certain such combinations – he cannot say in an analytic way which such combinations – which does not depend on subject matter, period, authorship or virtuoso technique.

Bell's aesthetic is more austere than any sceptic's need be. But having so restricted what can properly determine our aesthetic appreciation of paintings, he can give no other justification of our differences in feelings about copies and originals except in terms of necessarily existing more or less minute visual differences between them. (I am suggesting, of course, that these necessary differences are other sorts of differences translated into terms which Bell can accept as being relevant.) His overall position would seem to be more consistent and plausible if he admitted that copies and originals can be visually indistinguishable (and even when distinguishable not always identifiable; consider the various *Mona Lisas*) and when they are, they are aesthetically indistinguishable. But he cannot bring himself to accept a conclusion which the sceptic appears to relish.

An aesthetician who does accept this conclusion in Monroe Beardsley,[7] though here I see the acceptance as heroic, made in defence of his general theory. He writes:

suppose, instead of saying that x and y [two paintings] do not differ in any way, he [someone] says that there *is* a difference in their origin – one is a 'fake' – but no difference in their internal characteristics, so no one could tell them apart just by looking at them. Then, I suggest, this amounts to saying that there is no *aesthetic* reason for the judgement, though there may be another kind of reason; and the critic's word 'good' no longer can refer to aesthetic value, but only to some other species of value.

In my use of the term 'aesthetic value' – and I claim that this rule is actually in effect in the critical use of 'good' – two objects that do not differ in any observable qualities cannot differ in aesthetic value.[8]

Unlike Bell, Beardsley attempts to deal with the following objection to his thesis, which also appears to provide a solution to our problem. 'Surely,' one wants to say, 'the difference – the necessary difference – between a fake and an original is that the original is perhaps *original*, in subject matter, composition, lighting, colouring, technique, materials, and so on, and the fake, particularly when it is a mere copy, cannot be. Indeed the more nearly perfect the fake is as a copy, the less room for originality. So, however perfect as a copy, aesthetically the fake is necessarily different from, and inferior to, its original, to the extent that it lacks originality and to the extent that the original possesses it.' (We are leaving room here for the possibility that a fake might have originality and other merits in its own right, greater than those possessed by any painting of which it may be a, presumably poor, copy.)

Beardsley's way of dealing with this objection is to distinguish 'genetic considerations', which refer to 'something existing before the work, to the manner in which it was produced'[9] from 'objective reasons' which refer to 'some characteristic – that is, some quality of internal relation, or set of qualities and relations – within the work itself',[10] and it is, of course, only the latter which bear on the work's aesthetic merit. So when we praise the original for its originality and treat the copy as a lesser work we are guilty of a confusion. If

the paintings are visually indistinguishable, they are as paintings indistinguishable and so aesthetically equal. Our judgement is really of the painter.[11] It is he or she who deserves our
praise for originality. And here too we must remember that
mere originality is not a virtue in an artist; it contributes to the
artist's standing only to the extent that originality manifests
itself in works possessing aesthetic virtues (that is, intensity,
complexity and unity).

Now this last point, which is intended to strengthen
Beardsley's position by reducing the aesthetic dimensions of
originality to 'internal characteristics', that is, visible features
of paintings, fatally weakens it. Because although it tries to
persuade us to admit that 'strictly speaking' originality belongs
to artists rather than works, it concedes that originality is
manifested in the works. So the notion of originality, *like so
many critical concepts*, brings together people and work.

It also makes reference to a feature of the sceptic's definition
of a work of art that is abandoned in his account of aesthetic
merit, namely that paintings are *man-made* objects, and so
objects that appear at a certain time. Now we do not stand
aesthetically to works as we do to natural objects, and our
aesthetic appreciation of and interest in the former is not
reducible to our aesthetic interest in the latter. But it is that
sort of reductivism that Bell is committed to, though he does
not realise it, and so is Beardsley, though he tries to deny it.
But why should we accept this reductive aesthetic, the nature
and implications of which are not fully appreciated by either
proponent?

Beardsley may feel that he can, indeed *must* eschew originality as an aesthetic merit because it, unlike composition
say, is manifested by works but not manifest in them. That is,
one cannot literally see that a work is original because the
judgement involves claims not only about when the work was
produced but (even if we think age is visible) claims about
the non-existence of similar works which antedate that under
consideration. But why should we believe that only those
properties that we can see when we know nothing of the
object confronting us are aesthetically relevant? Of course,

Bell and others may have a very formal interest in and response to art (Bell's aesthetic appetites indicate that he did). But those whose aesthetic responses are determined by other factors are not therefore guilty of incoherence, inconsistency, dishonesty, and so on, and for what it is worth, these persons are using the word 'aesthetic' in the way in which it is actually used.

I turn now to Nelson Goodman. He is not worried if his definition of 'aesthetic' does not square with its ordinary usage[12] but he is properly contemptuous of what he hilariously calls the 'Tingle-Immersion' theory:

> which tells us that the proper behaviour on encountering a work of art is to strip ourselves of all the vestments of knowledge and experience . . . then submerge ourselves completely and gauge the aesthetic potency of the work by the intensity and duration of the resulting tingle. The theory is absurd on the face of it and useless for dealing with any of the important problems of aesthetics; but it has become part of the fabric of our common nonsense.[13]

This quote comes from his chapter on fakes (during which he mentions the Van Meegeren case) and after being much more sophisticated than, as I shall argue, I need be about visual indistinguishability, poses our question in this way:

> is there any aesthetic difference between the two pictures for x at t, where t is a suitable period of time, if we cannot tell them apart by merely looking at them at t?[14]

His answer is yes:

> the fact that the left-hand one is the original and the right-hand one a forgery constitutes an aesthetic difference between them for me now because knowledge of this fact (1) stands as evidence that there may be a difference between them that I can learn to perceive, (2) assigns the present looking a role as training towards such a perceptual discrimination and (3) makes consequent demands that modify and differentiate my present experience in looking at the two pictures.[15]

This last remark looks highly suggestive, though it is also gnomic, and he goes on to say that

> since the exercise, training, and development of our powers of discriminating among works of art are plainly aesthetic activities, the aesthetic properties of a picture include not only those found by looking at it but those that determine how it is to be looked at.[16]

The difficulty here is simply that it leaves us with our original question, namely which properties should determine how we look at, and see pictures? (Goodman makes in the above quote the same point, and passes the same buck as he made and passed in an earlier footnote on p. 105.) If I understand him, he is claiming that attribution matters because knowledge of attribution enables us to develop our discriminative powers. And this of course is true. But surely he is not suggesting that this is the only reason why attribution matters, even when we find two pictures indistinguishable? Yet, as if dealing with the question, he says that visual indistinguishability is an ultra-hypothetical notion[17] and continues:

> we may be faced with the protest that the vast aesthetic difference thought to obtain between the Rembrandt and the forgery cannot be accounted for in terms of the search for, or even the discovery of, perceptual differences so slight that they can be made out, if at all, only after long practise. This objection can be dismissed at once; for minute perceptual differences can bear enormous weight . . . Extremely subtle changes can alter the whole design, feeling or expression of a painting.[18]

Of course they can, but do they *always*? Would they *always* be of such a sort as to explain and justify our invariable change in feelings? Doesn't this remark show that Goodman is ultimately a reductivist (along with Bell, Beardsley and the sceptic), looking in the wrong direction for an explanation and justification of our feelings about fakes? Let me try to explain why by going back to the sceptics: it will be remembered that they allow that when critics discover that what they thought to be a Vermeer turns out to be a fake, the painting may indeed look different to them but insist that it shouldn't. But if what the sceptic allows to be a relevant difference between fakes and originals is too restricted, then perhaps that a painting we thought was an original looks different, at least to some of us, after we learn that it is a fake, is not simply the product of snobbery, confusion or self-deception. Neither can it be explained, as Goodman seemed to do, as the result, or perhaps the indicator, of a developing ability to see, for example, weaknesses of composition and technique, which were always there to be seen. For one thing, the change in our feelings and the change in the appearance of the painting follows immediately on the discovery that it is fake. For another, the forgery does not always exhibit faults in composition or defective technique.

I am suggesting then that even if the *Meeting at Emmaus* did not exhibit the faults in composition which are apparently now so patent; even if its technique were so Vermeerish we could not in fact tell it to be a fake without the aid of scientific tests, many of us who are interested in painting would feel differently about it on discovering it to be a fake, and, as a result of our change in feelings, it would *look different*. And, to anticipate an objection I shall deal with: this 'looking different' cannot be dismissed by calling it an 'illusion'.

In arguing this claim I shall look at two other cases first.

Case one

I see a man, perhaps someone I know, and am struck by how healthy he looks. I then learn that he has TB and now his fine colour looks different – *hectic*. A skilled diagnostician may be able to recognise the flush for what it is, but though I could not do so, *after* I learn what the colour means, that is, what caused it, it looks different to me, and so does the man.

Perhaps a sceptic will say that this 'looking different' is an 'illusion'. But what does this means? That the TB sufferer does *not* look different to the observer! Or does it mean that he *shouldn't* look different? But why not? Presumably because, the sceptic feels, the only proper determinants of how things look are their physical properties, in particular, their propensity to reflect light, and this has not changed in this case; all that has changed is the observer's beliefs and knowledge about the TB sufferer.

But it is a fact that we are so constituted that other factors do affect the way things look to us. It is a fact surely too well established to require my illustrating it further that how things look to us is not simply a function of how they are illuminated, their shapes, and their colours (hues, intensities and saturations).

The sceptic's thesis is not generally true, so he must restrict it, as Bell tends to do with this doctrine of 'significant form', to paintings.

I therefore turn to the second case.

Case two

A sophisticated painter – not a primitive – paints, with great care and after much research, in the style of 10-year-old. Critics disagree about her work, but those who like it acclaim the 'achieved innocence of vision' and the technique that conveys it. But then they learn that one of her most celebrated canvasses is not hers at all, but a 10-year-old child's. At least some of these critics will now feel differently about the painting and it may look different to them. But why? Because the child's painting *is* different. Although physically, photographically, the painting is the same as it was before the discovery – and perhaps very little different from some of the artist's own canvasses – the critics now know it to be quite different from what they thought it was. Here there is no, or very little, skill, or skill of a quite different sort; here no, or very little, art; and here, certainly, no 'achieved innocence of vision'. These aesthetic differences cannot be reduced to or explained in terms of more-or-less minute differences in visible technique between the woman's work and the child's, even if we concede that such differences will exist and are in principle detectable. The aesthetic differences between the woman's work and the child's depend on their different genesis.

Case three

I return finally to Van Meegeren's *Meeting at Emmaus*, and, to make my points, we will suppose that in composition and technique it matched Vermeer's own best work. On discovering this hypothetical painting to be a fake, would we feel differently about it? And might it look different to us? May it properly do so? For many of us at any rate, the answer must be that though we would continue to admire the painting, we could not but see its splendid composition and technique as imitative of Vermeer's and so lesser than, and different from, what it would be if it were original and genuine. We should also, of course, see and admire it as we do not see the originals, namely as a marvellous imitation of them. Indeed, this aspect of Van Meegeren's work might even make us laugh (especially if we saw it as providing a trap for the critics – and ourselves), delighting in a skill which is so like Vermeer's and *yet so different.* But if we see it as a deceitful painting, this may have consequences for our appreciation of its content: instead of seeing it as a consummate expression of an earlier Christian faith, it may seem suffused by hollowness and pretence – and one would not have to be a Christian to feel this.

If persons interested in art do feel like this – and, I am claiming, they do – it is no good the sceptic or any other aesthetic theorists calling such changes in feelings about paintings and changes in how they look to us, 'illusions'. These 'illusions', like so many illusions, are real, public phenomena. All the sceptic can mean is that our responses should not change as they do. But why not? Paintings can be – some of them are – expressions of Christian faith and are appreciated as paintings as such. More generally, they are, and are seen and appreciated as being, *works*, that is, objects that are the produce of a particular person's inspiration and skill and which are made at a certain time and place. So forgeries, no matter how perfect as simulacra, are different as works from originals and will be seen as such.

Of course, to anticipate an objection: some information about works of art is irrelevant to their standing as works of art, and if for whatever idiosyncratic reason such information had consequences for how we saw a work, we should regret it. But could information of the sorts I have discussed be said to be of this kind? Yet the sceptic and other aestheticians have insisted that, in painting, anything but physical, visible differences are irrelevant to paintings and our appreciation of them.

I conclude by pointing out that I am not presenting a monolithic thesis about fakes. Sometimes, though rarely, the discovery that a painting is a fake might not affect our apprehension or appreciation at all. Neither am I suggesting that there could not be a culture in which attribution did not matter, or that our culture might not be improved in certain ways if we weren't so interested in genesis. Nor am I arguing that what we say about traditional painting in so far as we say one thing, is what we should say about all modern works.

What I do say is that we can make an aesthetic distinction between certain paintings even when we can't tell them apart and they don't look different at all *until after we know when they were painted or who painted them.* And seeking to establish this claim involves examining both the nature of paintings – what kinds of thing they are – and the nature of, and in particular what determines, our aesthetic responses to them.

Notes

1. This article first appeared in *Mind*, LXXVII, 345 (1978).
2. For information concerning the Van Meegeren case see, for example, John Jacob and Puro Biancori, *The Complete Paintings of Vermeer*, Weidenfeld & Nicolson, 1970, Appendix.
3. Such as, more recently, and locally, Tom Keating, and more problematically, Elmyr de Hory.

4. Even so, such a change in attitude may strike us a fishy and rationalising, particularly when it emanates from a critic. Fishy because, for example, weakness or strength of a composition ought to be identifiable independently of identification of creator; rationalising, because if the features, whatever they might be, are important enough to matter, they should have been noticed. So either they are not sufficiently important or the critic's original interest was insufficiently serious or not genuine.

5. Clive Bell, *Art*, Grey Arrow, 1976, pp. 64–5.

6. Of a like sort is his explanatory hypothesis that these minute differences must stem from, and reflect, the differing mental states of the original painter and his imitator. But obviously – tautologically – there is independent reason for believing in the existence of these differing mental states, and a different and cogent reason for thinking that such biographical factors affect our appreciation.

7. See. *Aesthetics*, Harcourt, Brace, 1958.

8. Ibid., p. 503.

9. Ibid., p. 457.

10. Ibid., p. 462.

11. Ibid., p. 458.

12. Nelson Goodman, *Language of Art*, Oxford University Press, 1969, p. 254.

13. Ibid., p. 112.

14. Ibid., p. 102.

15. Ibid., p. 105.

16. Ibid., pp. 111–12.

17. Ibid., pp. 106–8, 101.

18. Ibid., p. 108.

HOW CAN WE BE MOVED BY THE FATE
OF ANNA KARENINA?

INTRODUCTION

It was in 1967, 24 hours before I was due to read a paper about Freud to the University of California, Berkeley Campus Philosophy Society that, suddenly, bored with Freud, and paying attention to a niggle I had been having for some time, I wrote the following paper.

Fictional characters are not real, and we adults know that. (And if characters in a work of fiction are real, and some are, what happens to them isn't. Or, if it is, then we do not treat what we read about these happenings as history, but fiction. Or if we do treat it in some ways as history . . .!) So how can we be moved by what happens to them? That there is indeed a problem here is spelt out in the paper, and I therein conclude that in being moved by what happens to characters we know to be fictional, we are irrational, incoherent, inconsistent.

When I published the paper (in 1975), it called down on my head all kinds of criticism, and prompted all kinds of solutions to the paradox which, it was claimed, I had not only propounded but invented. Philosophers – at any rate, those who have gone into print on the issue – are strongly disinclined to believe that any way of carrying on which is institutionalised, widespread, practised by sane, normal – indeed cultured – people, can be irrational, inconsistent, incoherent. I find this a surprisingly unphilosophical view, and a vigorous, not to say forthright debate continues in the professional journals.[1]

HOW CAN WE BE MOVED BY THE FATE OF
ANNA KARENINA?

What's Hecuba to him, or he to Hecuba,
That he should weep for her?
Hamlet, Act 2 Scene 2

That human beings feel concern for the fate of others, that
they have some interest, and a warm and benevolent one in
what happens to at least some other human beings, may be
simply a brute fact about them, though a happy one. By this
I mean that we can conceive that they might have been different in this respect, and so it is possible for us to be puzzled by
the fact that they are not different. In a situation where people
did not feel concern for others, children might be nurtured only
because mothers could not stand the pain of not feeding
them, or because it gave them pleasure to do this and to play
with them, or because they were a source of pride. So that if
a child died, a mother might have the kind of feeling the
owner of a car has if the car is stolen and wrecked. He doesn't
feel anything for the car, unless he is a sentimentalist, and yet
he is sorry and depressed when it happens.

Of course there may be good biological reasons why we
should have concern for each other, or at least some others,
but that is not to the point. The present point, a conceptual
one, is that we can conceive that all of us might have been as
some of us are, namely, devoid of any feeling for anyone but
ourselves, whereas we cannot conceive, for example, what all
language users might (always) be what some are, chronic
liars.

So concern and related feelings are in this sense brute. But
what are they? What is it to be moved by something's happening to someone?

Anything like a complete story here is a very long one, and
in any case I have a particular interest. Suppose then that you
read an account of the terrible sufferings of a group of people.
If you are at all humane, you are unlikely to be unmoved by

what you read. The account is likely to awaken or reawaken feelings of anger, horror, dismay or outrage and, if you are tenderhearted, you may well be moved to tears. You may even grieve.

But now suppose you discover that the account is false. If the account had caused you to grieve, you could not continue to grieve. If as the account sank in, you were told and believed that it was false this would make tears impossible, unless they were tears of rage. If you learned later that the account was false, you would feel that in being moved to tears you had been fooled, duped.

It would seem then that I can only be moved by someone's plight if I believe that something terrible has happened to her or him. If I did not believe that someone has not and is not suffering or whatever, I cannot grieve or be moved to tears.

It is not only seeing a person's torment that torments us, it is also, as we say, the thought of his torment which torments, or upsets or moves us. But here thought implies belief. We have to believe in his torment to be tormented by it. When we say that the thought of his plight moves us to tears or grieves us, it is thinking of or contemplating suffering which we believe to be actual or likely that does it.

The direction of my argument should now be fairly clear. Moving closer to its goal: suppose that you have a drink with a man who proceeds to tell you a harrowing story about his sister and you are harrowed. After enjoying your reaction he then tells you that he doesn't have a sister, that he has invented the story. In his case, unlike the previous one, we might say that the 'heroine' of the account is fictitious. None the less, and again, once you have been told this you can no longer feel harrowed. Indeed, it is possible that you may be embarrassed by your reaction precisely because it so clearly indicates that you were taken in – and you may also feel embarrassed for the story-teller that he could behave in such a way. But the possibility of your being harrowed again seems to require that you believe that someone suffered.

Of course, if the man tells you in advance that he is going to tell you a story, you may reach for your hat, but you may stay and be moved. But this is too quick.

Moving closer still: an actor friend invites you to watch him simulate extreme pain, agony. He writhes about and moans. Knowing that he is only acting, could you be moved to tears? Surely not. Of course you may be embarrassed, and after some time you may even get faintly worried 'Is he really acting, or is he really in pain? Is he off his head?' But as long as you are convinced that he is only acting and is not really suffering, you cannot be moved by his suffering, and it seems unlikely as well as – as it were – unintelligible that you might be moved to tears by his portrayal of agony. If seems that you could only perhaps applaud it if it were realistic or convincing, and criticise if it were not.

But not suppose, horribly, that he acts or re-enacts the death agonies of a friend, or a Vietcong that he killed and tells you this. Then you might be horrified.

If this account is correct, there is no problem about being moved by historical novels or plays, documentary films, and so on, for these works depict and forcibly remind us of the real plight and of the real sufferings of real people, and it is for these persons that we feel.[2]

What seems unintelligible is how we could have a similar reaction to the fate of Anna Karenina, the plight of Madame Bovary or the death of Mercutio. Yet we do. We weep, we pity Anna Karenina, we blink hard when Mercutio is dying and absurdly wish that he had not been so impetuous.

Or do we? If we are seized by this problem, it is tempting for us to argue that, since we cannot be anguished or moved by what happens to Anna Karenina, since we cannot pity Madame Bovary and since we cannot grieve at the marvellous Mercutio's death, we do not do so.

This is a tempting thesis especially because, having arrived at it, we have then to think more carefully about our reactions to and feelings about, for example, the death of Mercutio, and these investigations reveal – how could they do otherwise? – that our response to Mercutio's death differs massively from our response to the untimely death of someone we know. As we watch Mercutio die the tears run down our cheeks, but as O.K. Bouwsma has pointed out,[3] the cigarettes and chocolates go in our mouths too, and we may mutter, if not to each other, then to ourselves 'How marvellous! How sublime!' and even 'How moving!'

'Now,' one might say, 'if one really is *moved*, one surely cannot comment on this and in admiring tones? Surely being moved to tears is a massive response which tends to interfere with saying much, even to oneself? And surely the nature of the response is such that any comments made that do not advert to what gives rise to the feeling but to the person experiencing it tend to suggest that the response isn't really felt? Compare this with leaning over to a friend in a theatre and saying "I am completely absorbed (enchanted, spellbound) by this!"'

But although we cannot truly grieve for Mercutio, we can be moved by his death, and are. If and when one says 'How moving' in an admiring tone, one can be moved at the theatre. One's admiration is for the play or the performance, and one can admire or be impressed by this and avow this while being moved by it.

So we cannot say that we do not feel for fictional characters, that we are not sometimes moved by what happens to them. We shed real tears for Mercutio. They are not crocodile tears, they are dragged from us and they are not the sort of tears that are produced by cigarette smoke in the theatre. There is a lump in our throats, and it's not the sort of lump that is produced by swallowing a fishbone. We are appalled when we realise what may happen, and are horrified when it does. Indeed, we may be so appalled at the prospect of what we think is going to happen to a character in a novel or a play that some of us can't go on. We avert the impending tragedy in the only way we can, by closing the book, or leaving the theatre.

This may be an inadequate response, and we may also feel silly or shamefaced at our tears. But this is not because they are always inappropriate and sentimental, as, for example, is giving one's dog a birthday party, but rather because we feel them to be unseemly. They may be excusable though still embarrassing on the occasion of a real death, but should be contained for anything less.

Of course we are not only moved by fictional tragedies but impressed and even delighted by them. But I have tried to explain this, and that we are other things does not seem to be the point. What is worrying is that we are moved by the death of Mercutio and we weep while knowing that no one has really died, that no young man has been cut off in the flower of his youth.[4]

So if we can be and if some of us are indeed moved to tears at Mercutio's untimely death, feel pity for Anna Karenina and so on, how can this be explained? How can the seeming incongruity of our doing this be explained and explained away?

First solution

When we read the book or better when we watch the play and it works, we are 'caught up' and respond and we 'forget' or are no longer aware that we are only reading a book or watching a play. In particular, we forget that Anna Karenina, Madame Bovary, Mercutio, and so on are not real persons.

But this won't do. It turns adults into children. It is true that, for example, when children are first taken to pantomimes they are unclear about what is going on. The young ones are genuinely and unambiguously terrified when the giant comes to kill Jack. The bolder ones shout 'Look out!' and even try to get on the stage to interfere.

But do we do this? Do we shout and try to get on the stage when, watching *Romeo and Juliet*, we see that Tybalt is going to kill Mercutio? We do not. Or if we do, this is extravagant and unnecessary for our being moved. If we really did think someone was really being slain, either a person called 'Mercutio' or the actor playing that role, we would try to do something or think that we should. We would, if you like, be genuinely appalled.[5]

So we are not unaware that we are 'only' watching a play involving fictional characters, and the problem remains.

Second solution

Of course we don't ever forget that Mercutio is only a character in a play, but we 'suspend our disbelief' in his reality. The theatre management and the producer connive at this. They dim the lights and try to find good actors. They, and we, frown on other members of the audience who draw attention to themselves and distract us by coughing, and if, during a scene, say, a stage-hand steals on, picks up a chair that should have been removed and sheepishly departs, our response is destroyed. The 'illusion' is shattered.

All this is true but the paradox remains. When we watch a play we do not direct our thoughts to its only being a play. We don't continually remind ourselves of this – unless we are trying to reduce the effect of the work on us. None the less, and as we have seen, we are never unaware that we are watching a play, and one about fictional characters even at the most exciting and moving moments. So the paradox is not solved by invoking 'suspension of disbelief', though it occurs and is connived at.

Third solution

It's just another brute fact about human beings that they can be moved by stories about fictional characters and events. That is, human beings might not have been like this (and a lot of them are not; a lot of people do not read books or go to the theatre, and are bored if they do).

But our problem is that people *can* be moved by fictional

suffering given their brute behaviour in other contexts where belief in the reality of the suffering described or witnessed is necessary for the response.

Fourth solution

This thesis about behaviour in non-fictional contexts is too strong. The paradox arises only because my examples are handpicked ones in which there is this requirement. But there are plenty of situations in which we can be moved to tears or feel a lump in the throat without thinking that anyone will, or that anyone is even likely to, suffer or die an untimely death, or whatever.

But are there? A mother hears that one of her friend's children has been killed in a street accident. When her own children return from school she grabs them in relief and hugs them, almost with a kind of anger. (Is it because they have frightened her?) Their reaction is 'What's wrong with you?' They won't get a coherent answer perhaps, but surely the explanation is obvious. The death of a friend's child 'brings home', 'makes real' and perhaps strengthens the mother's awareness of the likelihood of her own children being maimed or killed. We must try another case. A man's attention wanders from the paper he is reading in his study. He thinks of his sister and, with a jolt, realises that she will soon be flying to the States. Perhaps because he is terrified of flying he thinks of her flying and of her plane crashing and shudders. He imagines how this would affect their mother. She would be desolated, inconsolable. Tears prick his eyes. His wife enters and wants to know what's up. He looks upset. Our man is embarrassed but says truthfully, 'I was thinking about Jean's flying to the States and, well, I thought how awful it would be if there were an accident – how awful it would be for my mother.' Wife: 'Don't be silly! How maudlin! And had you nearly reduced yourself to tears thinking about all this? Really, I don't know what's got into you', and so on, and so on.

In this case the man's response to his thoughts, his being appalled at the thought of his sister's crashing, *is* silly and maudlin, but it is intelligible and non-problematic. For it would be neither silly nor maudlin if flying were a more dangerous business than we are prone to think it is. Proof: change the example and suppose that the sister is seriously ill. She is not suffering yet, but she had cancer and her brother thinks about her dying and how her death will affect their mother. If that were the situation his wife would do well to offer comfort as well as advice.

So the man can be moved not only by what has happened to someone, by actual suffering and death, but by their prospect, and the greater the probability of the awful thing's happening, the more likely are we to sympathise, that is, to understand his response and even share it. The lesser the probability the more likely we are not to feel this way. And if what moves a man to tears is the contemplation of something that is most unlikely to happen, for example, the shooting of his sister, the more likely are we to find his behaviour worrying and puzzling. However, we can explain his divergent behaviour, and in various ways. We can do this in terms of his having false beliefs. He thinks a plane crash or a shooting is more likely than it is, which itself needs and can have an explanation. Or his threshold for worry is lower than average, and again this is non-problematic, that is, we understand what's going on. Or lastly, we may decide he gets some kind of pleasure from dwelling on such contingencies and appalling himself. Now this is, logically, puzzling, for how can a person get pleasure from pain? But if only because traces of masochism are present in many of us, we are more likely to find it simply offensive.

The point is that our man's behaviour is only more or less psychologically odd or morally worrying. There is no logical difficulty here, and the reason for this is that the suffering and anguish that he contemplates, however unlikely, is pain that some real person may really experience.

Testing this, let us suppose first that our man when asked 'What's up?', says 'I was thinking how awful it would have been if Jean had been unable to have children – she wanted them so much.' Wife: 'But she's got them. Six!' Husband: 'Yes,

I know, but suppose she hadn't?' 'My God! Yes it would have been but it didn't happen. How can you sit there and weep over the dreadful thing that didn't happen, and now cannot happen.' (She's getting philosophical. Sneeringly) 'What are you doing? Grieving for her? Feeling sorry for her?' Husband: 'All right! But thinking about it, it was so vivid I could imagine just how it would have been.' Wife: 'You began to snivel!' Husband: 'Yes.'

It is by making the man a sort of Walter Mitty, a man whose imagination is so powerful and vivid that, for a moment anyway, what he imagines seems real, that his tears are made intelligible, though of course not excusable.

So now suppose that the man thinks not of his sister but of a woman . . . that is, he makes up a story about a woman who flies to the States and is killed and whose mother grieves, and so on, and that this gives him a lump in his throat. It might appear that, if my thesis is correct, the man's response to the story he invents should be even more puzzling than his being moved by the thought of his sister's not having children. 'Yet,' one who was not seized by the philosophical problem might say, 'this case is really not puzzling. After all, he might be a writer who first gets some of his stories in this manner!'

But that is precisely why this example does not help. It is too close, too like what gives rise to the problem.[6]

Fifth solution

A solution suggested by an earlier remark: if and when we weep for Anna Karenina, we weep for the pain and anguish that a real persons might suffer and which real persons have suffered, and if her situation were not of that sort we should not be moved.

There is something in this, but not enough to make it a solution. For we do not really weep for the pain that a real person might suffer, and which real persons have suffered, when we weep for Anna Karenina, even if we should not be moved by her story if it were not of that sort. We weep for *her*. We are moved by what happens to her, by the situation she gets into, which is a pitiful one, but we do not feel pity for her state or fate, or her history or her situation, or even for others, that is, for real persons who might have or even have had such a history. We pity her, feel for her and our tears are shed for her. This thesis is even more compelling, perhaps, if we think about the death of Mercutio.

But all over again, how can we do this knowing that neither she nor Mercutio ever existed, that all their sufferings do not add one bit to the sufferings of the world?

Sixth solution

Perhaps there really is no problem. In non-fictional situations it may be necessary that in order for a person to be moved, he or she must believe that such a thing may indeed happen to someone. But, as I concede, being moved when reading a novel or watching a play is not exactly like being moved by what one believes happens in real life and, indeed, it is very different. So there are two sorts of being moved and, perhaps, two senses of 'being moved'. There is being moved (Sense 1) in real life and 'being moved' (Sense 2) by what happens to fictional characters. But since there are these two sorts and senses, it does not follow from the necessity of belief in the reality of the agony or whatever it is, for being moved (S.1), that belief in its reality is, or ought to be necessary for 'being moved' (S.2). So I have not shown that there is a genuine problem, which perhaps explains why I can find no solution.

But although being moved by what one believes is really happening is not exactly the same as being moved by what one believes is happening to fictional characters, it is not wholly different. And it is what is common to being moved in either situation which makes problematic one of the differences, namely, the fact that belief is not necessary in the fictional situation. As for the hesitant claim that there is a different sense here, this clearly does not follow from the fact that being moved by what happens in real life is different from being moved in the theatre or cinema or when reading a novel, and I find it counter-intuitive.[7] But even if the phrase did

have different senses for the different cases, it would not follow that there was no problem. It may be that 'being moved'
(S.2) is an incoherent notion so that we and our behaviour are
incoherent, when we are 'moved' (S.2).

When, as we say, Mercutio's death moves us, it appears to
do so in very much the same way as the unnecessary death
of a young man moves us and for the same reason. We see
the death as a waste, though of course it is really only a waste
in the real case, and as a 'tragedy', and we are, unambiguously – though problematically as I see it in the case of fiction
– saddened by the death. As we watch the play and realise
that Mercutio may die or, knowing the play, that he is about
to die, we may none the less and in either case say to ourselves 'Oh! No! Don't let it happen!' (It seems *absurd* to say
this, especially when we know the play; and yet we do. This is
part of what I see as the problem.) When he is run through we
wince and gasp and catch our breath, and as he dies the
more labile of us weep.

How would our behaviour differ if we believed that we were
watching the death of a real young man, perhaps of the actor
playing the part of Mercutio? First, seeing or fearing that the
actor playing the part of Tybalt is bent on killing the other
actor, we might try to get help. But if we are convinced that
we can do nothing, as we are when we watch the death of
Mercutio or read about Anna, and if we thought that our
watching was not improper, these irrelevant differences in our
behaviour would disappear. Once again, we would say to
ourselves – and, in this case also to each other since there is
no question of aesthetic pleasure – 'My God! How terrible!'
And as the actor lay dying, perhaps delivering Mercutio's
lines, either because he felt them to be appropriate or
because, unaware that he was actually dying, he felt that the
show must go on, we should again weep for the dying human
being and the pity of it. Secondly, but this is not irrelevant, our
response to the real death is likely to be more massive, more
intense and longer in duration for, after all, a real young man
has been killed, and it will not be alloyed – or allayed – by

aesthetic pleasure. But such differences do not destroy the similarity of the response and may even be said to require it.

So a similarity exists, and the essential similarity seems to be that we are saddened. But this is my difficulty. For we *are* saddened, but how can we be? What are we sad *about*? How can we feel genuinely and involuntarily sad, and weep, as we do, knowing as we do that no one has suffered or died?

To insist that there is this similarity between being moved and 'being moved' is not to deny that there are other differences between them besides the necessary presence of belief in the one case and its puzzling absence in the other. Yet, as I have already indicated, some of the peculiar features of 'being moved' add to the problem it presents. Not *any* difference between being moved and 'being moved', over and above the difference in belief, has the effect of reducing the conceptual problem presented by the latter, as is suggested by this sixth solution. For example, when we hope that Mercutio will not get killed, we may realise, knowing the play, that he must be killed, unless the play is altered or the performance is interrupted and we may not wish for that. So not only is our hope vain, for he must die and we know this,[8] but it exists alongside a wish that he *will* die! After the death, in retrospect, our behaviour differs. In the case of the real man, we should continue to be moved and to regret that happened. With Mercutio we are unlikely to do this and, in talking about his death later, we might only be moved to say 'How moving it was!' For we are no longer at the performance or responding directly to it. We do not so much realise later as appropriately remind ourselves later that Mercutio is only a character and that, being a character, he will, as it were, be born again to die again at the next performance. Mercutio is not lost to us, when he dies, as the actor is when he dies.

Our response to Mercutio's death is, then, different from our response to the death of the actor. We do not entirely or simply hope that it will not happen, our response is partly aesthetic, the anguish at his death is not perhaps as intense, and it tends not to survive the performance.

Perhaps we are and can be moved by the death of Mercutio only to the extent that, at the time of the performance, we are 'caught up' in the play, and see the characters as persons, real persons, though to see them as real persons is not to believe that they are real persons. If we wholly believe, our response is indistinguishable from our response to the real thing, for we believe it to be the real thing. If we are always and fully aware that these are only actors mouthing rehearsed lines, we are not caught up in the play at all and can only respond to the beauty and tragedy of the poetry and not to the death of the character. The difficulty is, however – and it remains – that the belief, to say the least, is never complete. Or, better, even when we are caught up, we are still aware that we are watching a play and that Mercutio is 'only' a character. We may become like children, but this is not necessary for our tears.

So the problem remains. The strength of our response may be proportionate to, *inter alia*, our 'belief' in Mercutio. But we do not and need not at any time believe that he is a real person to weep for him. So that what is necessary in other contexts, namely, belief, for being moved, is not necessary here and, all over again, how can we be saddened by and cry over Mercutio's death knowing as we do that when he dies no one really dies?

I am left with the conclusion that our being moved in certain ways by works of art, though very 'natural' to us and in that way only too intelligible, involves us in inconsistency and so incoherence.

It may be some sort of comfort, as well as support for my thesis, to realise that there are other sorts of situations in which we are similarly inconsistent, that is, in which, while knowing that something is or is not so, we spontaneously behave, or even may be unable to stop ourselves behaving, as if we believed the contrary. Thus, a tennis player who sees his or her shot going into the net will often give a little involuntary jump to lift it over. Because he knows that this can have no effect, it is tempting to say that the jump is purely expressive.

But almost anyone who has played tennis will know that this is not true. Or again, though human beings have increasingly come to think of death as a dreamless sleep, it was pointed out long ago – was it by Dr Johnson or David Hume?[9] – that they still fear it. Some may say that this fear is not incoherent, for what appals such persons is not their also thinking of death as an unpleasant state, but the prospect of their non-existence. But how can this appal? There is, literally, nothing to fear. The incoherence of fearing the sleep of death for all that it will cause one to miss is even clearer. We do not participate in life when we are dead, but we are not then endlessly wishing to do so. None the less, we fear the endless, dreamless sleep of death and fear it for all that we shall miss.

Notes

1. This article first appeared in the *Proceedings of the Aristotelian Society*, Supp. vol. XLIX (1975).
2. Not for the performance which elicits this feeling or for the actor – for those we feel admiration, are impressed and so on. This may help to explain how we can enjoy tragedy. Besides the actor's skill and the producer's, we also enjoy the skill of the writer. What is difficult is that we weep. This turns the usual problem upside down. People are more often puzzled about how we can enjoy a tragedy, not how it can harrow us, cf. Hume's essay, 'On tragedy'.
3. In 'The expression theory of art', collected in his *Philosophical Essays,* University of Nebraska Press, 1965, p. 29.
4. Though why that should worry us is another worry. There may be some who still feel that there really is no problem, so consider the following case. A man has a genre painting. It shows a young man being slain in battle (but it is not a historical picture, that is, of the death of some particular real young man who was killed in a particular battle). He says that he finds the picture moving and we understand, even if we do not agree. But then he says that, when he looks at the picture, he feels pity, sorrow, and so on, for *the young man in the picture.* Surely this very odd response would be extremely puzzling? How *can*

he feel sorry for the young man in the painting? But now suppose that the picture is a moving picture, that is, a movie, and
it tells a story. In this case we *do* say that we feel sorry for the
young man in the film who is killed. But is there a difference
between these two cases which not only explains but justifies
our differing responses? Is it, perhaps, simply because most of
us do respond in this way to films that we do not find our doing
so puzzling?

5. Cf. 'The delight of tragedy proceeds from our consciousness of
    fiction; if we thought murders and treasons real, they would
    please no more' (Johnson, *Preface to Shakespeare*).

6. Incidentally, and to avoid misunderstanding, I do not have a
    monolithic view about aesthetic response. I am not saying, for
    example, that we must believe a story about Margaret Thatcher
    to find it *funny*. I am saying that, with the paradoxical excep-
    tion of watching plays, films, and so on, including those about
    Margaret Thatcher, we need to believe the story to weep for her,
    to feel pity for her.

7. Does 'killed' have a different sense in 'Reagan has been killed'
    and 'Mercutio has been killed'?

8. Of course, seeing a clip from the newsreel of President Kennedy's
    assassination may elicit the same response 'Don't let him get
    killed!', and here we do realise that our response is silly, is
    incompatible with our knowledge that he is dead and we are
    watching a film of his death. But there is in the theatre nothing
    analogous to actually witnessing Kennedy's death. The death
    of a character is always irrevocable, out of reach, and out of our
    control.

9. Either could have made such an observation, though Hume
    regarded death with phlegm, Johnson with horror. But in fact it
    was their contemporary, Miss Seward. 'There is one mode of
    the fear of death which is certainly absurd; and that is the dread
    of annihilation, which is only a pleasing sleep without a dream'
    (Boswell, *Life of Johnson,* for 1778).

PART THREE:

PLAY(S)

INTRODUCTION

As I have suggested in the earlier parts of this book, paintings and literature and, indeed, the other art forms, and the ways in which we respond to them, raise many and various philosophical problems. For example, in music, which I have not discussed, some of the music that we most treasure we would characterise as 'sad'. But how can music be sad? If part of what we mean is that is *sounds* sad, does it not also and therefore make us feel sad? (Certainly Beethoven's last quartets don't make us smile or snap our fingers, or get up and dance, as does some other music.) But if it does make us feel sad, why on earth should we choose to listen to it?

Some philosophers have been so impressed by this point that they have argued that such music does not and cannot make its devotees feel sad. They have suggested that it doesn't make listeners *really* feel sad, but 'quasi-sad' or 'sad'. Of course such remarks could only be the beginning of or indeed the preface to a solution of this puzzle.

Is it perhaps that 'sad' is really not quite the right word, and perhaps 'sombre', 'reflective', might be more precise? Or is 'sad' right but the music which inspires it offers delights which could not be had without the sadness? (Rather, perhaps, as the satisfaction of achieving something which cannot be had without the effort involved in preparing for and in bringing off the achievement.) Yet if 'sad' is, sometimes, the right word, what does the music make us sad about? How?

In his *Republic*, Plato seems to regard music as being a 'representation'. Just as sculptures and paintings represent persons, or gods, or places, events, and so on, music represents human emotions. If you are not sure what this means,

211

or whether what Plato appears to be saying is true, perhaps this is because although it seems as if pieces of sculpture and paintings represent what they are of, that is, their subjects, in rather similar ways, if music represents human feelings and emotions it does so in a very different way or ways, and what these are is not immediately clear. Wouldn't it be better to say, as Plato also says, that music, or at least some music, gives *expression* to human feelings and emotions – though, of course, we should not want to say that composers must feel sad when composing sad music or gay when composing gay music. (Perhaps their main 'feeling' is always concern with the task of composition itself: a composer having difficulty in writing a piece of music expressing and conveying a feeling of tranquillity might feel agitated until he had finished it.) Yet in those late Beethoven quartets, it does seem that there are passages of almost unbearable poignancy where the cadences and rhythm of the music sound rather like those of a voice breaking under emotion, others that sound rather like a solemn conversation as the melody modulates and moves from one instrument to another, while the rest murmur in the background or are silent. The music then does seem to echo and imitate, in that way, those sounds, and perhaps that is an important part of its expressive character and how it achieves its effects.

Plato certainly thought of all art as imitation, and that, being an imitation, it was inferior to what it imitates! Perhaps only respect for such a great thinker and the fact that our texts may be corrupt and that all texts require interpretation, prevent us from noticing that Plato's view here is exactly like the philistine's who is puzzled why anyone might pay such a huge amount of money for a painting of fruit when he might have bought the fruit itself for a minute fraction of that money!

Some of you may have been struck by the fact that Plato's account of art as representation and imitation overlooks abstract art, or perhaps, if only by implication, denies that such 'art' is art at all. Of course there are people who – at least in regard to painting and sculpture – agree with that view and would welcome this implication, and they are not all of them persons who lack any real interest in, or knowledge of, art. Defenders of Plato who do accept that fine art can be non-representational would have to argue that Plato's notions of representation and imitation are such that we can say, in those terms, that not only pure music but abstract art is representation and imitation, and that saying this is illuminating. I am inclined to the less profound view that Plato's account of art as representation may be explained at one level as encouraged by there being (virtually) no abstract art and perhaps no pure music, in Ancient Greece. (By 'pure music' I mean here music that was not an accompaniment to dancing or singing.) This lack of diversity fitted very well with the monolithic view he gave of art (and which he gave of much else).

So art and our responses give rise to many philosophical problems. This is not to say that these problems are raised in the art itself, though that can happen too. Since philosophy is discursive and – if not always, often – analytic, this occurs more often in literature than the fine arts or music; indeed it might seem that, as the other arts are not discursive (unless a text is included in them), they cannot raise philosophical problems. But this is not quite true. To the extent that paintings and music can and do draw attention to their own nature, their relation as particular works of art to whatever they may happen to represent, or their relationship with what is now fashionable to call their 'consumers', that is, the persons who work at or listen to them, they can be philosophical. Many of Escher's works; Mozart's philosophical joke (used, wittingly or not, as the theme music the now defunct BBC TV's 'Horse of the Year' programmes); perhaps his 'Dissonance' string quartet (K 465); possibly some of Beethoven's protracted conclusions to certain movements in his symphonies; Haydn's surprise in his symphony thus called; even Jan van Eyck's claim 'Jan was here' written in Latin above the mirror in the painting known as 'The Arnolfini' which inscription, like a signature, is not in the represented room; Vermeer's turning his back to us in the only painting we have by him which contains a representation if not a portrait of the artist; the reflection in Velasquez's *Las Meninas*; almost any painting by Magritte;

much if not perhaps most of modern fine art; Holbein's skull in 'forced perspective' which stretches across the front, that is, in front of the Dutch Ambassadors in the painting that goes by that name; so much of its iconography and symbolism, and the iconography and symbolism in so many Renaissance and indeed medieval paintings – all, intentionally or not, draw attention to the work of art *as* a work of art and encourage its audience to reflect on this and their relation and response to the work.

Even so, we would expect and do find the most explicit, detailed and protracted discussions, explorations, dramatic representations or recreations of philosophical issues in literature, that is to say, in novels, sagas, stories, poems, plays, myths, sacred texts. The examples here are so many that it is difficult to know where to start or what to nominate to illustrate the claim. One of the earliest and the most completely and directly philosophical is Plato's *Symposium* – if indeed it was written as a play (which is possible, even if the play is an attempt to recreate an actual party attended by Socrates *et al.*).

So literature not only raises, but discusses philosophical problems. However, the manner in which the *Symposium* does so is unusual. That is to say, the ways in which works of literature pursue, present and discuss philosophical problems is not that of the philosopher. Muriel Spark in her first and, I think, her most brilliant novel, *The Comforters*, is concerned to explore the relation between fiction and reality, between fictional characters and real persons, and does so by writing a novel about a young woman undergoing a mental and emotional crisis who believes that she is the creation of some hidden author who, despite being her creator, is writing a novel through her by recording what she thinks on a typewriter, the tapping of which she can hear. (The novel does not itself tell us, but notes accompanying the novel do, that Muriel Spark herself experienced a breakdown around the time she was abandoning her life as a critic and embarking on creative writing; she was also being received into the Catholic Church and ending a relationship with a man, and this is also echoed in the novel.) In doing this, Spark is also at the same time exploring an issue which arises for any believer and perhaps especially strongly for a Catholic. The sceptic and the atheist attach no meaning to the vicissitudes of life. They just happen and have no meaning beyond the mere contingencies of life and the unproblematic facts that the things we do may have their causes and may certainly have consequences. But for those who believe in God, their creator, everything is what it is (as Bishop Butler said) and is another thing as well: it has *significance*. And of course the same is true of what happens in fiction. If we are told of, or presented with, something in a novel, however mundane that incident, then the mere fact that we are privy to it suggests to us that it is important, it will matter as the story develops, it is significant. (If it doesn't, we are puzzled, think that the writing and editing is slipshod, or that the author is writing an experimental work. In *War and Peace*, there are inconsistencies in Natasha's age. Those who notice these inconsistencies tend to assume, surely rightly, that Tolstoy nodded, not that he *meant* something by them. Had he written the work one hundred years later we might not feel quite so sure.)

But Muriel Spark's examination, her 'discussion' of the relation between fiction and reality, real persons and fictional ones, 'meaning' in the world and in the novel, are of course literary rather than philosophical. That is to say, she is concerned to excite our interest, provoke us, produce something beautiful, disturbing, funny, puzzling, which leaves us with a frown of puzzlement and delight. She is not tackling the issues she raises directly, literally, eschewing distractions and side-issues, denying herself the pleasure and opportunity of writing so brilliantly that both the brilliance and the minutiae of her story may distract us from a sober, analytic examination of the philosophical issues raised by her story. Like Laurence Sterne, who is always interrupting the story, and in so doing, drawing attention to its only being a story, that is not really a history, and doing so again, and again, until you have lost sight of what he was purporting to tell us, and why, Spark is not just examining a philosophical problem. Yes, she is doing that, but she has other, perhaps, larger, to some tastes juicier, and certainly more glittering, iridescent fish to fry. That is why we feel uncertain about the status of the *Symposium*.

So the pieces in this part of the book, being literary (except, perhaps, for the first), raise philosophical problems, but, being the work of a philosopher, do – some of them – pursue philosophical problems, though not in the way that philosophers do in their professional writings. Thus: the passages in 'The seminar' in which Professor Rea muses about necessary and sufficient conditions, and in which Jack (the giantkiller?) argues about meaning, are not merely an imitation of philosophical arguments, they *are* philosophical arguments. But, as this is a play, and the subject is arcane, this is not their justification. Of course, as author, I, a philosopher, am pleased that they do make philosophical sense and raise problems which have been raised and discussed in such terms by philosophers. But, in a play, that cannot be their first or main justification. What is crucial is that someone seeing a production of this play should be persuaded that philosophers do talk like this, do raise and dispute problems, the importance and resolution of which should be apparent to the professional disputants.

All this is by way of saying that the literary pieces which follow in this part of the book, if they work, work, as they must, primarily as literature (and, if that sounds somewhat solemn, or even pretentious, I would remind you, and myself, that jokes, anecdotes and sketches, as much as stories and plays, are literary productions). In other words, the philosophical problems which they raise are raised primarily, not *in* the work, but *by* the work.

Now it is a fact, and one of which I have been reminded by so many of the best students on a course I taught for years with my friend and colleague Tony Skillen, 'Truth in fiction', that even students who enjoy a work of literature, and, as critics, have many acute comments to make about the work, may be embarrassed by the question, 'But what *philosophical* questions are raised by this work?' It is for this reason that I feel that it may be helpful not to write introductions to the pieces, as I did with the articles in Part Two, but append post-scripts to the various pieces, in which I encourage and, I hope, conspire with the reader to ask what philosophical questions, if any, are raised by the piece, and what philosophical work does it do that might not have been done, and better done, by a philosophical article.

8

THE UNEXPECTED EXAMINATION

ADRIAN: When you were doing physics this afternoon, Foggy said we were going to have an exam next week.

BEATRICE [*shocked*]: *What in?*

CELIA [*shocked*]: *When?*

A: He didn't say that. Any subject; English, Maths, Biology, Fr—

B: —'s not *fair!*

C: *When? Which day?*

A: Oh, we won't know before. We won't know until the day of the exam.

B: That's ruined my weekend.

[*Pause*]

C: So it can't be Friday.

A: Why not?

B: Because if we haven't had it by Thursday –

C: – we'd know after school it was going to be Friday.

A: Oh *yea!* So it can't be Friday.

C: But that means it can't be Thursday, either.

B: Why not?

A: Because if it can't be Friday, if we haven't had it by Wednesday, it's got to be Thursday and we'd know that Wednesday, so it can't be Thursday.

B: So it can't be Wednesday, either. Or . . .

C: Tuesday, or . . .

A: Monday. [*Pause*] So we won't be getting an exam next week!

B: That's *mad!* I'll bet we do!

A: We *can't!* Not an *unexpected* one.

C: Oh yes we can.

A: How?

C: We can have it any day.

A: How?

C: Suppose we go in Monday and he tells us we're having the exam. Won't that be a surprise?

B: Not altogether.

C: Yes, but you won't know until you get in. Same with Tuesday, Wednesday, and so on.

A: But how about *Friday*? If we haven't had it by Thursday, we know it'll be Friday and then it won't be a surprise.

C: So we won't be able to have it on Friday?

A: *No.*

B: Hmm?

C: So when we get it on Friday it'll be a really big surprise then, won't it?

POSTSCRIPT

The philosophical problem raised in this sketch is an old one and you may be familiar with it. But is Celia's solution (first offered, I believe, by the famous American philosopher W. V. O. Quine) wholly convincing? Is there not something profoundly puzzling about it?

I think there is, and I think it's this. Suppose the Celia/ Quine solution is correct, and not only Celia but Adrian and Beatrice accept that it is correct. Then by the time Thursday evening comes and they still haven't had an examination, A, B and C will know that, if they are to have an exam that week, they must have it tomorrow, Friday. But if they know this on Thursday they cannot have an unexpected exam on Friday.

So Celia's solution is self-destructive. The only surprise that the students can have on Friday is not having an exam at all. They cannot have an exam and one that is unexpected on Friday. They can have an expected exam or be surprised by not having one at all. Either way their teacher's statement is not true (see below).

But if he cannot leave the exam until Friday without falsifying what he told the students, can he leave it until Thursday? Are we not back in our original mess? Of course if only the teacher had said, 'You may have an exam next week, and it may be on any day', there wouldn't have been a problem. But he didn't, and there still is.

As to the philosophical problems raised *by* the sketch, there are virtually none, and it might almost as well be written out in the form of a statement of the problem. But, having three imaginary characters work their way through the problem may do two things: it may make the problem clearer, perhaps, and the solution offered more dramatic; secondly, however minimally, the three protagonists begin to emerge as different characters. Celia is quick and bright, Beatrice is much slower but thoughtful, Adrian is rather brash. This may give the sketch an interest that would be lacking in a straight philosophical article, but not so great as to distract from the problem itself. Which may explain why, for example, Lewis Carroll used this form in his hilarious, 'What the Tortoise said to Achilles' (which was published in the most venerable British philosophical journal, *Mind*, in 1895).

I enjoy this way of presenting philosophical problems, and, since 'Adrian', 'Beatrice' and 'Celia' pleasingly contract phonetically into A, B and C, I have used these names in other articles. I am beginning to feel that they are developing characters in such a way as to prevent me, for example, making C say stupid things. Real writers often say that their characters take on a life of their own and disrupt the author's plans for them and the work as a whole. And this itself creates a philosophical problem. Since imaginary characters in plays and stories are the inventions of the author how can they have, or even appear to have, a being and nature which resists the author's intentions and plans for them?

Part of what may be going on here is that, having developed a certain type of personality, what the author does, that is, writes, subsequently, is constrained by this knowledge and the picture he or she has built up of them. Writers create characters, but even in the work in which they are created, they begin to take on an existence independent of their creators, of their wishes and plans for them, and their beliefs about them.

I said above that a problem remains: indeed, it might be argued that the *original* problem remains, not merely that a related problem remains about whether the teacher could set his unexpected exam on Thursday or the days preceding it. This argument runs: A, B and C first argue, 'prove', that they cannot have an unexpected examination on Friday, and then apply the same argument back through the days of the week. Celia then argues that, having thus proved that they cannot have an unexpected examination on Friday, they can only be surprised if and when Foggy sets them an exam on that or any other day.

It is not true, then, that they can only be surprised if they do not get an examination at all on Friday. They may get an exam, but they may not; so, if they do, it will be unpredictable, a surprise therefore, and the regression back through the week cannot get started. So, apparently, Foggy wins. Yet I argued above, that once Celia proves that they can have an unexpected exam on Friday, it will, therefore, not be a surprise, and the only surprise they can have is no examination at all. Celia's argument is self-destructive. But it is also *unstable.* Because once we have shown that it succeeds, in so doing, it fails. *But having shown that it fails, it then succeeds.*

Anyone who has followed the argument thus far might argue that, given the proof of the instability of Celia's argument, Foggy still wins, and so, therefore, must Celia and the Celia/Quine argument. But now suppose that Adrian, say, is unwilling or unable to follow the argument to this level. If *he* gets an examination on Friday it will be no less than he expected! He will only be surprised if he and the others do not get an examination, and not getting an examination is not the surprise that Foggy threatened them with. The unwelcome result of this argument is that Adrian's brashness succeeds, reason is endless and defeats itself!

As someone trying to write a book intended to stimulate interest in philosophical argument, I am now presented with a practical problem. If I go on discussing this paradox and its ramifications I may – probably will – sicken the appetite and interest that I wish to stimulate. But, if I stop, I may disappoint those whose interest and appetite is keenest. The problem is practical and so is my solution. I shall go on, but say to those who have had enough: not all philosophical problems are of this sort; they do not all demand this sort of interest or the minute (I mean fine, detailed, 'nice' – in the old sense) intelligence which feeds it. These persons, if they have not already given up, should do so now and go on to the next chapter in this part of the book.

Returning then to the problem which, originally, I brashly suggested was the only problem that remained, namely could the teacher set his unexpected examination on any day other than Friday: only Adrian's truncated argument means that there cannot be an unexpected examination on Friday. Celia's argument that there can be such an examination, being unstable, yields the conclusion that there can be one on Friday just as there can be on any other day. But reason now owes brashness an account of why it is that when A, B and C go into school on Monday, Tuesday and Wednesday, and do not get examined, the situation looks different to them on Thursday and, if they don't get an examination then, *very* different on Friday. Can reasoning, and so philosophy, really show us that these feelings are confused and illusory?

Being a paradox, this paradox resembles some better known, really ancient paradoxes, including that known as 'the liar'. The ancients' form of this was known as the 'Epimenides', and ran: 'Epimenides, the Cretan, says that all Cretans are liars. This must be understood as making the unlikely and, I think, incoherent claim, not that all Cretans sometimes lie, but that all Cretans *always* lie. Construed thus, the paradox is immediate and pretty obvious: if what Epimenides says is true, then it is false, because Epimenides is a Cretan and he has told the truth. Conversely; if Epimenides lied in asserting that all Cretans are liars, his lie supports the truth of what he lyingly asserts. It doesn't prove the truth of his claim that all Cretans always lie, because other Cretans may not always lie, in which case when he lyingly asserts that all Cretans always lie, what he says is none the less false.

These blemishes in the classical liar paradox may have led to its modern reformulation. This runs: 'This statement is false.' So if it is false, it is true, and vice versa. But as Gilbert Ryle pointed out in his exquisitely named essay, 'The namely rider', the defect with this formulation of the ancient problem is very apparent: if we ask 'Which statement is false?', we get an endless, empty regression. Where it is said that this statement is false, what purports to be a reference to a statement is empty. When we try to cash it out we get, first: 'This statement, namely this statement is false, is false.' At the second stage we get, 'This statement, namely this statement, namely this statement is false, is false, is false.' No further stages are necessary to make Ryle's point that the namely rider involves us in a vicious, empty regress.

The paradox of the unexpected examination is therefore more complex than the ancient and modern versions of the liar paradox, and differs from them in presenting us with a challenge which cannot be met as can the liar's. In this way it more closely resembles Russell's celebrated 'Class of all classes' paradox. Regrettably, I cannot discuss it or its ramifications here, but anyone who is intrigued will find discussions in many textbooks on philosophical logic and the philosophy of mathematics. The really keen will want to join in such discussions and may do so by attending extramural courses on these topics offered by their local colleges and universities. (For suggestions on how to do this, see the last part of the book, the Conclusion.)

Even those who have a great appetite for trying to sort out paradoxes may suspect that, though paradoxes have a certain interest, they are not important in any way, either theoretically or practically. Russell and Wittgenstein both worried about whether they were of any theoretical interest. Russell finally decided that they were important in the philosophy of mathematics and logic, Wittgenstein that they were of no importance or significance.

Perhaps this final example may throw some light on Wittgenstein's position. A colleague once turned to me accusingly and said, 'Why do you always disagree with me?' I replied, 'I don't.' Only later did I realise that this was a version of the liar paradox. Until I was struck, it seemed to me that the conversation made perfectly good, clear sense. Indeed, I want to say that it did and does make perfectly good sense. In which case the paradox would seem to be a product of a philosopher's too literal construing of what was said. My colleague was referring to past occasions and, when replying, so was I. The paradox only arises if I over-ingeniously construe and hence misconstrue my reply as referring or applying to itself. But I did not intend it in this way.

9

THE ANGEL

The term 'angelic' – which is somewhat hackneyed in its application to children – can rarely have been applied with more point than it was to Peter Jordan: that is, to Peter as a small boy. And to him as a small boy, it was applied often.

Our ideas about angels being what they are, it is not difficult to guess that Peter as a child, and indeed as an adult, was fair almost to transparency, delicate, and the obviously unwitting possessor of the biggest, bluest, and most innocent eyes. He was a forward, tractable child, and had he not taken to biting his nails almost as soon as he produced his pearly white teeth, his mother's heart would have burst with maternal pride. As it was, she nightly thanked God for his goodness and bound Peter's hands in bandages. No matter what she threatened he would have the bandages and vestigial nails off by morning.

This bad habit and his perversity in it alone gave Mrs Jordan doubts as to her son's evident perfection, that is, until he reached the age of 4. His birthday very nearly coincided with Christmas Day, which Mrs Jordan thought – and prayed that her doing so was not blasphemous – was very probably significant.

She had noticed that he kept looking up the kitchen chimney and asked him what he was looking for. 'Father Christmas', was the charming answer. Her sister, who was without children, thought it 'perfectly sweet' and gave him the sweets *and* the teddy bear. After Christmas, Peter again looked up the chimney. Mrs Jordan's sister, who was staying with them, asked rather nervously – for she was not well off and Peter, not to be denied equal rights with his sisters, always had a birthday treat on New Year's Day – what he was looking for.

He replied, 'The hole; and it's too small. I don't think Father Christmas did bring my toys.' This shocked Mrs Jordan and her sister, though *she* was sent packing when she dared to criticise. Perhaps he was just growing up; though the girls still wrote their letters to Father Christmas. Peter *was* forward; even so it seemed to show a certain lack of faith and trust on his part. This so common feature of childhood, by its very commonness seemed almost . . . well, almost a fall from grace.

She was even more disturbed the following Christmas by Peter's saying (after he had failed to get the roller-skates he had asked for 'what with him being so young and them being so dangerous') that he had never believed in Father Christmas. 'How could he be all over the world at once?' he shouted, and having lost both front teeth looked almost daemonic as he did so.

At 6 Peter declared that he did not believe in fairies. This was a matter about which Mrs Jordan had never really made up her mind. He could not think of a knock-down argument as he had in the case of Father Christmas but his scepticism and teasing were enough to disenchant his sisters.

Giants were the next to go, though their being banished from Peter's world was not justified till a much later date. 'Their thigh bones would have to be about two feet thick, and their connective tissue couldn't stand the strain. Their stomachs would fall out on to the floor. You know, the way the vicar's looks as though it's going to do.'

It was this last remark that horrified Mrs Jordan. It lifted the scales from her eyes. There had been a lull in the list of denunciations and she *knew* what would be next. He would corrupt the others. She felt panicky, she must send him to the confirmation classes immediately.

About a month later the vicar called on Mrs Jordan. He made the routine enquiries about her temporal state, the sort of question which is required of our spiritual guardians, and then came to the point. 'Mrs Jordan,' he began in a heavy cadence, 'I am afraid that I cannot confirm Peter this year.' 'Why not?' She could guess the broad outline of what must have happened but did not intend to spare the vicar his duty or admit to having failed in hers. 'He does not believe in God.' The old man looked very uncomfortable and seeing that Mrs Jordan was gathering herself for an outburst hurried on. 'And it is not merely that he does not believe in God' – the solecism bothered him but he ploughed on – 'He glories, yes, he glories in his lack of faith. I have had many boys to the confirmation classes who have lacked a firm belief in God, but they felt their loss. And I have confirmed many whom, I am sorry to say, were never exercised by the matter at all, in spite of everything I said.' The vicar paused as his mind dwelt on the many village children who had sat mute and red in his study, conscious only of their desire to rush from the room to laugh and laugh with the relief from tension. The cold eye of Mrs Jordan made him grope for the thread of what he had to say. 'Ah! yes. But your son glories in his atheism and', and final blow, 'I simply cannot allow the other children to run the risk of being influenced by his opinions, with which, Mrs Jordan, he is very ready.'

Mrs Jordan fought to change the vicar's mind but he was strangely adamant. He even insisted that although Peter's treble voice had not yet broken he should leave the choir. Peter should come to see him once a week he suggested, but did not sound happy in doing so; he seemed almost to dread any further contact with her son, whose pink ear and fair head were pressed close against the other side of the door.

Between Peter's leaving school at the age of 18 and his going up to the university, he married. He did so without his mother's prior knowledge and in a registry office. The girl, Terry, was a quiet, nondescript, seemingly well-mannered girl and Mrs Jordan tried to comfort herself with the thought that it could have been so much worse. Terry, Peter told her, was a lapsed Roman Catholic.

Though very hurt by his action, Peter's mother allowed her son and his wife to live with her until it was time for him to leave for his first term at Cambridge. She was not surprised by his saying that he intended to take Terry with him, provided that they could find somewhere to live. 'Of course I'll have to

explain that I don't want to live in college. Sounds a bit fishy,
I suppose, but women aren't allowed in and anyway, undergraduates aren't allowed to be married. An inducement to
immorality,' he mused, 'perhaps the Fellows have shares in
the local . . .', but his wife would not let him continue.

They had great difficulty in finding anywhere to live and it
was not until Peter advertised for a flat in return for domestic
help (from his wife) that they received any reply. It was from
a rectory. 'Oh! what joy!' shouted Peter on hearing the news.
'Absolutely heaven sent.' His mother tushed. He held his
slender white hands in an attitude of prayer and looked at the
ceiling. 'Living amongst the Holies. God, what sport.'

The rector and his wife turned out to be an elderly, childless
couple. They were kind in an ineffectual way to the young
couple but to Peter's annoyance kept themselves very much
to themselves. After a couple of months Peter had still got no
further than saying 'God morning' to the rector on the infre-
quent occasions they met in the drive, and though Terry spent
much of her time with his wife their conversation was limited
entirely to domestic matters.

'You know, he might as well be a bank clerk for all his
blasted religion affects his life,' Peter complained one night.
'Except, of course, he'd have to do more if he were a bank
clerk. Lazy old devil! I can't see much sense of vocation in his
case.' Peter had very advanced ideas about what constituted
the religious life. 'We haven't been to church once since we've
been here and neither he nor his wife have as much as mentioned it – not even dropped any hints.' He got up and began
to mince up and down the room rubbing his hands together.
'"Ah! Good mo-orning, Mr Jordan. Bea-utiful day is it not? And
how is your good wife" – just as if I had a bad one somewhere
– "I don't seem to have seen you amongst my congregation
these last few Sundays. But of course, you owe your first
allegiance to your college chapel. But do send your good lady
along; we would be so pleased to see her. Well, I must not
detain you. Go-ood morning", and then off like a dose of
liquorice before you can tell him what he can do with his

Sunday-morning service. Not even a hit-and-run attack like that. How about our immortal souls? I've a damn good mind to write to his bishop and tell him that old Gale's on the other bloody side.'

He dropped into a chair and began biting his nails.

After a further couple of months Peter managed to engineer several chats with the old man. He returned to his wife after these encounters so choked with rage that she wondered why on earth he so desired them.

'By God,' he exploded after the third exchange, 'it would be pathetic if it weren't so sickening. You know he's not one scrap interested in or bothered by the problems of religion. He just laughs when I show him that he hasn't got a leg to stand on and says things like "Oh! I've no doubt that you could prove black's white without much difficulty but nothing you can say, my boy, can alter the fact that God exists and he loves us", and it's he that proves – well, assumes – that black is white: all the time. "You must have faith", he tells me, but he can't tell me why. Either he can prove that God exists, in which case the exhortation to have faith is superfluous, or he cannot, in which case it is unreasonable. At least the RCs can see this. But it doesn't bother him. He spends a lot of time, from the look of that study, reading detective stories. And it's not as if he lived the good, bloody life. Sherry – the best; lying about all day when he's not telling people what miserable bloody sinners they are and they'll never go to heaven unless they pull their fingers out. Blimey, what an ethic that is! And if he gets to heaven; well, all I can say is that there will be standing room only.' He was silent for a moment and then continued, 'What gets me is that he should set himself up as the moral guide and spiritual leader of his fourteen or fifteen hundred so-called parishioners. And if one of them begins to say what he thinks, the old man knows just enough to shut him up, or the rest come down on him like a ton of bricks. I've seen it happen. They prefer apathy to honest-to-God concern and interest. And he gets paid for it. Jesus!'

'I know.' Peter sat up and grinned wickedly at his wife. 'I've just thought of a scheme which will shake the old man's ideas up. If he swallows it it'll prove him to be the fool I think he is, and if he doesn't without seeing through it – and I'll take good care to see he doesn't – then I shall know at least that he has as much of the faith he's always appealing to as my left boot.' He looked at this and wriggled his toes with glee.

'What are you going to do?' His wife was anxious. 'Don't do anything stupid or cruel, please Peter. I hate you in this sort of mood, and Mr and Mrs Gale have been very good to us.'

'That's not quite the point, is it? He doesn't set himself up to be just an ordinary run-of-the-mill sort of chap, but as a representative of God. And anyway you haven't heard what I intend to do. It's not cruel, in fact it could do the old chap a great deal of good. He's just ripe for a spiritual booster.'

He rose to his feet and fluffed out his extravagantly long and yellow hair. Clasping his hands in front of him and assuming a saintly expression he took a quick look at his wife, resumed his pose and asked 'What do I look like?'

'As if you were going to burst into 'Oh! Ho-ow wonderful they are, the little lordly ones, who-o dwell, who-o dw– '

'No, no –answer the question. What do I look like, not what do I look as if I'm going to do.'

'I suppose a bit more angelic than usual. Very misleading. What do you want me to say?'

'That will do; and congratulate yourself on your stereotyping. It's been very unfortunate for me that most people have that idea; you know, that an angel looks like a sort of golden-haired pre-Raphaelitish lover in a swoon. Perhaps that's where the idea originated. I wonder what a Chinese angel looks like? But to business; old Gale's sure to have the same idea. He's very conventional and literal. Now then; half these holy men are arrogant enough to have the thought tucked away at the backs of their minds that God or one of his emissaries will one day make them a visit: for services rendered.'

'I thought you said . . .'

'I know, but even so they have. Listen.'

'Well,' said Terry afterwards, 'I think you underestimate Mr

Gale, and the difficulties; oh! and the unpleasantness when he finds out. And supposing he did swallow it? It might even unhinge him.'

'I doubt it, and anyway, it's worth the risk even if it's only to find out just what does happen.'

After arguing along these lines for some time Peter persuaded Terry to help him. She even began to get excited about the idea.

'I'll cover most of me with that white, figured, satin bedspread. You can pin it in place so as to keep it secure and give me enough to hold up on either side like wings, I won't wear anything on my feet but will rub a lot of talcum into them so as to make them look ethereal and stop them sticking to the lino. I must make sure that I don't leave any un-angelic tracks. The other thing is to stick a piece of tissue paper behind the glass of the bicycle lamp and somehow tie it behind my neck. Then at the psychological moment I'll switch it on and make my appearance complete with halo.'

'Then what?'

'The getaway: I think the best place and time is at the top of the main stairs when he comes to bed. He's likely to be in a receptive frame of mind at that time of night and the light's very poor. No one will be about – the old lady will be in bed – and we will make sure that they know that we have gone to bed. They can't very well come barging into our bedroom saying that Gale's seen an angel and what do we know about it. I'll go through the door of the bathroom that separates our flat from their part at about half past ten. You had better unlock it when you are cleaning up there tomorrow. Then I'll wait on the landing out of sight until I hear him coming. When he reaches the landing I'll tiptoe to the head of the stairs and switch on the lamp. I'll wait just long enough for him to get the full impact, then off with the lamp, tiptoe back to the far wall, and then a silent and invisible bolt for the bathroom door. I must remember to leave the door ajar. Once inside, I'll go through the door that's usually kept bolted and be back in our bedroom before he reaches the top of the stairs.'

'Supposing he goes into the bathroom and notices that the bolt on the other door is unlocked? That would give the show away.'

'Hm! Ah! There's a keyhole under the bolt isn't there? You pop a trace of oil on the bolt – some soap from the bath would do the trick – tomorrow. If I push a piece of bent wire or a bent nail through the keyhole I can open it, go through, and then close it directly I get back. That is unless he comes into the bathroom like a shot, and if he does that'll mean he's smelt a rat anyway. I'd better practise that part of the manoeuvre.'

They practised the deception that night on their own, on what had been in earlier times the servants' stairs. Peter looked truly awful. Perfecting the management of the lamp was difficult and delayed their putting their plan into operation for two nights, during which time Peter carefully timed the old couple's movements.

The nights were cold and as Terry adjusted the bedspread she felt Peter shudder.

'Cold?'

'And nervous. Give me that powder.'

'Don't you think it would be wiser to call it off?'

'You sound just like my mother when you say things like that. No; it's mostly anticipatory thrills. How do I look?'

'Turn the light on. Ugh! Awful; but there's no mistaking what you're supposed to be.'

'What I am as far as old Gale's concerned. I'd better be going, it's nearly ten-thirty. Give me a kiss.'

He disappeared along the passage and she heard him slip through the bathroom door.

As Peter crept out on to the landing he broke into a cold sweat. The landing in the pale light of a fifteen-watt bulb looked cold and sinister. The broad, darkly varnished stairs plunged out of sight to the hallway and study below. The silence was intense, and Peter became aware of the throb of blood in his ears which strained to move as a floor board creaked behind him. It became oppressive, then he started violently as the silence was broken by a groan that came from the bedroom to his left. Mrs Gale stirring in her sleep. Supposing she were to come out on to the landing? His heart thudded: he hadn't thought of this contingency. He heard her turn but then she became quiet again and as Peter strained his ears for noises from the study he heard a wheeze at the bottom of the stairs. The grandfather clock struck the quarter. Perhaps the old man was already in bed. He broke into a violent shiver and pulled at the satin which clung to his clammy body. He ought to give it up and go back to bed. No! He filled with rage at the thought of the rector comfortable and smug – *smug* – in his study below, no doubt drinking sherry. No! He would shake the man to the very core of his being or — Peter heard the sound of someone's walking across a room and a door's being opened and then closed. He heard the person below lock and double bolt the front door. His lips curled at the old swine's trust in human nature and fear for his worldly goods. He trembled with cold, excitement and venom as the old man approached the foot of the stairs and slowly began to mount them. The climber paused for breath on the landing. Peter waited for him to start again and his hand stole shakily to the lamp. From the landing there came the hiss of a sharp intake of breath and in his mind's eye Peter saw the old man start up the second flight of stairs. He stepped forwards to the head of the stairs and turned on the lamp. His shadow sprang huge on the opposite wall, he stared at it and slowly lowered his eyes.

What he saw stilled the blood in his veins. Instead of the solid, soberly dressed body, and ruddy, bespectacled face of the rector his gaze fell on a bent, withered figure, wrapped in a soiled brocade dressing gown. Its bony, veined hand clutched the banister and a white, collapsed face was turned up, open-mouthed towards his. It was the rector, *sans* teeth, *sans* glasses, *sans* cloth. Peter felt his nostrils quiver and eyes begin to smart as he looked down at the man, who gave a sob. The face looked incongruously like a very young animal. It was naked, defenceless, and swayed from side to side as it peered blindly and now trustingly up at him. Peter felt himself drop one arm and then raise it above his head. He brought it down to waist level and then moved it, first one way and then the other, across his body. The figure below slumped to its knees and bowed its head. Peter stared down at the grovelling, mumbling thing. He backed away, turned, and fled through the half-open bathroom door.

He was met by Terry, whose 'How did you get on?' and conspiratorial grin somehow shocked him.

'All right. Sh!' He slid the bolt home, removed the nail and listened at the keyhole.

'How did he take it?'

He looked at the floor and sighed. 'On the chin, I think.' Once more he bent to the keyhole. 'And from the sound of things he still hasn't got up.'

After some time – a minute perhaps – during which time Peter began to feel that Terry's worst fears had been realised, he heard the muffled throbs of the rector labouring up the last few stairs. Peter turned, pushed his wife in front of him and they rushed into their bedroom. Peter closed the door, bolted it, and, leaning up against it, began to shake with silent, tremulous laughter.

The following morning it was Saturday, Terry's day off, and a day on which Peter stayed at home. They sat in their downstairs room and talked endlessly about what effect the night's happenings must have had on the rector. Both longed, but neither dared, to go on some pretext to the Gales' side of the house. By nightfall, after seeing neither the incumbent nor his wife, both felt flat.

'Well,' said Peter as he began to undress for bed, 'it obviously hasn't deranged the old bloke, and it even looks as if he hasn't said anything to his wife'.

'Perhaps he won't let on at all.'

'Old hypocrite; and after all our efforts. I expect he's frightened that if he says anything they'll lock him up. Senile decay or religious mania or something. And I'll bet the keenest lot to give him the push if he did say anything would be the religiosos. It's not done in this day and age to have, and claim, direct contact with God. Come on, let's go to bed.'

The church was visible from the Jordans' bedroom window and as Peter rose on Sunday he noticed that about fifteen people, obviously the bulk of the eleven o'clock congregation, were gathered and talking excitedly in front of the lychgate. Peter felt a Hobbesian laugh, the laugh of 'sudden victory', rise from the pit of his stomach. He was sure he knew what kept them outside the church at twenty minutes to one.

He ran to tell his wife.

They watched the congregation arrive for the six o'clock service. It was, Terry said, a little larger than usual and it did not reappear until seven thirty-five p.m. Once again its bulk gathered in an excited group by the lychgate. By now Peter was convinced that the rector had spoken: but as to what he had said about his experience Peter was unsure and desperately curious. He felt that neither he nor Terry could attend a service without arousing suspicion – at least, not until the fact that something unusual had happened was generally known. In the meantime he told Terry he would try to drum up a conversation with one of the villagers he knew by sight, and make do with that.

But this turned out to be unnecessary. In the village shop the next day, the proprietor quietly told him that the rector had preached 'fire and brimstone on Sunday and offended a good many of the local folk, though a good many liked it.' Not unexpectedly, or so thought Peter, the next Sunday's congregations were even larger and the next's larger still. People were beginning to attend from the surrounding parishes. Peter and Terry went to church.

The rector conducted the service badly. He was abstracted and gave the impression of being bored. He muffed his responses, gabbled the prayers, and did not join in the hymns. Either he forgot to read his text or he did without one. His sermon was remarkable. For some minutes after having mounted the pulpit he gazed at the congregation with what seemed to be pity or contempt. His audience grew restive and the nerve of an unfortunate lady sitting near Peter in the back row, broke. She half-rose in her pew and began to edge sideways towards the door. She was immobilised by the rector's suddenly leaning over the pulpit and hissing, 'We are all running away from God.' There followed another silence shorter than the first, the suspense of which was heightened by a baby's beginning to whimper.

'Even I,' Peter remembered the rector's saying, 'even I, one of His ministers, was running away from God. But the mercy of God is great – no-o – INFINITE – and once again He comes' – his voice dropped to a caress – 'He comes to offer us His blessings and forgiveness. I am an unworthy creature, lazy, pleasure-loving, fearing, and even refusing to recognise, any disturbance of my comfortable life, even if that which threatens to disturb my sloth is God Himself,' his voice, which had risen to a shout, dropped to a sob, 'and perhaps just because I am a wretched, miserable sinner, a creature like each one of you here today, like those who are not here, it is required of me that I should lead those of you who have strayed, back to the paths of righteousness and the ways of God.'

This sermon, which, Peter was told near the lychgate after the service, had been preached six times by the rector with only minor alterations, lasted fifty-five minutes. Little was materially added to what he had said in the first three, yet this latter part impressed some of his listeners (especially those few who had happened to come in from the town) more than the first. In it the old man became calmer though no less forthright. He showed that he was far from being unaware of the dangers of claims such as his. He realised that even if his listeners were to acknowledge the purity of his motives, then, whether Christian or non-Christian, they might still find suspect what they had heard. He agreed that what he desired, namely 'a complete and general acceptance of God', must seem impossible of achievement and argued that for this very reason it must be striven for the harder. 'For,' he concluded, 'if God exists – and who can deny in his heart that He does? – and if He loves us (and how could the good God not?), then our first and last duty is to serve Him. My brethren, there can be no other proof of these things than that God shew Himself to us; He has shewn Himself to me.' And though Peter became angry and muttered 'Which has to be proved', he felt shaken and, absurdly, impressed.

'Well,' said Terry as they at last walked away from the

group, 'that was horrible. It looks as if you have started a revivalist movement. Was that part of your plan?'

Not a month later it seemed indeed that Peter had precipitated a religious revival. So large were the village congregations that the services were relayed to the village hall. The rector was invited to preach at fashionable churches in the nearby university town. His superiors interviewed him and he won their approval. His success was sealed when he was taken up by a popular Sunday newspaper. The rectory received a constant stream of visitors and a torrent of mail.

At first Peter pretended to Terry and to himself that the turn of events amused him. They proved if anything did what a hoax – he became fond of this word, it seemed so appropriate – religion was. He made jokes about not just looking an angel. Later he began to demur. It had not been his intention to delude all these people, quite the opposite, in fact. He had wanted to discover whether Gale was a complete fool, a knave, or both; though now it seemed as if he didn't quite fit any of these categories. Finally, he decided he must speak to the man. Terry begged him not to. Mr Gale's experience had affected him profoundly, he had committed himself to it completely, he was an old man. It would be the greatest cruelty to shatter his public and religious life. It might even kill him or send him out of his mind; so argued Terry. Peter, unusually, was not disposed to argue his case. Gale, under a delusion, was misleading a great number of people, including himself, on a matter of the very last importance. He must be disabused.

The following morning Peter asked Mrs Gale if he could speak to the rector. Mrs Gale showed her surprise but said she was sure that the rector would be delighted to see Peter in the evening, when he was free. Peter wanted to tell her that what she was thinking was quite wrong.

The day dragged for Peter. He felt nervous and angry and tried to pass the time in rehearsing his denunciation. Suddenly it accelerated; it was seven o'clock and time to go. He felt like an ill-prepared examination candidate and the rector suddenly seemed a harsh examiner. Again Terry wished him luck.

'Come in.' The voice that bade him enter was as weak, oily

and rehearsed as ever. Anger entered Peter with his deep, preparatory breath; he opened the door and his anger was heightened by a wall of warmth that made him prickle. The rest of the house was like a mausoleum. He closed the door and turned to face the rector.

The warmth, Peter noted, was the huge square room's only luxury. Its scanty furniture was old and ugly, the inadequate carpet threadbare and patched with rugs worn to a uniform dun colour. Gale was seated at a mess of papers which almost hid a roll-top desk situated beside the fire. He looked, surprisingly, his usual self.

'Ah! Peter. My wife told me to expect you. Do sit down my boy.' He waved towards what was obviously his customary seat, a large wing easy chair the other side of the fire. 'My goodness, is it an especially cold February or do old bones feel the cold? We'll have some more coke on the fire, I think.' After a short pause, 'It must be very unpleasant cycling into the college?'

'Not really.' Peter felt he could not be drawn into this sort of conversation. Another short silence in which the rector recovered his seat and breath brought him to the point.

'Is there anything in particular you want to see me about, Peter?' A lifetime of this sort of thing, thought Peter, and even now he gets embarrassed.

'Yes Mr Gale, there's something I must say to you. It's about . . . well, about . . .'

'. . . about my experience? But of course. I thought you might like to discuss it with me. Such a very wonderful thing to happen you know, Peter; to an old man. And such a wonderful reception. I confess I was extremely loath to speak of it but it was my duty to do so and my unworthy fears have turned out to be quite groundless, quite groundless – as you probably know? Yes, there was a great fountain of faith among these people that was simply waiting to be released. My su—'

'Mr Gale, I have something I must say to you. My beliefs too force me to speak when for a variety of reasons I would rather remain silent.'

'Yes. What is it?'

'I hoaxed you. I was the angel.'

Gale said nothing.

Peter began the explanation he had rehearsed but on looking at the rector he stopped. 'I'm sorry. It would be difficult to explain why I did it – let alone justify it; but I did. I'm sorry, I was the angel.'

'Don't distress yourself.' The rector was curiously calm. 'I know. I've known for some time.'

Again there was a pause. Peter felt numbed. 'What in heaven's name do you mean?'

'Well, I did not realise for some days after the visitation tha—'

'The what-tt?'

'The visitation; ah! ah, that you had played any part in it, but when I met you one morning in the drive it was obvious, unmistakable.'

'But; but', Peter's senses reeled. 'My God! you knew all the time; and you've had the brass, bloody neck to get on your hind legs and tell everyone that – that God has sent one of his angels to bless you?'

'But He did. I cannot explain why I should have been chosen, but there was great work to be done, and He did.'

'This is fantastic. Look, I thought of it, I planned it, *I* did it; *I* – *I* did it, you old twister. You know I did.' Peter was infuriated by the rector's calm, by his – his stupid, wicked duplicity!

'My boy,' the rector's voice was tinged with asperity. 'I believe you are quite a clever young man, but you seem to have some curiously primitive and rigid ideas about religious experience, God, and the ways He chooses to reveal Himself. God may move in a mysterious way, and why He chose either of us for these tasks we shall probably never quite know, but it is entirely consistent that He should have chosen to execute His will and secure this great end with the means at hand. We are all of us instruments of His will: *you* were the instrument of God; and for some moments you *were* an angel.'

POSTSCRIPT

The philosophical problem raised in this story is, again, one discussed in Part One, namely the nature of religious belief and the arguments that are used to articulate and defend it. Peter discovers to his surprise – and, I hope, the reader's – that not only had the rector worked out that Peter had played the part of the angel but this realisation had not undermined his faith, or even made him feel foolish. On the contrary; he feels blessed because, though Peter believed himself to be pretending to be an angel, the rector believes that he was – or was *also* – briefly, and perhaps only partly, an angel, and the unwitting, instrument of God. The story leaves one to ponder the nature and merit of what the rector says to Peter.

I am sufficiently distanced from my own disbelief, and Peter's, to suggest that it is not as clear as Peter thinks – or the rector. If God exists, the rector's understanding of what happened could well be correct. If he does not, Peter's no-non-sense view is correct. But if the existence of God is something which can neither be proved nor disproved, neither under-standing of what happened can be shown to be correct or incorrect, though they cannot both be correct.

Perhaps because of my own beliefs (though they are no longer as fierce as Peter's) I would like to put in a word for Peter, the victim and anti-hero of the story. What should we think of an hypothesis – in this case, the God hypothesis – if anything which, to a dispassionate observer, seemed to tell against the hypothesis, is miraculously construed by its advocates as evidence in favour of it?

But these remarks send me back to the story and the ques-tion of what philosophical problems are raised *by* it and our response to it. Peter is not an attractive character. He is cer-tainly clever, though the denouement of the story may suggest that he is not as clever as he thinks he is. But his cleverness is in the service of his unkindness, egocentricity, brash self-confidence. He delights in attacking the no doubt conventional but sincerely held beliefs of those around him. He continually upsets his poor mother and simply makes use of his wife, and both women are treated by Peter, and the story, as ciphers. They have and are given no individuality, no existence independently of Peter.

Why? As the author of the story, it may seem that I must know the explanations. But this does not follow, and it is not always true that authors know why they put in this, or omitted that, or presented this in this way, and do on. In any case, I am not trying to provide just an explanation of Peter's character and behaviour, but also a justification. Perhaps it is this: having described the rector through Peter's eyes as lazy, selfish, thoughtless, I did not want these, the only account we have of the rector's character, to bias the reader in favour of Peter. Moreover, it is a fact, and one I personally regret, that sceptics do often relish and glory in their scepticism. They are, or can be, prone to revel in their cleverness and its discomfiting their more conventionally-minded fellows. So, having given Peter the best of the arguments about Father Christmas, fairies, giants, and do on, I wanted to ensure that when the debate was about the more serious and living issue, the reader would not be unduly sympathetic to Peter, whose character and views so closely resemble those of the person who wrote the story. To echo a profound but puzzling remark of D. H. Lawrence, I did not want to 'do dirt' on the rector or 'put my finger in the pan' in which Peter is balanced in the story.

10

RONALD, THE RELUCTANT RHINOCEROS

Ronnie had never cared for being a rhino, not from the first; not from the time that, like Narcissus, seeing himself in a pool, he saw himself, so unlike Narcissus.

'It's worse than I thought,' he muttered hopelessly, 'a face like a large, old boot, and *two* disgusting horns.' He was indeed, a large, lumbering quadruped, and the fact that it said so in the *Shorter Oxford English Dictionary*, seemed to make it worse.

But it wasn't just his appearance that appalled Ron. Far from it. There were the habits of the rhinoceros. Many of these are so crude that merely to mention them would embarrass and upset my reader, and they certainly embarrassed and upset Ronald.

'But I am a rhino,' he thought, as he wandered out of the public library, smashing a chair with a swing of his head, crashing over the whole section of books on antiques with a sad shrug, and inadvertently defecating on the parquet floor by the issue desk, 'and shall no doubt behave like one.' In a sudden, desperate, rhino fury, he charged the double entrance doors, and emerged, wreathed in them, feeling defeated and yet vindicated by this immediate confirmation of his thought.

Besides the trammel of horrid habits, there was, much worse, the obscene interest that humans had in rhinos. I certainly shan't detail this, but Ronnie had been aware of it in outline from the time that his horns had started to appear and his anxious mother had told him to run if a human appeared.

Yet, far worse than mere appearance or mortifying habit, was a lack, of which, rather curiously, humans had made Ronnie more fully aware.

A human being is usually not just that, that is, a man or

woman, and so a son or daughter, and perhaps a brother or sister, father or mother, but is perhaps another thing as well, a game warden, librarian, truck driver, shop assistant, traffic warden, psychiatrist, and so on. But a rhino usually *is* just a rhino, and Ronnie felt trapped and pointless.

'I know what I am,' he said to his mother, when he had got back from his trip to the library, 'but what shall I become?'

'Boring?' said his sarcastic father.

'A nice, big grown-up rhino, with a nice mate, and a few nice young rhinos', said his mother, comfortably. She was not an existentialist.

Ronnie charged and impaled himself on a nearby tree, and his parents sent him to see a psychiatrist.

After a lengthy discussion, the psychiatrist leaned back, lit his pipe, and looked kindly at his young patient.

'Well,' he said, 'what would you really like to be?' Ronnie looked hard at the psychiatrist, then dropped his gaze.

'I *think* I'd like to be *you*', he muttered.

'Then you shall be', he said, and knocked out his pipe. There was a pause.

'I don't understand', said – Ronnie?

'We have just become each other', said Professor Williams.

'That's silly,' said the young rhino, who knew himself still to be Ronnie, 'absolutely nothing has changed.'

'But if *everything* has changed,' said Professor Williams enthusiastically, 'if you in your entirety become I in mine, and I in my entirety become you in yours, what change could anyone notice?!'

Ronnie thought about this. 'None, I suppose', he said at last.

'Exactly!' shouted the triumphant psychiatrist. 'I think it's time I had my sedative. Nurse!' A young rhino appeared, holding a syringe the size of an elephant gun, gave Ronnie a sweet smile, and the psychiatrist a shot in his right shoulder, and left. 'Aagh!' said the psychiatrist, 'That's better. Right then. Are your problems solved?'

'Yours may be,' said Ronnie, 'but since, as you say, if everything has changed, it will seem that nothing has, and as nothing may have changed, of course – the answer is and seems to be no.'

'You know, you really are a philosopher', said Professor Williams.

'Am I?' said Ronnie, feeling patronised, yet excited. 'What is that? What do philosophers do?'

'Well, they *think*. They think about the really big questions.'

'I *hate* long division', said Ronnie.

'Oh – no. Not big questions like that. Not mechanical questions. Questions like – "What is the meaning of life?", and "What is the meaning of a word?"'

'That sounds fascinating,' said Ronnie, but he had a common sense streak, 'Do they get paid?'

'Oh yes. It is a profession. If you can get a job in a university, you can earn a very respectable salary.'

'Just sitting around *thinking*?' said an incredulous Ronnie.

'Well, you might have to do a bit of teaching, but there's not much demand for pure philosophy. You could become an eco-philosopher, or interest yourself in speciesism. You know – do elephants have moral rights, as rhinos do? Is it as bad to kill a human being as it is to kill a fellow rhinoceros? That's very in, now.'

'No, I'm not really interested in popular stuff,' said Ronnie, 'or teaching, really.'

'Well,' said Professor Williams, 'That's where the jobs are, these days.'

'Never mind,' said Ronnie, 'where's the nearest university?'

'Witwatersrand', said the psychiatrist, and rang his bell.

Ronnie walked two hundred miles to Witwatersrand. He got past the porters' gate and, with some difficulty, found the department of philosophy. His appearance terrified the secretary, and the department, who fled into and barricaded the professor's room, which was the biggest. They phoned the campus police, two of whom came armed with elephant guns, and shot Ronnie.

'I must try to be philosophical about this,' thought Ronnie, as he lay dying against the secretary's desk, 'otherwise my life will have been a failure.'

But he could not be, the pain and disappointment were too great. Ronnie died a rhino, but in trying to be philosophical, he also died a philosopher.

The consolations, then, of philosophy, are not great, and are not always available to philosophers.

<h2 style="text-align:center">POSTSCRIPT</h2>

Could Ronald and Professor Williams swap identities? That is to say: could Professor Williams become Ronald and Ronald Professor Williams? About the only thing that is clear here is that unless this total change were instantaneous, we, if not the two involved in the change, would certainly notice the change taking place. Presumably, if it were gradual, Ronald's rhinoceros form would seem to melt, so would Professor Williams's human form, and what was and, as it were, looked like Ronald (do each of us look like ourselves?) would end up looking like Professor Williams and vice versa. This sort of thing does not happen, except in sci-fi movies and stories, but it seems to be conceivable, imaginable, describable. And in the insect world, we actually are confronted by perhaps even larger transmutations between the larva and pupa stages of insects and their emerging as an imago, the mature insect.

But if such a melting and *transposing* of appearances were to take place in our fictional case, would Ronald have become Professor Williams and vice versa? Of course, we can imagine that the end results of this process, for example, the figure that ends up looking like Ronald might even believe that he were Ronald and, similarly, the figure that ends up looking like Professor Williams might think of himself as Professor Williams. But would they not both be mistaken? After all, the creature that ends up looking like and believing himself to be Ronnie was not born of a rhinoceros, so he is not Ronnie, despite his looking just as Ronnie did before the melt-down and his believing that he was born, as Ronnie, of Ronnie's mother. Professor Williams is quite right to insist that the change, if it takes place, must be instantaneous.

But not only must the change be instantaneous, both he and Ronnie assume (I think) that the change would not result in the creature that looks like Ronnie suddenly, immediately looking like Professor Williams and vice versa. Because if that were to happen – so that if you filmed the event it would look as if the film were badly edited and a length had been edited out – it would appear that Ronnie and Professor Williams would have suddenly swapped positions, and that is something which, for example, Professor Williams's assistant could have noted. Could this happen?

Unless you have grown tired of being required to imagine such stuff, in which case you are not a philosopher or are a philosopher who believes that the only real problems are raised by science and hence by its subject matter, namely what actually happens, you may – and will, if you are a philosopher – object. You will object that although human beings, animals, plants, material things of whatever sort, do not suddenly disappear and then immediately reappear somewhere else, they might and could.

But if we agree that that could happen, as we must, we could also imagine that, for example, when Ronnie disappears from one side of Professor Williams's desk, two 'Ronnies' might appear on the other. But if this were to happen, which would be Ronnie? Since both have an equal claim, and Ronnie is a unique individual, the answer must be that neither is Ronnie. (And that is a result established many years ago by Professor Bernard Williams – which is why I gave the psychiatrist in the sketch that name.) So, if we lived in such a world, our concept of being the very same x, rhinoceros or human being, would have to undergo a profound change or, if it did not, we would not – as we do not or should not – say that the rhinoceros that appears on Professor Williams's side of the desk is Ronnie.

Both Ronnie, Professor Williams, and, I suspect, the reader, suppose that the total change is total and instantaneous, that is, that nothing detectable changes, that Ronnie does not end up looking like Professor Williams and vice versa. Indeed,

DRIVING TO CALIFORNIA

Ronnie asserts and Professor Williams seems to agree that as, or if, everything changes, nothing changes. But if nothing changes – nothing changes!

What is really going on here I suspect is an unvoiced, unthought and hence unexamined idea, namely that of the self, the ego, the real, unchanging me or you which, none the less, can and does undergo so many changes, a featureless but particular thing, the equivalent of the bare particular discussed in Part One.

What is, perhaps, of greater interest, is that the philosophical problem raised in the sketch, though scarcely pursued there, is not raised *by* the sketch. Or, rather: it *is* raised by the sketch, but we do not therefore allow its difficulties to distract us from the story and its interest. What happens to poor Ronnie? If the story works as a story, that must concern its audience more than the philosophical problem raised in it. Or, at least, it must do so as long as we read the story.

If we do start thinking about the philosophical problems raised in this story after we have read it, the story itself is of no help in sorting them out. But as J. L. Austin once tartly observed (in a philosophical article), the task of philosophy is not to start hares but to split them. How ironic that, in proposing the nature of the philosophic enquiry, Austin could not resist a literary stroke and one depending, moreover, on a conflation.

11

THE APPOINTMENT

OFFICIAL: Excuse me, sir!

SPEEDY PASSER-BY: What d'you want?

OFF: I wonder if you would mind helping us out?

SPB: Well . . .

OFF: Thank you sir. Just come this way sir.

SPB: Oh! Oh, well . . . I got an appointment.

OFF [*jovially, disbelievingly*]: I'm sure you have, sir!

SPB: Yes. I got an appointment already. I –

OFF: I'm sure you have sir. But not as important an appointment as this!

SPB: I gotta –

OFF: This way, sir; please!

SPB: Oh!

[*Follows*]

OFF: Now, then, sir. If you'd just like to remove that . . .

[*Attempts to remove SPB's cloth cap*]

SPB: Eh! Watch it!

OFF: Come along sir. Please!

SPB: Get out!

OFF: Well. How about this, sir?

[*Produces dark overcoat, tries to remove SPB's greasy
mackintosh*]

SPB [*struggling*]: Wass the bloody idea, then? Get out!

OFF [*panting slightly*]: Frankly sir, the way you're dressed –
you look a bit seedy, sir!

SPB: Bloody sauce!

OFF: Well, we want to be fair, sir.

SPB: Wass that!

OFF: Well, the rest of them look fairly respectable sir. Wouldn't want you standing out *unfairly*, sir.

SPB [*thoroughly alarmed*]: Now look 'ere. Wass the bloody game?

OFF: D'you want to try these on sir?

[*Tries to offer Homburg and dark overcoat to SPB*]

SPB: Get out – now, look 'ere! Wass the *game*?

OFF: Well, sir. Well – we're looking – we're looking for – well it's not against the rules to tell you, I suppose. We're looking for a professor of philosophy.

SPB: Jesus Chr—

OFF: Now, it's all right –

SPB: I'm not a bloody professor of philosophy!

OFF: '*Course* you're not sir! I know that.

SPB: Well, then?

OFF: We just want someone to make up the numbers. You know – give 'em something to pick from.

SPB: Oh! [*Pause*] How much?

OFF [*ignoring this*]: Come along, then, sir! Sure you won't have that coat and the Homburg?

SPB: No bloody fear. Think I'm stupid? [*Official chuckles*] 'Ere. Wass he done?

OFF: What's who done?

SPB: This professor of philosophy. Wass 'e done?

OFF: Done, sir? Oh – he won't have done much sir, don't worry. Not people like him sir. A lot of 'em are fond of the old ergo. Some of them seem to specialise in I-E-ing. That sort of caper. Nothing very remarkable, sir

[*Turns away*]

SPB: Aggro? I-E-ing? I-E-ing? [*Pause*] Indecent exposure! Oh, my Christ!

OFF: Now come along sir!

[*SPB shambles after official. He is very nervous. They reach a line of three men all dressed in Homburgs and dark coats.*]

OFF: On the end sir, if you wouldn't mind. Thank you. Just try to stand up straight, sir. Thank you. Now d'you want to change your mind about the hat and – right sir! This won't take very long gentlemen. [*Turns, calls*] Right! Thank you!

[*Man comes on stage. Looks at official who nods. Man walks up and down looking at line. He starts visibly at sight of SPB, turns walks back up line to official and surreptitiously nods over shoulder at SPB. SPB starts to shake*]

OFF [*loud whisper*]: Would you mind touching him, sir?
MAN: *Touch* him?
OFF: Regulations sir.
MAN: Must I?
OFF: Oh yes, sir.

[*Man walks nervously up to SPB and with great distaste touches him on the shoulder, SPB gasps*]

OFF: Thank you sir. [*The man exits.*] Right! [*A second man enters*] Off you go, sir. [*The second man wanders up and down the line, shows interest in the now distraught SPB, and then returns to the official. He is hesitant. He and the official confer in whispers*] Right, gentlemen. Now we'd like you each to say something. [*The second man pulls the official by the shoulder*] Yes. Something philosophical. Keep it short. Yes.
1ST IN LINE-UP [*clears throat, nervously*]: Aristotle is greater than Plato!

[*Pause*]

2ND IN LINE-UP: Plato's greater than Aristotle!
3RD IN LINE-UP: Kant is a very great philosopher, too.

[*Pause*]

SPB: Why am I here?
OFF: Very good! Thank you!

[*He looks at the second man who nods at the SPB*]

OFF [*bored*]: Touch him, sir! Yes.

[*The SPB cringes with horror and fear as he is touched. He whimpers and the second man exits*]

OFF: Thank you. Next!

[*A third man enters. He exchanges nods with the official and walks to the line-up. He wanders up and down, peers at the SPB, who tries to look unconcerned. The third man returns to the official and they whisper briefly*]

OFF: And again, gentlemen, if you would not mind. Something philosophical. Keep it short.

1ST IN LINE-UP [*defiantly*]: Plato's better than Aristotle.

2ND IN LINE-UP: I said that!

OFF: Please! Something philosophical. We don't want –

2ND IN LINE-UP: Plato is better than Aristotle!

OFF [*to third man*]: Is that . . . ? No sir. Something else. And don't shout sir. Conversational tones we want, sir. Thank you.

2ND IN LINE-UP: If A says something and B says what A says and if A says 'I said that', what does the 'that' refer to? Is —

OFF: Please!

2ND IN LINE-UP: Imitation is the sincerest form of flattery.

OFF: Thank you.

2ND IN LINE-UP: Too many cooks spoil the —

OFF: Quiet please, sir. If you can't behave properly sir, I shall have to charge you with creating a disturbance. Now then. Next please.

3RD IN LINE-UP: Kant was really a very great philosopher. But so was Plato. And Aristotle. In fact —

OFF: Thank you. Next.

SPB: What does all this mean?

OFF: Very good indeed. Right!

[*He looks expectantly at the third man who wanders up and down the line-up. He peers at the SPB carefully and then goes and looks again at the second in the line-up. The SPB is sweating and trembling. The third man*]

returns to the official who after a whispered conversa-
tion shakes his head vigorously. Making up his mind
the third man marches up to the SPB, who moans as he
is clasped on the shoulder]

OFF: Thank you sir! [*The third man exits*] Thank you gentlemen!

[*The others in the line-up trail off, a couple of them dump-*
ing their hats and coats as they go. They grumble and
mumble to each other as they exit]

OFF [*Walking up to SPB he stops before him, beams, clasps*
his hands behind his back. The SPB grovels]. Well there
you are, sir. Looks like it's you, sir.
SPB: Oh my God!
OFF: There was a bit of doubt sir, there, just at the end. Nearly
fooled he was. That last chap [*SPB snivels*] 'Too many
cooks' . . . ! Bloody rubbish – if you'll pardon my saying so,
sir.
SPB: Please!

[*He falls on knees and clutches official round legs*]

OFF: Bit surprised are we, sir?
SPB: Please! [*broken*] I've done nothing. NOTHING, d'you
hear me. Nothing . . .
OFF: Exactly, sir. That's what I told you. Brasses me off too
sometimes, sir. Anyway, apart from that bit of hesitation,
and he soon got over that.
SPB: Nothing.
OFF: These gentlemen think they've found their man, sir.
SPB: Oh no!
OFF: And, come to think of it, you do *look* the part.
SPB: Oh *no*!
OFF: Oh, it's not so bad, sir. [*Pause*] I should concentrate on
the money, sir.
SPB: What?
OFF: Yes. And the hours are very good, too. Yes [*encourag-*
ingly] you can manage it. Forty thousand a year? [*He*

*invites the SPB to consider the offer then, in more busi-
ness-like manner]* Now, I expect you can read, sir? [*The
SPB nods dazedly and climbs on his feet*] Good, appearances are very important, but it helps considerably if you
can actually read. [*He turns to go, and the SPB follows
him*] Well – just come with me and we'll give you a start.

[*The SPB follows him. His now dazed condition is returning to its original anger*]

SPB: 'Ere. Now wait a minute!
OFF: Yes, sir?
SPB: Wait a bloody minute. Professor of bloody philosophy?
OFF: Yes, sir. As I said, you —
SPB: Look, I'm a professor of bloody sociology already!
OFF: Oh shit! [*Very brief pause*] I might have known it. Well —
SPB: Well?
OFF: Could you manage it on the side?
SPB: Well . . . ? [*doubtfully*]
OFF [*with growing confidence and enthusiasm*]: I'm sure
you can manage the pair, sir. Mornings at Magdalen, after-
noons at . . . ?
SPB: Somerville.
OFF: Really? [*quizzically*] Very nice, sir. Well —

[*Exeunt*]

FINIS

POSTSCRIPT

The second man in the line-up's desperate attempt to say
something philosophical, 'If A says something and B says
what A says and if A says "I said that", what does the "that"
refer to?' raises an interesting question in philosophical logic.
But, in the context in which he produces it, his question
sounds trivial, prolix, ridiculous. Conversely, the SPB's desperate but mundane requests to know why he is there and what
it all means are treated as existential profundities. Which
shows that how a remark is understood, indeed, according to

Wittgenstein, what a remark means, depends on the situation in which it is made. (The SPB misunderstands the situation and so he is misunderstood.) Here, the dramatic form is beginning both to take on substance and to do some real philosophical work. Construed as existential profundities, Wittgenstein may well have held that such questions have no answers; are, therefore, not real questions, and so are not profound at all. (They just sound, that is, strike us, as profound.) This may add to the absurdity of the SPB's getting, and the way in which he gets, the appointment.

A philosophical problem raised by this sketch is if it *is* funny, *why* is it funny? To some extent the answer, or answers, are obvious. For example: called 'The appointment', the sketch turns on a pun; this word has more than one meaning, and we do not realise until the end of the sketch what it means. But this raises a philosophical question: if this strikes us as funny, why does it do so? Or again: everyone in the sketch behaves badly – even the unnamed MAN, who does not wish to touch the SPB (but, perhaps, not – or not only – because he has an understandable reluctance to 'finger' someone). But why should this be funny?

Philosophers have attempted to answer such questions and, virtually all of them, have striven to give a single answer, in terms of incongruities, or the opportunity which what we find risible gives us to feel superior, and so on. Anyone who finds the sketch funny at more than one place, should be suspicious of any monolithic answer. Things strike us as funny in different ways for different 'reasons'. However, the reasons we can adduce as to why they do strike us funny are incomplete. For example, if those who loved Oliver Hardy were asked why they found him funny, they might very well mention his particular comic character, his appearance, and his 'timing'. But are these not merely verbal gestures which, of course, fail to specify not only just what is loved but why it is funny?

In any case, what do we mean by 'funny'? Don't say, 'What makes us laugh', because we laugh for many different 'reasons', that is in different situations, expressing different reactions. We laugh with relief, pleasure, triumph (which Hobbes confused with laughter at something funny), incongruously, in shock or disappointment, and so on, and our inappropriate laughter is not itself funny at all.

I don't know if any of these questions have answers or, if they do, what they would look like. But even if I were persuaded (how?) that they had no answers, I should not therefore agree with Wittgenstein that we are confused, if puzzled by them.

12

THE SEMINAR

NOTE TO THE DIRECTOR

In this play I was anxious to show what might be said to be really going on, when academics engage in professional disagreements, to those who may have little knowledge of or, indeed, interest in the discipline – in this case philosophy – that is their medium.

My basic idea, and of course I write as someone professionally involved, is that these arguments are not primarily intellectual things. (The belief that they are is itself a bit of academic mythology.) During classes, in seminars, in disputes in learned journals, a polite tone is maintained but participants are fighting for their lives, attacking and damaging one another, being attacked and maimed, suffering, gloating, and so on. 'Having one's head chopped off', 'getting slaughtered', 'the fight going on in *Mind*', and so on are metaphors but they do almost literally describe some of the things that happen when we get to work. In this play I have presented the metaphors literally.

Much of the dialogue in the play is very difficult, and, therefore, demanding, clever, and echoes many things which actual philosophers have said, still say, might say. But much of it is also rather silly and – ostensibly, anyway – pointless. Meaningless, one might be tempted to say. (That's part of the reason I decided to have them talk about meaning.) The production should therefore concentrate on the other aspects and significance of the speakers' performances and the actors should deliver their lines at the academics' own frantic and bemusing pace.

But although their conflicts are quite horrible, they are

fought in accordance with rigid conventions and are highly stylised. Moreover, the academic life is very medieval in flavour; indeed its locale, garb and much of philosophy's technical vocabulary are actually medieval. So I have presented these unacknowledged battles as unacknowledged, medieval battles in which men attack with swords whose existence seems to go unnoticed, defend with armour they apparently pretend they do not wear, and suffer terrible wounds they do not recognise or cannot acknowledge.

And lastly, like all such conflicts, they promise, and are presented as continuing into, an indefinite future.

THE SEMINAR (A PLAY WRITTEN FOR TELEVISION)

Cast

Jack	:	a young man
Jack's Girl Friend	:	a young woman
Professor Rea	:	a middle-aged man
Issue	:	another middle-aged man
Dr Allein	:	an old lonely man
Dr T. T. Error	:	a youngish man
Girl	:	Error's pupil
Tom Style	:	a grand old man
Chairman	:	a mature man
Makeweight	:	an older man

Members of the seminar audience
First, second, third, fourth and fifth Members

Jack's Friends
First, second, third and fourth Friends

Non-speaking parts
Extras at seminar

Following standard practice, CU is used throughout
for 'close up', and OOV for 'out of view'.

SCENE 1   *INTERIOR. JACK'S DOOR. LATE EVENING.*

> [*Shot of Jack's door. It has 'Jack' on it. Track in. CU of name*]

> *Mix to –*

INTERIOR. JACK'S ROOM. LATE AFTERNOON.

> [*CU of Jack's sweating, contorted face. He is chanting in a strained, high-pitched voice. There is music in background, perhaps something mournful and classical for small wind and string ensemble. As camera tracks back, Jack is seen to be pressing a heavy barbell*]

JACK: I shall argue that the doctrine that meaning is use is hopelessly vague and, secondly, that in as far as it presents a discernible thesis, this thesis is incompatible with the major discovery of its author. For —

> [*He pauses, drops the barbell and rushes to a typescript lying on a table. He peers at it, scribbles some note on it*]

JACK: Yes! [*rushes back to barbell and starts curling it*] Is incompatible with the major discovery of its author. For, I shall argue, 'meaning' has many meanings or, if you like, many uses.

> [*He puts the barbell down, inhales triumphantly, skips about and pirouettes and then postures in front of a full-length mirror. He admires his beautiful and powerful body, his achievement*]

JACK [*exhaling*]: Marvellous! [*Picks up barbell and starts 'upright rowing'*] As to the first part of my thesis, I think the proof of it is —

JACK'S GIRL FRIEND: (*OOV*) Why do you do it?
JACK [*surprised, stopping his chanting*]: What?
JGF: (*OOV*) Why do you —
JACK: Tsst! Don't interrupt! [*Begins to squat*] As
   to the —

Cut to –

SCENE 3 *INTERIOR*. JACK'S ROOM. LATE AFTERNOON.

[*JGF, a decorative girl with a cutting well-bred
   voice and manner lolls in a chair appraising
   Jack*]

JGF: Well, why? I should really like to know.

Cut to –

SCENE 4 *INTERIOR*. JACK'S ROOM. LATE AFTERNOON.

[*Jack rests, and stares at the girl. His irritation
   gives way to consideration*]

JACK: I enjoy it.
JGF: You don't. [*Triumphantly*] You hate it. Or at
   least that's what you say.
JACK [*still panting*]: Yes, but —
JGF: You always moan when you have to do it,
   you put it off . . .
JACK: Ah! But I keep on with it, and that's the test
   of appetite. And I get very fed up if I haven't
   done any for a few days. [*Pauses*] I think I love
   it because it's so hard. I'm frightened by it,
   appalled . . . I tremble at its awful prospect.
   And quite rightly too because it completely
   exhausts me . . .
JGF [*irritated*]: Don't I know!
JACK: You know what O. Wilde thing said about
   smoking? [*JGF looks at him coolly*] Cigarettes
   are a perfect pleasure, they are exquisite and

leave one unsatisfied. [*JGF cannot totally suppress a smirk*] And it's the same with this. One is never totally satisfied, things are never *quite* perfect.

[*He looks at himself in the mirror*]

JGF: Well I think you're mad! And what's the *point* of it? Apart from amusing you, what real good does all this . . . [*She waves her hands in the general direction of typescript – and barbell*] . . . *effort* produce?

JACK [*flexing muscles and looking in the mirror*]: Well, obviously, it makes one very powerful. I mean I don't think any one who hasn't been through the training can compete with anyone who has.

JGF: But what do you want to be powerful for? You —

JACK: You can *cr-rush* people.

[*He grabs her*]

JGF [*escaping*]: Well, you haven't crushed me. Not yet anyway. And that's my point. You never crush anyone. Your kind never do. All you do is fight each other and get nowhere.

JACK: You don't really think we would compete against non-professionals do you, or take part in their crude public contests? That would be vulgar and boring. [*He turns away*] As we lack low cunning it might conceivably be humiliating as well. [*He laughs*] Notice I don't say we're not dishonest or even stupid enough – or not sufficiently *vicious* [*he karate chops a punchball and sways aside as it comes swinging back. Moodily –*] We are all of that.

JGF: Well then why do it? All that work wasted. You could – well, earn a lot of money if you spent all that energy on doing something useful.

JACK: You don't understand. It's satisfying.

JGF: But it's useless – and so – so *unreal.*

JACK: I could ask you what you mean or deny it, but I won't. I'll agree – and that's part of its satisfaction.

JGF: How self-indulgent!

JACK: Yes.

JGF: It's just narcissism!

JACK: Not just narcissism. You must leave room for the self-indulgence you just mentioned.

JGF: Typical! That's typical.

JACK: But correct.

JGF: Y-es, but —

JACK: Somehow irrelevant?

JGF: Yes!

JACK: Trifling?

JGF: Yes.

JACK: But you must admit, it can produce something very beautiful?

JGF [*reluctantly*] I suppose so.

[*They stare at each other*]

JACK: Yes you do. Now go away. I *must* finish this.

[*She goes to the door and turns*]

JGF: May I come tonight?

JACK: You'll be bored.

JGF: No, really.

JACK: Yes, really. Strange seedy old men bickering endlessly about the precise import of the imprecise and unimportant things some of them said before yesterday.

JGF: But I'd like to go.

JACK: Go then.

[*She goes. Jack turns away, pauses, and then begins to march up and down the room swinging and punching the air. He declaims*]

JACK: As to the second part of my thesis, that the doctrine is incompatible with the major discovery of its author . . .

Fade out music. Mix to –

SCENE 4   *INTERIOR.* PROFESSOR REA'S ROOM. LATE AFTERNOON.

[*CU of Professor Rea*]

Cut to –

SCENE 5   *INTERIOR.* PROFESSOR REA'S ROOM. LATE AFTERNOON.

[*A small, dapper man of about 50 stands before a mirror flickering a rapier. His face is worn and scarred. He weaves a pattern in the glass.*]

PROFESSOR REA [*in a thin, clipped voice*]: It is a sufficient condition of B's being a necessary condition of A, that A should be a sufficient condition of B. [*Pause*] It is also a necessary condition, too!

[*He grins wolfishly at himself in the glass, lunges at himself*]

PROFESSOR REA: *Touché!*

Cut to –

SCENE 6   *INTERIOR.* ISSUE'S DOOR. LATE AFTERNOON.

[*CU of Issue*]

Mix to –

SCENE 7   *INTERIOR.* ISSUE'S ROOM. LATER AFTERNOON.

[*An intense man feverishly polishing armour –*

particularly a gigantic helmet. As he does so he mutters –]

ISSUE: I have *never* said that the meaning of word is to be identified with the criteria for its application; which criteria may, of course, vary with the occasion of its use. So those who have said that I have said, or implied, that, for example, 'big' changes its meaning or that 'real' does, because I have said that the criteria for their application vary depending on whether one is talking about mice or elephants, pearls, or threats, or men, *themselves* accept the mistaken theory of meaning they mistakenly impute to me.

[*He blinks and sniffs*]

ISSUE: What I have said . . .

Cut to –

SCENE 8   *INTERIOR*. ALLEIN'S DOOR. LATE AFTERNOON.

[*CU of 'Dr Allein' on door*]

Mix to –

SCENE 9   *INTERIOR*. ALLEIN'S ROOM. LATE AFTERNOON.

[*An old man is grinding an axe. He grumbles away in a German accent*]

DR ALLEIN: It is apparently now generally accepted that many words are vague or, as one might say, that language is reticulated; full of gaps or holes where there are no lines of application drawn – and none necessary or even desirable. The mesh is irregular, fine and even in some places for minute specimens, coarse and strong in other for rough, everyday work. But though it is many years now since I first drew attention to this feature of language, and it is a picture generally accepted, it is only accepted with the *mouth*, not with the understanding. Essences are still being looked for, necessary and sufficient conditions are spoken of and pursued [*Gradually fade*] as if linguistic vagueness were just a blurring or blunting of the edges of much-used words . . .

Fade out

SCENE 10 *INTERIOR*. ERROR'S DOOR. LATE AFTER-NOON.

[*CU of Dr T. T. Error. Suddenly a girl's laugh OOV comes from within the room*]

Cut to –

SCENE 11 *INTERIOR*. ERROR'S ROOM. LATER AFTER-NOON.

[*Error, a younger version of Rea, is sitting on a settee, a girl of about 20 wearing an academic gown sits in an arm chair, between them is a coffee table with tea things*]

ERROR: But if you want to do something and you have no reason for not doing it, then how can you possibly not do it? I mean, providing no one prevents you and you don't change your mind?

GIRL: But suppose you *don't* want to as well?

ERROR: But this is very strange. Unless you simply mean that you're not *sure* that you want to do – whatever it is, the point is a quite general one of course – I simply don't understand. You say that you *are* sure you want to?

GIRL: Yes, but I don't want to as well.

ERROR: Then you are *not* sure you want to.

GIRL: I am.

ERROR: In that case you don't *not* want to.

GIRL: It doesn't feel like that.

ERROR: Well, if *per impossibile*, you did not want to as well as being sure that you did, what reasons have you for not wanting to?

GIRL: Oh? None!

ERROR: None?

GIRL: No, I don't think so.

ERROR: But you must have some.

GIRL: One doesn't have to have a reason for not wanting to do something.

ERROR: Generally, no. But if you also want to do it and have reasons for wanting to do it, you cannot be said not to want to do it unless you have reasons for not wanting.

GIRL: But, why not?

ERROR: Well, unless you've got reasons we can't speak of your not wanting to do it – only perhaps of your feeling that you can't or perhaps shouldn't do it.

GIRL: I suppose it's my upbringing.

ERROR: Yes, and of course that's not a *reason* for your not wanting, it's a *cause* of your not wanting.

GIRL: Yes.

ERROR: And you're not really sure that you do want to, are you?

GIRL: I *know* I want to!

ERROR [*raising eyebrows, staring and after some two seconds*]: Hmm! Perhaps there's an ambiguity in the notion of wanting to do something. [*The girl scribbles a note*] Well, you think about it.

GIRL [*preparing to leave*]: Yes, you must be wanting – hah! – to think about this meeting tonight.

ERROR: Well, this has all been about meaning of course.

GIRL [*standing*]: It feels like analysis.

ERROR [*standing*]: Yes, it *is*, and in the sense you mean it's been said before. [*Pause*] We'll go on to wishing next week, shall we?

GIRL [*enthusiastically*]: Oh yes!

ERROR: And perhaps hoping after that?

GIRL: Yes. [*She walks to the door*] Do you know Henry Green's work?

ERROR [*amused*]: Oh yes. Still, I can't see our getting as far as *loving* this term, can you? [*Girl looks confused and disappointed*] Look, come and have a drink tonight when this meeting's over?

GIRL: Oh, that would be nice. Yes.

ERROR: Good. Well, we'll meet at the Seminar then?

[*He smiles, there is the sound of the girl leaving and then Error does an exultant* entrechat *and spins round his large, exquisitely furnished room*]

Mix to -

SCENE 12 INTERIOR. STYLE'S EMPTY ROOM. EARLY EVENING.

[*The camera sweeps the room*]

Cut to –

SCENE 13 INTERIOR. STYLE'S DOOR. EARLY EVENING.

[*CU of Style. A hand comes into vision and knocks on door*]

STYLE'S VOICE: (*OOV*) Come!

[*Professor Rea opens door and enters room. He*

is carrying a gown. Style is sitting in an armchair smoking a pipe and reading a book]

PROFESSOR REA: Hullo Tom.

STYLE: Hullo!

REA: Are you coming to hear Jack?

STYLE: Jack, Ah – I suppose I should. What's he talking about?

REA: Meaning as use. [*Style sighs*] I know how you feel.

STYLE [*knocking out pipe*]: Now that's a far more interesting thesis. Why doesn't he talk about that?

REA: Ha! No one else is at the moment.

STYLE: In that case how do we ever start talking about new topics?

REA: We don't.

STYLE: Cheap! *And* inconsistent. [*Rea grins*] Yes, I'll come. I'll sit by the door.

REA: We'll have to hurry. It starts at quarter to!

STYLE: Eight! Well, that's original.

[*He picks up a gown*]

REA: And we don't like it.

[*They make for the door*]

Cut to –

SCENE 14 EXTERIOR. A QUAD. EVENING.

[*Shot from above of academics hurrying to a doorway, gowns flying behind them*]

Cut to –

SCENE 15 EXTERIOR. DOORWAY. EVENING.

[*CU of dons hurrying through doorway. Some un-gowned younger persons go past. Allein*

*lumbers past by himself. Issue stalks to the
door, eyes staring at the ground. Jack
arrives with girl friend. They stop. He
motions her through the door and nods
farewell. Rea and Style arrive, panting. They
exchange nods. Style goes through the doorway. He immediately looks for a seat, Rea
passes further into the room. Error arrives
with the Chairman and the Girl he was
teaching. She passes into the room; Error,
the Chairman, and Jack stand back from
the door nodding at each other and watching late arrivals hurrying past. After about
30 seconds and no new arrivals they nod at
each other, adjust their gowns and pass
through the doorway]*

SCENE 16 *INTERIOR*. THE SEMINAR ROOM. EVENING.

[*A large medieval room. Seated round three
sides is the audience – the impression
should be of about 80 persons. The camera
studies them as they peer about and preen
and twitter like so many starlings. There
should be a suggestion of steel, a half-
glimpse of a helmet, a breastplate briefly
and partially exposed by the adjusting of a
gown*]

[*When the camera reaches the door, the
Chairman followed by Error and Jack, each
armed at all points, march – or better, ride –
perhaps on hobby-horses – into the room
and up to a table at the far end. If the effect
can be bizarre, slightly disquieting and ludicrous that would be precisely appropriate.
These three sit, and after a little preliminary
wriggling and grimacing and interchanging
of glances, the Chairman removes his*

breastplate, lays down his mace and picks up a gavel. He of course is a non-combatant. During his speech the camera should wander round the audience]

CHAIRMAN: Perhaps we may take the minutes of the previous meeting as read? [*Error nods*] Tonight we are to be addressed by Mr Jack.

[*He looks at Jack. Shot of Jack looking nervous and struggling to draw a sword from its scabbard. Camera moves on to the audience*]

CHAIRMAN: (*OOV*) His topic is the old but important one, the nature of meaning, and his paper is called 'Meaning as use'.

[*The audience is seen to be paying no attention. Its members are getting out their hatchets, spears, and so on. Issue is pulling on his absurdly large helmet, and his neighbours have to edge away to avoid his contortions. Issue wears his helmet for the rest of the meeting. It blurs and distorts whatever he has to say. Only Style is still – so still that were it not for a blink of an eyelid he might be unconscious or dead*]

CHAIRMAN: (*OOV*) The reply will be by Dr Error [*he pronounces this 'Err or'*] I don't know if we shall want an interval after the papers. No? [*The audience takes no notice*] No! Well then I shall ask . . .

Cut to –

SCENE 17 INTERIOR. THE SEMINAR ROOM. EVENING.

CHAIRMAN: Ah . . . I shall ask Mr Jack to give us his paper.

JACK [*rising to his feet and giving some pre-*

liminary swings of his sword]: I shall argue in this paper that the doctrine that meaning is use is, firstly, hopelessly vague; and, secondly, that in as far as it presents a discernible thesis it is incompatible with the major discovery of its author.

As to the first part of my thesis, I think the proof of it is that those who used to chant what of course is essentially a slogan stopped when virtually everyone else had joined in and began to ask themselves just what their slogan meant. And we have had a whole series of answers to this question, most of them demonstrably wrong.

For example, Mr Makeweight has construed 'use' – and hence 'meaning' – as 'utility'. [*Brief glimpse of Makeweight looking intently at Jack. His neighbours, some grinning, edge away nervously from him*] So the meaning of a word or phrase – his thesis is intended to cover both – is its utility. But testing this, suppose I wish to keep some children out of a nearby river, I might say to them either 'The river is full of germs' or perhaps, 'The river is full of snakes.' In either event we may suppose that the children keep away – or don't. So these differing remarks could be made for the same reason and achieve the same desired result. But would anyone – even Mr Makeweight –

Cut to –

SCENE 18 *INTERIOR*. THE SEMINAR ROOM. EVENING.

[*Jack standing before Makeweight and prodding him with his sword*]

JACK: – want to say that, either in general or even on this particular occasion, these two sentences had the same *meaning* or that on this occasion 'germs' and 'snakes' have the same *meaning*? [*He slides the point of his sword up under Makeweight's chin and with slight rhythmic movements made in time with his delivery begins to cut Makeweight's throat. Makeweight groans slightly but does nothing to defend himself. His neighbours look bored or faintly amused and superior*] Conversely, if I say 'The river is polluted' to some children and the same thing to a man from the local drainage board, I may intend to achieve and succeed in achieving very different results with my differing addresses. But shall we say [*He sneers at poor Makeweight*] that the self-same remark then has two entirely different meanings? How could we, for how could it?

[*He leans on his sword and pushes it through Makeweight's throat. Makeweight groans*]

Cut to –

SCENE 19 *INTERIOR.* THE SEMINAR ROOM. EVENING.

[*Jack is standing behind the table once again, a blood-stained sword in his hand*]

JACK [*looking towards Makeweight*]: There are many more objections to utility interpretations of the slogan, but as the ones I have made are I think fatal [*Makeweight, anyway, looks as if he is dying*] let us decently avert our eyes and focus them on a second interpretation.

[*He decently averts his eyes from Makeweight and looks at his notes. Some of his audience are grinning*]

Cut to –

SCENE 20 INTERIOR. THE SEMINAR ROOM. EVENING.

MAKEWEIGHT [*now on his feet, bleeding from the throat but voice unimpaired*]: If Mr Jack has finished with me, perhaps I might get this issue out of the way now.

SCENE 21 INTERIOR. THE SEMINAR ROOM. EVENING.

ISSUE [*looking startled through his visor and half-rising*]: I don't think I . . .

[*He peers about and subsides. Some grin, others ignore him*]

Cut to –

SCENE 22 INTERIOR. THE SEMINAR ROOM. EVENING.

[*Makeweight looks at the Chairman who looks at Jack who half-shrugs. Jack sits down*]

MAKEWEIGHT: Well – very briefly – *of course* mine is a general thesis. And it is because in general 'germs' and – what was it ' snakes' do *not* have the same utility that they differ in meaning.[*He strikes Jack with a cudgel. Jack leans back in his chair with closed eyes and sighs*] But that doesn't mean that they cannot have the same effect on particular occasions! So my thesis is unscathed!

[*He slashes downward at Jack but misses completely. Some members of the audience grin and whisper*]

Cut to –

SCENE 23 INTERIOR. THE SEMINAR ROOM. EVENING.

[*Jack stands over Makeweight, now slumped in his chair*]

JACK: But you will then have to say that words have the same meaning on those occasions that they have the same effect or achieve the same desired end. [*He takes paper from Makeweight's hand on which the latter had been making notes. He crumples it into a ball*] And conversely that one and the same word or remark can have two completely different meanings if it achieves two different – but perhaps intended – effects. But this [*he flicks out Makeweight's tie*] is surely wrong, absurd even. It confuses the meaning of a word or remark with those varying factors that determine reactions to its utterance. For example [*Rolling the ball of notes between the palms of his hands*], on your thesis 'communism' has roughly the same meaning to the Americans as 'capitalism' has for the Russians.

MAKEWEIGHT [*stoutly*]: At the moment, surely that's correct!

JACK: No, not at this moment or any other. You confuse the meanings of words or even perhaps what those words identify with the attitudes that persons have both to what they identify and, by extension, to the words themselves.

[*He stuffs the ball of paper into Makeweight's mouth and looks at him. Makeweight shakes his head slightly but is silenced. He slumps forward*]

Cut to –

SCENE 24 INTERIOR. THE SEMINAR ROOM. EVENING.

[*Jack standing behind table yet again*]

JACK [*almost gaily*]: Moving on to the next interpretation of the slogan, this one identifies use
with usage. Now we have been most adequately
and elegantly warned against this insidious and
widespread vulgarisation – [*bows to an inert
Style*] so it needs no further attack from me.
But the very existence of such a widespread
confusion lends support to my first contention
– that the doctrine is vague – and, furthermore,
it is no wonder that this confusion *is* vulgar in
the sense of being widespread, for, in fact,
usage and meaning *are* very closely connected.

For – taking yet a third interpretation – I cannot know the meaning of a word, that is to say,
I cannot know how to use a word unless
the word *is* used in some particular way, i.e.,
unless there is some more or less widespread
and standard usage for me to know – and
which, incidentally, a dictionary will inform me
of if I look up the word's meaning. We tend to
miss the point if we forget that knowing the
meaning of a word involves being able to
understand what others say when they use it.
Moreover, if people start to use a word in a different way then of course – that is to say – the
word's usage changes and so of course does
its meaning. So if we seek to identify meaning
and identify it as use, it cannot be always or
wholly wrong to identify, that is, to construe,
use as usage.

[*He lobs a gauntlet at Style*]

Cut to –

SCENE 25 *INTERIOR*. THE SEMINAR ROOM. EVENING.

[*Style wearily picks up the gauntlet. He is
unarmed, but as he rises massively to*

*answer Jack he should look as if he were
made of burnished steel. His jaw is like a
gin-trap, and yet his voice has a rotundity
and maturity the other academics lack*]

STYLE: Well, some small points. The identification
of use and usage while perhaps not wholly
wrong is not wholly right either – and that is
what I want to say. And indeed if, as Jack says,
no one could know what a word meant until he
knew how others used it, it would be a complete mystery how language ever got started or
how new words are ever introduced into language or how old words get new meanings.
What Jack omits or forgets is that one can create a use but one cannot create a usage. One
can give a word a meaning by using it in a new
way or by redefining it, but one cannot similarly
create a usage simply by making a decision.

Cut to –

SCENE 26 *INTERIOR.* THE SEMINAR ROOM. EVENING.

[*Jack rises to speak. His manner is respectful
and reasonable. He gets a little warmer and
moves closer to Style as the speech proceeds*]

JACK: Well, I don't see the start of language or
even the emergence of a new usage as something happening at a given moment in time,
which is what you seem to imply. As to your
other point, that you can't create a usage by an
act of will: the same is true of giving a word a
meaning. I don't succeed in giving a new word
a meaning, even in a restricted context, unless
and until I start using the word in a certain way
and unless and until someone – if only myself

– understands what I say when I so use it. Until such times the word has no meaning – only a definition – and if the word is used in some way that does *not* square with the definition then what is at fault is the definition.

STYLE [*rising*]: But *that* is to admit that the definition *can* bestow meaning; though of course it can fail to do this. [*He lazily cuffs Jack and sends him – literally – spinning back across the room and behind the table where he collapses into his chair*] And if I do define a new word, indicate how it should be used, say what it means, it then has a meaning though, never having been used, it lacks a usage.

Cut to –

SCENE 27 INTERIOR. THE SEMINAR ROOM. EVENING.

[*Jack raises his head, its left side is bruised and broken from temple to jaw. He pushes himself to his feet*]

JACK [*tremulously, earnestly*]: What I am trying to say is that meaning is very much a matter of practice, of a common activity. Usage draws attention to this feature, 'use' if construed as 'being able to use' does not. [*Recovering his spirit somewhat*] And what I think your counter-example founders on is the fact that definitions *themselves* involve in their *definiens* words which must have a common usage if the definition is to succeed in specifying how the word is to be used. [*He looks enquiringly at Style but Style has returned to immobility. Jack, very nervous now, peers at his notes. The next part of his paper is delivered in a gabble*] Well – [*licks lips*] – in discussing use and usage I have already mentioned a third

and what is, I suppose, the favoured interpretation of the slogan, namely that to know the
meaning of a word is to know how to use it.
They are perhaps minor objections to this
thesis that one can know how to use a word
without knowing what it means – I successfully
used the word 'egregious' for many years without having anything but the faintest idea what
it meant – and, conversely, that one can know
what a word means, having looked it up in the
dictionary, and yet still not be able to use it –
'captious' is a personal example. [*Members of
the audience sneer and grow restive. Jack's
nervousness increases*] But my main difficulty
with this interpretation is that the slogan, thus
construed, sounds all right only because it is
so imprecise. Let me illustrate this with reference to the problem of *difference* of meaning.
If a word can be used in different ways, it surely ought then to have different meanings,
according to the doctrine. But if one word
could have different meanings in this way, how
could it be one word and not merely a series of
punning homonyms? The doctrine on slightly
closer examination is seen here to be actively
unhelpful.

Let me consider one last difficulty where it
is simply no help at all. If I say that a mistake
is a big one I condemn whatever it is I call a
mistake more strongly than if I call it a small
one. If, on the other hand, I say that an
achievement is a big one, I praise it strongly
whereas if I call it a small one, if I praise it at
all, I do so with very faint praise. But if I call an
elephant a big one I don't praise it or dispraise
it at all – unless the circumstances are special.
Now, am I using 'big' differently in these differing contexts? Certainly I do, and intend to do,

and say, and imply something different in each case. Certainly too my tests, though not perhaps my criteria, for determining whether an achievement, a mistake, or an elephant is a big one are different. But am I using the word 'big' differently?

Now I don't think that this is a clear question, for it is not clear what if anything turns on its answer. But if deciding to answer 'Yes' commits us to the view that 'big' has a different sense or meaning or even force in these differing contexts, we are I think likely to answer 'No' instead. In other words, it is our prior intuitions about meaning which determine our view that the word is, or in this case is not being, used differently. (Though what these intuitions are intuitions of I am not sure.) And, once again, this example raises the question 'What would count as two correct though differing uses of a word which would indicate or constitute a variation of sense?'

The notion of use then on which our third interpretation of the slogan depends is itself vague and perhaps counterintuitive, and with this point I bring the first part of my paper to an end.

[*He splashes water from a carafe into a glass and gulps at it, spilling water on to himself, his papers and the table. His audience are glazed with boredom and disdain. Style looks at his watch, rises, nods to Jack and exits. A couple of others follow. Jack plunges back into his paper. As he does so Issue rises*]

JACK: My first contention has been that . . .
ISSUE: I wonder if I might . . .

[*Jack looks up wildly and grabs for his sword lying on the table. He sees Issue swaying under the weight of his armour and a lance that he is struggling to level, not at Jack, but the audience. After some hesitation, Jack gratefully sits down*]

Cut to –

SCENE 28 INTERIOR. THE SEMINAR ROOM. EVENING.

ISSUE: As there has been a lot of misunderstanding on this point about meaning and criteria, I wonder if I might just try to get one point clear on this important – ah – matter about meaning and criteria. These *are* confused, but I certainly have never wanted to say that because the criteria for the application of such words as 'big' and 'real' vary, their meanings vary. But only those who themselves conflate meaning and criteria can say that I have said, therefore, that the meanings of these words change. I agree with Jack that they don't, at least not in such contexts as he mentions. Perhaps –

JACK: Well, I'm not even sure their criteria change, their tests do.

ISSUE: Oh! [*He swings round to face Jack but the end of his lance has gone limp*] Oh? Yes, you distinguish, but . . .

JACK: Yes, because I think the criterion for something's being a big one is always the same – roughly, its being appreciably larger than the average member of the class of comparison. But the actual *tests* you would carry out to *determine* this would vary from context to context. You see, I am inclined to identify meaning and criteria here and say *neither* change.

ISSUE: Yes, but . . .

[*A member of the audience, a young man,
rises. He is very nervous and armed only
with a child's sword which he points at
Jack as, speaking, he advances towards
him*]

FIRST MEMBER OF AUDIENCE: But couldn't you
equally well argue that the test too is always
the same. You see if the object is larger than
the average member of the class of comparison. I mean, I don't see why the same argument doesn't apply here.

JACK [*contemptuously disarming him*]: Well,
something changes and it's not the meaning
or criteria. The operations you would carry out
are what change and these are what I'm calling the tests.

FIRST MEMBER OF AUDIENCE [*collapsing into his
chair, mutters defiantly*]: They're always the
same.

REA: (*OOV*) I'm unhappy with your definition of
'big' because it involves the cognate compara-
tive 'larger'.

[*Jack, surprised, swings to face Rea. In the
ensuing exchange he suffers a few slight
cuts about the face*]

REA: But leaving that aside, how would Mr Jack
make his distinction between criteria and tests
in the case of 'real'?

JACK: I – well. I – no, well I don't suppose it can
be made quite generally. But as far as 'big'
goes and other similar attributives, whether
you make the distinction I do or identify tests
and criteria as does Mr Issue, you say that
something changes – but *not* the meaning.

REA: Well, you might. But how about 'a good
dinner'? Suppose your criteria, your necessary

and sufficient conditions for something's being a good dinner, are that the food should be of high quality and mine that it should be edible and a lot of it. Wouldn't you say that we meant something very different by 'good dinner'?

[*Laughter*]

JACK: Well, I . . .

ISSUE [*stepping between them, firmly*]: I don't think we should bring 'good' into this. It's as difficult a notion as 'real'. The question is, does Rea think that 'big' means something different in 'This is a big mouse' and 'That is a big elephant'?

REA [*lightly*]: I think this is something we might well say. And *do*.

[*Laughter. Issue winces as from a low blow. He drops his lance and his visor drops. He sits down. Allein wearily shakes his head*]

JACK [*after a slight pause*]: Well – my first contention has been that 'meaning is use' is almost hopelessly vague. My second is that in as far as it can be made to yield various theses, even the best favoured is incompatible with the major discovery of its author. For each suggests, almost irresistibly, that meaning has an essence which it identifies. That the slogan does have this misleading connotation might be denied by pointing out that it *is* merely a slogan – but then my first objection remains, namely that it is vague; and in any case and all over again, in as far as it does yield various more precise interpretations each is likely to mislead by suggesting that meaning has an essence. If it is argued that this second charge, of essentialism, itself presupposes what is false, viz. that 'use' has an essence, my reply would be that the slogan, which has the form of an identity proposition, is not misleading if, and only if, the penumbra of 'meaning' and 'use', coincide. But, as we have seen, they do not seem to do this, and the lack of coincidence seems particularly marked where the notion of meaning relates to etymology. And, more importantly, our looking to use however and wherever we do this, though solving some meaning-problems does not solve all and, as I have tried to show, actively interferes in the proper solution of at least some.

It is then in my view time to forget the slogan and time to march forward into those unexplored territories the general nature of whose terrain was indicated by other remarks from the same author and which have received far less and too little attention.

[*Jack sheaths his sword and sits down. There is some very sporadic applause*]

Cut to –

SCENE 29 *INTERIOR*. THE SEMINAR ROOM. EVENING.

ERROR [*urbane, incisive*]: Mr Jack makes two criticisms of the doctrine that meaning is use. The first is that it is vague, the second that in as far as it can be made to yield more specific theses each and any of these is incompatible with the doctrine of family resemblances and is therefore incorrect. He concludes that we should forget the slogan and get down to some detailed work guided by the family-resemblance notion – which, his time being short, he quite properly neither expounds nor defends.

In proof of his first criticism he shows that the assertion that meaning is use has been variously construed and proceeds to argue that one such construction is wrong, one popular interpretation thought to be wrong is *not* – or not wholly wrong, and a third, that knowing the meaning of a word consists in knowing how to use it, is itself vague, foundering on the vagueness of the notion of use, and in as far as it is not vague is doubtful of truth. [*He now draws his rapier with a hiss*]

What he has to say about the so-called vulgar error of constructing use as usage, namely that it is vulgar but not erroneous or not wholly so, would seem to threaten his general position – that every particular interpretation of the doctrine is and must necessarily be either wrong in what it specifically asserts or wrong in the *kind* of thing it asserts, namely that meaning has an essence which it purports to identify *of any kind at all*. [*He thrusts at Jack but holds back at the last moment*]

I imagine that Mr Jack would meet this objection by saying that he was only trying to show that the identification of use and usage and meaning is not wholly wrong. [*Jack wearily nods*] But if *that* is a defence of this view it is equally a defence of the third and first interpretations if they are partial truths, and his criticisms of them and perhaps of the slogan itself need reformulation.

Cut to –

SCENE 30 *INTERIOR*. THE SEMINAR ROOM. EVENING.

[*Blood trickles from a wound running across Jack's right cheek*]

Cut to –

SCENE 31 INTERIOR. THE SEMINAR ROOM. EVENING.

    ERROR: After all, if what is admittedly a slogan yields various partial truths where there are no whole truths, the slogan can scarcely be criticised.

    Cut to –

SCENE 32 INTERIOR. THE SEMINAR ROOM. EVENING.

    [*Blood trickles from a wound running across Jack's forehead*]

    Cut to –

SCENE 33 INTERIOR. THE SEMINAR ROOM. EVENING.

    ERROR: Again, I must anticipate Mr Jack's reply. I think he would say that the interpretation of use as utility is not even partially true, but wholly false.

    [*He turns to look at Jack*]

    Cut to –

SCENE 34 INTERIOR. THE SEMINAR ROOM. EVENING.

    [*Jack, eyes closed, nods very slightly. It could be his head trembling; but his two most recent wounds have already stopped bleeding*]

    Cut to –

SCENE 35 INTERIOR. THE SEMINAR ROOM. EVENING.

    ERROR: Now this I think is much too strong a claim. I do not see how we could give an account of, for example, indexical words – such words as 'I', 'this', 'that', 'here', 'now', and so on, without mentioning the fact that these words enable us to refer to, to talk about, various parts of our environment by a method akin to, but more sophisticated and flexible than pointing. [*Slight pause*] That is their use and utility.

Cut to–

SCENE 36 *INTERIOR*. THE SEMINAR ROOM. EVENING.

[*Jack's head is bowed. The two wounds have reopened and bleed profusely*]

Cut to –

SCENE 37 *INTERIOR*. THE SEMINAR ROOM. EVENING.

[*Makeweight stares coolly at Jack*]

Cut to –

SCENE 38 *INTERIOR*. THE SEMINAR ROOM. EVENING.

ERROR [*still urbane*]: His criticism of the third interpretation is that the notion of use to which it makes appeal is itself hopelessly vague and, in as far as its sense can be discerned, it is either discerned through our prior, intuitive understanding of the notion of meaning itself which it therefore does nothing to elucidate, or, when it is not so discerned, it tends to upset our intuitive notion and hence is counterintuitive. His argument here is that if, as is surely the case, one word has a variety of uses, the doctrine commits us to the paradoxical view that the word has a variety of meanings and its varying occurrences would then amount to a collection of punning homonyms.

This surely, is a bad argument. If meaning is use it doesn't follow that if a word has a variety of uses, it has a variety of meanings. Its use and of course its meaning comprises its variety of uses. That this is the correct line to take is made especially clear by the third formulation of the doctrine which Jack is attacking, 'Knowing the meaning of a word is knowing how to use it.' There is no suggestion here that for every use I know there is a meaning I know. Indeed, one only gets this kind of conclusion and criticism by assuming the very view that Jack wishes, quite rightly, to dispel, namely that meaning has some kind of essence. Here the view, though slightly more complicated, is essentially – ah, hah – [*he smiles*] the same, namely, that meaning comes in discrete chunks and these can be identified with discrete uses.

Of course [*turning slightly towards Jack and away again*], I do not wish to be understood as claiming that the notion of use that we make appeal to here is a clear one. It isn't. It is vague and extremely protean. But this [*He places his rapier against Jack's breastplate and begins to lean on it*], is its strongest – or at least a necessary part – of its claim to comprise whatever it is we allude to when we speak of meaning.

[*The rapier pierces the metal and slides into Jack's heart. He grimaces in agony*]

Cut to –

SCENE 39 INTERIOR. THE SEMINAR ROOM. EVENING.

[*Jack's Girl Friend seated in the audience is looking with some concern towards the front of the room*]
Cut to –

SCENE 40 INTERIOR. THE SEMINAR ROOM. EVENING.

ERROR: (*OOV*) . . . when we speak of meaning.

[*Jack, without sword or armour, grimaces as Error concludes his remark*]

Cut to –

SCENE 41 INTERIOR. THE SEMINAR ROOM. EVENING.

ERROR [*armed as before, bloodstained rapier in hand*]: This view, like Jack's, argues that we should get down to some detailed work on the notion of meaning, but it is more charitable than his both to the slogan itself and perhaps to the notion of use.

Indeed, if I had to make a general criticism of his paper it would be that it lacks charity – and it is this lack which is responsible for the feeling of strain, of an almost aggressive unwillingness to understand, that makes his paper uncomfortable and his position contorted and uneasy. [*Jack is contorted in his seat*] Intelligence is a moral quality. [*Error throws off this last remark*]

After all, slogans are just that. They exhort us to action, but they cannot be expected to give us detailed instructions as to strategy or tactics. How *should* the workers unite? [*He raises his eyebrows. There are a few guffaws*] And it is surely no proper way to treat a slogan to construe it as an ambiguous statement and then to say that each interpretation of the statement is necessarily incorrect in what it asserts.

[*Still urbane, Error wipes his rapier on his gown, sheaths it, and sits down. There is warm applause*]

Cut to –

SCENE 42 *INTERIOR.* THE SEMINAR ROOM. EVENING.

> CHAIRMAN [*turning to Jack. Quietly*]: Would you like to – ah – *answer* any of – ah – Error's points, or shall we – ah –
>
> [*He gestures to the audience, members of which are preparing themselves for action*]
>
> JACK: Well – [*Then, deciding to say something, in his public voice*] Well, there is one thing. I just don't see that Error has said anything to show that the notion of use isn't vague *or* counterintuitive in the way I claimed in my paper.
>
> ERROR [*surprised, putting down a cigarette he has just lit*]: Oh? Ah, well – ah – well, take another example. If I say, if I say – ah – yes! If I say – as a slogan – 'Health is exercise' I haven't committed myself to the view that for every exercise there is a health.
>
> [*He looks at Jack who is frowning in thought. Suddenly Jack reaches for his sword. As he begins his reply a couple of people from the audience try to speak as well but they give way to Jack*]
>
> JACK: Well, I don't like your example. It's clearly an aphorism, I mean it's metaphorical, it couldn't be construed literally. In any case, another way in which it's not like 'Meaning is use' is that there is just *health*, healthy people, but there isn't just *meaning*, there are *many* meanings, different ones. So your example won't do. And unless there *is* some connection between different uses and different meanings we could never determine what a word means,

and how it differs from another, by seeing how it is used and comparing this with the way in which the other one is used.

[*Jack has scored a palpable hit on Error and it staggers him*]

ERROR [*faintly*]: Yes, my example is a bad one. But . . .

JACK: So I still say that if a word has different uses, it remains entirely mysterious that these different uses don't – or, anyway, needn't – yield a difference in meaning whereas between *different* words they do. 'Use' must itself be being used differently here.

REA: Then the problem is solved! Different uses yielding different senses are found within one word, the word 'use'! [*Banteringly*]

JACK [*trying to avoid the flickering tip of Rea's teasing rapier and making a counter-thrust*]: But why then *one* word? And what about those uses that don't yield a difference of sense?

REA [*easily avoiding the thrust and rapping Jack's knuckles*]: Family resemblance! Where the uses are similar we discern no difference in sense, where they are not so similar we do, but they are not so different, so unrelated, as to warrant our saying they are uses of different words.

FIRST MEMBER OF AUDIENCE: Could Professor Rea give an example of this?

REA [*whirls round, parries and runs the questioner through*]: Of course. If I say *A* and *B* are the same, I may mean either that they are exactly similar – like two peas – or are one and the same – are one pea. 'Same' has these two very different uses and senses, but clearly they are related.

SECOND MEMBER OF AUDIENCE [*young, diffident*]: Perhaps Mr Jack's – perhaps Mr Jack was worried by the ambiguity of what is supposed to be a technical word?

[*No one takes up this point. Abashed he sinks back down among the people surrounding him*]

THIRD MEMBER OF AUDIENCE [*young, cocky. As he makes his point he sticks out a very long stringy neck*]: It seems that everyone here takes this notion of family resemblance seriously. Am I alone in thinking . . .

ALLEIN [*goaded beyond endurance*]: Young man! [*He rises*] Permit me. You must not make the mistake of thinking that because you are in a minority you are right. [*He swings his axe and chops off the previous speaker's head. There is some laughter and applause. Allein waits for this to stop*] I have three things. The first: it surprises me greatly that neither Mr Jack – who of course is very young – nor Dr Error nor Professor Rea – who after all are not so young – [*a few laughs*] have tried to understand this meaning-dictum in its history. Here is another dictum for all of you: if you want to know what it means, look at the context – the times – in which it was said. And what did they say about meaning then? What did Professor Rea say? Well, he can tell you – or, better still, you can read what he said. [*There are a few giggles. Rea seems to have shrunk*] Of course we were brash young men then. [*Laughter*]

Second: where are the *examples*? Have I heard *two* tonight? And *they* were illustrations. Yes, you say you understand, you talk as if you do – in one sense – but you do not behave as people who understand. Now, which do you prefer as a guide to answer this question? You!

[*He points at a young man in the audience*]

FOURTH MEMBER OF AUDIENCE: Behaviour.

ALLEIN: Yes, you have learnt something! [*a few titters*]

Third: everything that could be wrong with Mr Jack's paper *is* wrong with it. [*There is no expression on Jack's face*] Except two things. He is really puzzled – but he doesn't like to work. He prefers to theorise. [*Nodding, answering Jack's silent and invisible protest*] Yes, yes. And, second: he suspects the notion of use, he suspects that it may be

. . . [*he sketches this shape:*
 in the air with one hand] . . . this shape. And he's right. But it shouldn't make him unhappy! [*Titters*] That's a very good shape for a concept to be! [*Laughter*]

What he must do now is to map this shape closely – not criticise it for being complex.

[*He pauses, makes as if to say something else but changes his mind and sits down. After a pause there is scattered clapping. Allein's head nods*]

JACK: I'm not really interested in mapping 'use', I'm interested in mapping 'meaning'.

ALLEIN [*from his seat, nodding*]: Good! [*Then raising his voice slightly so all can hear, and wagging his finger*] Well, do it! [*Laughter*]

Cut to –

SCENE 43 INTERIOR. THE SEMINAR ROOM. EVENING.

[*Yet a Fifth Member of the Audience, a girl, wearing a gown and sitting next to the First Member rises. She has taken the toy sword from her companion and, as she attacks, it changes into a real and formidable weapon*]

FIFTH MEMBER OF AUDIENCE: I'm afraid I'm still not satisfied with Jack's answer about tests. Earlier he said that the criterion for something's being a big one didn't change, only the tests – what he called the operations you carried out to determine if something was a big one – changed. But surely the operation is always essentially the same, though it's true that the instruments – the weighing machines – vary somewhat. But *that's* not enough for what he wants to say.

Surely, all that really *is* different is the absolute size that a thing – an X – has to be in order to be a big X. But this variation only depends on – it's determined by – the size that Xs are. Surely, *this* is the only variable. The meaning of 'big', its criterion of application and what you do – in principle – to find out if an X is a big X are all constants.

Cut to –

SCENE 44 INTERIOR. THE SEMINAR ROOM. EVENING.

[*Jack, like all the participants apart from Allein, now looks very battered, and he is exhausted. He looks at his challenger then drops his eyes. His mouth is half-open*]

JACK [*shrugging, not rising*]: Well – er – perhaps.

Cut to –

SCENE 45 INTERIOR. THE SEMINAR ROOM. EVENING.

[*The girl gets to her feet and begins to talk again. But her voice is out of focus. Rea gets to his feet but again his voice is out of focus. No words can be discerned, only rise and fall and intonation. Jack, exhausted has left the field, and the battle now continues as a series of skirmishes and – literally – running fights between the indefatigable Rea and other members of the audience. At one point, very near the end, Issue is attacked on all sides. He defends valiantly from an impossible position but goes under. The film should be gradually accelerated. Just before the end one participant raises his voice. The audience is visibly embarrassed. Jack too must be shocked, for we hear the Chairman's words as he rebukes this speaker*]

CHAIRMAN: Please! [*The shouter subsides*] We share your enthusiasm Mr – ah– but please don't let it carry you away. We can't have our meetings get out of hand! [*Pause*] Perhaps this might be a good time to halt? [*He looks at Error who raises his eyebrows, nods and shrugs. Jack closes his eyes and nods*] Well, it only remains for me to thank our two speakers for their most – ah – *stimulating* papers.

[*He leads the ragged clapping. Jack opens his eyes*]

Cut to –

SCENE 46 INTERIOR. THE SEMINAR ROOM. EVENING.

[*Most of those who are still able to clap do so. Then the audience begins to stream out, dropping swords, armour, etc., as it goes and leaving behind one apparently dead man, another weeping, another who is half-carried away by two friends.*

Error and the Chairman, rid of all weapons and armour, stroll out smoking, chatting and laughing. Jack buries his face in his hands. But he hears a noise at the doorway and looks up]

Cut to –

SCENE 47 INTERIOR. THE SEMINAR ROOM. EVENING.

[Jack's Girl Friend is standing in the doorway. Behind her are three or four young men and a young woman]

JGF: Coming?

[Jack gets to his feet and swaggers towards her]

Cut to –

SCENE 48 EXTERIOR. OUTSIDE THE SEMINAR ROOM. EVENING.

[Jack is talking to his initially cautious, almost hostile friends. Half-armoured, he gestures mechanically with his sword]

JACK: Well, I don't think so! He never got to grips with the different use–different meaning thing!

FIRST FRIEND [*conciliatingly*]: That's true. [*He puts balm on one of Jack's many wounds. Jack appears not to notice*] Allein was good though!

JACK [*flinching*]: Just bloody patronising!

FIRST FRIEND: Yes, but he's good though.

JACK: Yes, good for a laugh! I've heard that monologue dozens of times.

FIRST FRIEND: Ha! [*He binds a wound*] True enough!

SECOND FRIEND [*giving Jack meat and drink*]: I should think Issue will shut up now about meaning and criteria.

JACK: Never! He'll think of something to say.

THIRD FRIEND: Well, I enjoyed that!

[*He gives Jack another drink. Jack drinks but shakes his head at this remark*]

[*Short pause*]

FOURTH FRIEND: Well, we're going for a beer. You coming?

JACK [*considers this*]: Ah – no. No – I'll – I might be along later.

[*They nod and turn away. JGF remains. He puts his arm around her shoulders and, using his sword as a stick, limps away*]

Mix to –

SCENE 49 *INTERIOR.* ERROR'S ROOM EVENING.

[*The door opens. Error and his girl pupil walk in. Error immediately, automatically, removes his gown. He turns to face the girl and then camera. His face is bloodstained*]

ERROR: Well, what did you think of it?

GIRL [*anxiously*]: Very interesting.

ERROR: Yes, there were some interesting points raised. Do sit down. What would you like to drink?

GIRL: Oh – Oh –

[*Having half-sat down she stands again*]

ERROR: Have a gin and tonic. I shall. Very nice.

GIRL [*sitting*]: Yes, yes. Thank you.

[*Error busies himself with the drinks*]

GIRL [*diffidently*]: You know – you look very tired?

ERROR: Oh? [*Amused, surprised. He walks towards her and places the drinks on the table*] I think I found it just a little tiresome tonight – in places.

GIRL: Yes. Thank you.

[*She is awkward and does not pick up her drink*]

ERROR: You know, I think you would be far more comfortable if you took off your gown.

[*The girl rises and half-turns away from Error in taking off her academic gown. As she does so Error passes a hand wearily across his face. The facial wounds disappear. He smiles at the girl and stretches out his arms towards her to take the gown*]

Cut to –

SCENE 50 INTERIOR. ISSUE'S ROOM. EVENING.

[*Issue, having removed the rest of his armour, tugs and twists and pulls off his dented helmet. He inspects it, turning it round in his hands*]

ISSUE: Well . . . [*He picks up a piece of wire wool and refurbishes some scratches*] I'm still inclined to say that the criteria of application for attributive words do vary. But even if we say they do not, the important point for my thesis, and one that remains, is that their meanings do *not* change. [*He picks up a ball-peen hammer and begins to hammer out the dents*] 'Big' does not have a different

meaning in 'big mistake' [*bang*], 'big elephant'
[*bang*], and 'big mouse' [*bang*]. Moreover,
criteria for the application of the *interesting*
attributive words – particularly 'good' and
'real' – *do* change. [*bang*] Just compare, for
example, 'real cream' [*bang*] and 'real oasis'.
[*bang. Muttering with satisfaction Issue
twists the helmet again – and his fingers
slip through a large hole. He stares fixedly
at this and it gradually disappears*] And
really *no one* would seriously claim that 'real'
has a different meaning in these two cases.
[*He hastily puts the helmet down and picks
up his breastplate, which he peers at, pats,
polishes, uttering and grimacing the while*]

Cut to –

SCENE 51 *INTERIOR*. ALLEIN'S ROOM. EVENING.

[*Allein squints along the bloodstained edge of
his axe. It is razor-sharp. He wipes the
blade, grunts with satisfaction and takes
the axe to a cupboard. He opens the cupboard door and places the axe inside. He
picks another axe from the ten or twelve
inside and begins to sharpen it on a grinding wheel*]

ALLEIN [*turning the wheel vigorously*]: It has
always seemed perfectly clear to me that there
can be no good philosophy done by those who
have no knowledge of science. Science and
philosophy –

Cut to –

SCENE 52 *INTERIOR*. REA'S ROOM. EVENING.

[*Rea, divested of armour and rapier is pouring

himself a stiff drink. He moves to an armchair, sits, stretches luxuriously and takes a
gulp. He leans back and closes his eyes.
Immediately he does this there is a whispering. It is Rea's own voice. The half-smile
of satisfaction on his face is replaced by a
look of horror]

REA'S VOICE [hesitantly at first]: A sufficient condition of a necessary condition's also being a
sufficient condition –

[Rea opens his eyes. He takes another large
drink and leans back in the chair. He closes
his eyes]

REA'S VOICE [gabble]: A sufficient condition of a
necessary condition's also being a sufficient
condition [now slower, thoughtful] is that the
sufficient condition of which the necessary
condition is a necessary condition

[There is a rapier in Rea's right hand. He tries
to shake it out of his hand. The rapier and
his voice disappear when he opens his
eyes. Having opened them he takes an even
bigger drink. Again he leans back in the
chair and determinedly closes his eyes. The
sword and voice reappear]

REA'S VOICE [gabbling]: – is that the sufficient
condition of which the necessary condition is
a necessary condition [more slowly] is itself a
necessary condition of the necessary condition.

[Rea tries to fling away the rapier. When he
opens his eyes it disappears, as does the
voice. Anxiously he sits on the front of his
chair. He screws up his eyes in thought]

REA: Hm.

[*He stands up, walks to his rapier lying on a table and then stands in front of his full-length mirror. As he speaks he begins to fence*]

REA: It is a *sufficient* condition of a necessary condition's also being a *sufficient* condition, that the sufficient condition of which the necessary condition is a necessary condition is *itself* a necessary condition of –

Cut to –

SCENE 53 INTERIOR. JACK'S ROOM. EVENING.

[*Jack is washing his face. He begins to strip, and though his many wounds are healing, he looks exhausted. JGF is there. She gazes at him. He pulls off his singlet, stretches and looks at her. She stares back, gets up and walks towards him. Jack's next speech should be completely and almost excessively naturalistic in treatment; in this it should contrast with everything else in the production*]

JACK: Well, I'll see you tomorrow then, shall I? I want to get this reply down on paper while it's still fresh in my mind.

[*JGF walks past Jack to the door. It is impossible to tell what she feels*]

JACK: About one in the Northgate?

[*JGF exits. Jack is momentarily puzzled, but quickly dismisses this puzzle. He walks to a record player, puts on a record, then he moves over to his barbell, picks it up and begins pressing it. As he does this he chants in the strange, artificial voice*]

JACK: There are those who wish to maintain both that the meaning of a word is its use and that – and perhaps, even, *therefore* – 'means' has a meaning, *one* meaning. I maintain, however, that 'means' – like 'use' itself – has many meanings, many uses, and in addition, that 'the meaning of a word' and cognate phrases have themselves many meanings, many uses, so that the doctrine as stated is not just – or *even* – *false*, but is ambiguous, misleading, and indeed self-stultifying.

[*He drops the bar. Exhausted, frustrated, he crouches over his burden, staring at the ground and shaking his head. A whispering starts. Immediately, Jack starts again*]

JACK: There are those who . . . etc., etc.

[*As he repeats his speech the whispers get louder. Now familiar voices are heard repeating their now-familiar set pieces. The voices get shriller, sobs are heard, then shrieks.*

The camera pans back, the picture fades and Jack seems to age. The cacophony of voices blend and begin to speak in unison. They say, in cool, clear, considered, detached tones]

VOICES: It was like this: the doctrine was not intended as a literal truth but as a corrective to the ever-tempting and then prevalent belief that the meaning of a word is and, indeed, must be, a thing. That is how it was . . .

[*But now other voices, new ones, talking about new topics fade in, and Jack's voice joins them. They are strident, aggressive and contradictory*]

NEW VOICES: Can we specify, in principle, sufficient conditions for human action?

Yes!

No!

The notion of cause in history is a nonsense!

It's just different!

Robots would be persons!

Given spare-part surgery, what identifies individuals?

How silly!

[The clash of steel is heard, thuds, shrieks, etc.]

Fade out –

FINIS

POSTSCRIPT

Today, critics would say that this play, though not the prefatory remarks, 'deconstructs' academic – or, at any rate,
academic philosophical – discussions, debates, seminars,
disagreements, work, life. The prefatory remarks, though not
using that later phrase, makes this point in order to explain
to the director or reader of the play the medieval, combative
symbols in it. The task of the director would be to convey the
meaning of this symbolism to the play's audience. When ITV
was regularly commissioning and producing one-off television
plays – there are, of course, very few such plays produced for
television these days – they offered me a £50 rewrite fee to
make the play more accessible to its viewers. I thought that
a director should be able to convey the meaning of the symbolism, and that an audience would not and did not need to
understand very much of what the disputants were saying in
order to understand what was happening, pocketed the fee,
and did nothing. The play was never produced.

What may be of interest now is not the historical situation in which the play was written, but the historical characters, the actual philosophers, on which the characters were based. Tom Style was based on – *is*, as I cannot but wrongly think – Gilbert Ryle, whose *Concept of Mind*, published in 1949, took the British, if not the entire English-speaking philosophical world by storm. Despite Ryle's protests, he was understood as offering a behaviouristic account of mind and, hence, of thought, consciousness, memory. In so doing he appeared to destroy the very phenomena of which he sought to give an account. That is why, when he is alone and doing nothing, that is not 'behaving', Tom Style ceases to exist. As to his name: the aforementioned Austin once said of Ryle, 'The style is Ryle.' The lovely aphorism expresses a truth about this philosopher and his thought, though whether that truth is available to philosophers who did not know Ryle, I am not sure.

Dr Allein (Dr 'Alone', in German) is based on Friedrich Waismann, a German *emigré* in Oxford after the Second World War, who had various misfortunes. One was that he was a contemporary and, until Wittgenstein banished him, a member of Wittgenstein's philosophical circle, to whom Wittgenstein dictated many of his thoughts. If he had not been a contemporary of Wittgenstein's, he would have been a great – or a very nearly great – philosopher; as it was, he was an acolyte who was charged with stealing his master's thoughts, mangling them or watering them down. Another misfortune was that he was, though not in consequence of his falling out with Wittgenstein, quite isolated at Oxford. He was proud, Jewish, and knew about mathematics and science. The Oxford philosophical world appeared to ignore him, and the undergraduates who, in fewer and fewer numbers, attended his lectures, tittered at his pomposities, sponge-bag trousers, poor jokes and ponderous, rather patronising delivery. When I heard him, his wife had already died and his son had committed suicide. His only book, *The Principles of Linguistic Philosophy*, was seen, rightly, as a reworking and, in a large part, a misunderstanding of what was to appear in 1953 as

Wittgenstein's *Philosophical Investigations*. (So was Ryle's *Concept of Mind*, but this was not appreciated until much later.) He was a fine man, erudite, serious, in love with philosophy, and I have worried if, in 'The seminar', I have done him less than justice.

Professor Rea (Professor 'A') and Dr T. T. Error are both based on Professor A. J. Ayer, a widely known, once-famous figure, presented as he appeared to me, and other young, ambitious philosophers in Oxford in the 1960s. Ayer, who, to be fair to him, never claimed to be original, had introduced the philosophical doctrine of logical positivism to the English-speaking world in 1935 with his precocious and iconoclastic *Language, Truth and Logic*. We postgraduate students thought he was a brilliant, superficial, anachronistic roué, and that is how Rea and Error are jointly presented in 'The seminar'. I can only say in excuse that I and my fellow postgraduate students *were* young, ambitious, and hypersensitive and responsive to what was then intellectually fashionable, which watered down logical positivism was not. Waismann, who had been involved with Wittgenstein as its leader (a role he later tried to deny) in the original logical positivistic movement, the so-called 'Vienna Circle' would have been mystified and irritated by Ayer's appointment to a professorship, a 'chair', at Oxford, and by his reputation. Honesty rather than generosity compels me to say that, whatever his other failings, Ayer had no intellectual 'side'. If a student attacked his work and Ayer thought – as he quite often did – that the attack was justified, he would not only say so but do so in a letter which his secretary would dispatch on the very same day, or, at the latest, the very next postal day, subsequent to the occasion of the attack. (I will add that ten years *after* I wrote this piece, the Aristotelian Society invited me to give a paper on 'Hoping and wishing'! When I got the invitation I thought I then completely understood Oscar Wilde's remark about nature imitating art.)

Makeweight is, that is, is based on, E. B. Braithwaite. I included him because Braithwaite had come from Cambridge, Wittgenstein's university, to deliver a paper in which he

explained that when Wittgenstein had instructed philosophers not to raise questions about the *meanings* of words, as
if meanings were things, but to ask themselves how the words
are used, by a word's use Wittgenstein meant its utility, that
is, its usefulness, what tasks are done with it. There are indeed
passages in the *Philosophical Investigations* which suggest
that Wittgenstein did think that there was a connection, but I
and my fellows listened to what we thought was vulgarity with
frozen embarrassment. The play gives expression to some of
the reasons why we felt such views were superficial, untenable
misunderstandings of Wittgenstein's thought. In retrospect I
want to say that Braithwaite's view was partly true, and
Wittgenstein himself, had he been capable of overcoming his
rage at what he always saw as the misunderstanding and
misrepresenting of his views by others, would have said – *did*
say – that, in some contexts, the identification of the use of
a word and its utility can be illuminating.

Issue is, or, rather, is based on, R. M. Hare who became the
professor of Moral Philosophy at Oxford. He bestrode philosophical discussions of morality like a Colossus, and rightly
so. But though he did so, and was not only irrefutable but
utterly scrupulous in debate, though he was the most committed and careful tutor one could have, he always thought,
and could not help himself from thinking, that if anyone crit-
icised his views and disagreed with them, the only possible
explanation of this was that he, Hare, had not expressed his
views with sufficient *clarity*. (This is a common ploy with
politicians.) Seen in one way, this is a remarkable humility,
but the way in which this reaction was construed by aspiring
philosophers, especially those working in moral philosophy,
was the flipside: Hare's remarkable arrogance. His critics
wanted to claim that they understood very well, only too well,
what Hare was saying, and what *they* were saying was that
he was wrong. Though not a moral philosopher (then)
myself, I was empathetic with my fellows who were: but,
again, honesty compels me to admit that when the chips
were down, the battle fought, the lists entered, the glove
thrown down and picked up – these are the metaphors which

still spring to my mind now after so many years – Hare was not bested. In some infuriating way, he always seemed to fight the battle on his terms and his ground. Experiencing this, more, I think, than anything else, led me to believe that although the pursuit of truth in philosophy may – sometimes must – involve a battle with opposing views, a necessary part and method of its pursuit involves withdrawal; contemplation; a cool, dispassionate, detached consideration of what is at issue; and, more important than all else, a willingness and ability to think oneself into, and in that sense to imagine, the position of the other, and an attempt to understand the factors and arguments which had led him or her to a contrary view. How difficult it can be to live one's beliefs.

Finally, Jack, the young man: Jack, of course, is me, but a much younger me – with a better physique! – and, like virtually all the other protagonists, is long dead.

CONCLUSION

I hope that by now I have shown you and persuaded you that, however unwittingly and however rarely, you do engage in philosophical thought and are in that sense a philosopher. (The same sense as the one in which you are a car driver or swimmer, however rarely you drive or swim.) Indeed, I hope to have shown you and persuaded you that you were a philosopher a long time before you read this book.

But would you like to be more of a philosopher? Even if you are not entirely sure, you will find out that you would if you go back to the book shelves marked 'Philosophy', flick through other texts, perhaps more specialised or technical than mine, and buy or borrow one of them as well. People discover interests, for example, when they see someone doing something, say mending an old clock, and think 'I'd like to do that!' But they can also discover that they have certain interests, perhaps in art history, when they realise that they often read books on art history; or in disasters, when they realise, somewhat sheepishly perhaps, that they always look at books on disasters in cheap book shops, though they never buy them for themselves, or their pulses quicken when they hear the siren of a police car, ambulance or fire engine, as it rushes by.

Now the philosophising which we engage in naturally is scarcely an interest, no more than keeping an appointments diary is an interest, though it can become one, as keeping the appointments diary scarcely could without the latter's seeming a quirk or minor obsession. But if it did become an interest I should be disappointed, paradoxical though this may seem. For describing something as an interest characterises an activity as something which a person does out of interest and for his or her amusement. Imagine someone practising surgery out of interest and as an interest!

I am not saying that philosophy is not interesting. Philosophical problems and puzzles can be fascinating, and working away at them can be a sort of joy – though of course it can also be exhausting and frustrating. But in a way in which we could not say of crossword puzzles, wrestling with philosophical problems is a pursuit of truth, knowledge and wisdom. Etymologically, it is somewhat fanciful to define philosophy as the love of wisdom, but the wisdom and understanding that philosophy can give is worthy of our love.

So if you are undecided, do have a look at some other books. You may find their content and approach more appealing than what you have found here. If you feel keen, even excited by the prospect of doing more philosophy, the opportunities are many. If you are about to go to college or university then, whatever you have chosen as your major subject, most universities will allow you to do at least one introductory course in philosophy and, if you like it, you will almost certainly be allowed to do more. If you are not about to go to college, there are many evening classes provided by local authorities, which will be advertised in local newspapers (and which tend to begin when the academic year begins, in September or October). There are diploma courses at universities, which are taught in the evening, and your local university would be pleased to answer your enquiry. There are even part-time degrees, which again people at work can do in the evenings which, in recognition of the students' other commitments, give them six years to complete, or more if they have to take a break ('intermit').

University libraries are, of course, a rich source of philosophy books and periodicals, though, with some exceptions, both books and articles have become rather technical and difficult. But if you would like to work at your own pace, in your own way, and at varying times to suit yourself, most university libraries will allow you access; some will allow you to borrow books; and there are still some who will not charge local ratepayers or taxpayers for this service. Indeed, if you fit that description, and already have a first degree, even in some other area, most universities will consider your application to work for a part-time higher degree, perhaps an MA. If you think you might like to go for that, I strongly encourage you to ring, not the admissions office, but the department, and ask the secretary, who will answer your call, if you may speak to the chairman or, failing that, whoever is in charge of the postgraduate programme, or, if that person isn't available either, to any senior member of the department. (Junior members cannot avoid being less helpful; they are less confident of what they can do or should do.) My prediction is that the person you speak to will be pleased to help someone wanting to do philosophy.

What about those who have decided that philosophy, at any rate, more philosophy, philosophy as something you pursue rather than something you can't always avoid, is not for them? Well, apart from those persons who always look at the end of a book – any book – first, most of those who have made this decision will have already closed this one and departed the scene. For those who have not: either you have decided that there are more amusing, or more worthwhile ways of spending whatever time you could spare than doing philosophy, or you feel that it is a luxury you cannot afford. You have to get a qualification that will enable you to earn a living, perhaps as a surveyor, or an actuary, or an aromatherapist. Perhaps you are so exhausted when you get back from work, you haven't got the strength to do anything that is going to make mental demands on you. For the latter sort I have nothing but sympathy. Ten hours' bus conducting left me too tired even to eat. I am amazed and impressed by the buildings, often rather grand buildings, which you can still find in many small towns in northern England, which have a date, often in the 1850s and 1860s, and above that, boldly emblazoned, an inscription, often in roman capitals, and in relief on the stone wall over the porched entrance, 'Workers' reading rooms', 'Working men's educational institute', 'Apprentices' study rooms'. Their energy and appetite for learning is even more impressive than their command of the plural possessive apostrophe. It is sad and paradoxical that in a society that is immeasurably richer than was theirs, those people who have work are worked so hard that they have nothing left for anything else, and others are demoralised and paralysed by poverty and the emptiness of their days. It is true that greater productivity means greater consumption and, in that sense, a higher standard of living. But what does it profit a person if he or she has a four track, a coupé, a Georgian or colonial, landscaped residence, and no time or energy left over from acquiring these things, except to holiday for a week or two in Hawaii or Turkey, and worry that greater drives to efficiency and productivity may lead to the loss of their middle-management job and income? Persons in such a state need philosophy, especially a political, social and economic philosophy.

But, and finally, how about those people who earn their livings as civil engineers. architects, farm workers, longshore fishermen, and would prefer to spend their free time bird watching, skiing, hang-gliding, ballroom dancing, biking, playing tennis, golfing? First, let me say that I love a lot of these activities, and I only wish that I were fit enough and brave enough to go hang-gliding. As to their jobs: a world in which everyone sat around doing philosophy would not only be impossible but intolerable. We need people to have different interests and aptitudes, not just instrumentally – because our whole way of life and culture would collapse if, as in subsistence economies, we all earned our livings in the same way – but because that diversity of occupations, interests, aptitudes, makes our world so rich in interest and distinguished in achievements and excellence.

So I cannot, and do not, wish that everyone were, or should aspire to be, a professional philosopher. But how about a non-professional and part-time philosopher, which latter is, of course, what even philosophers are? (Tom Stoppard, the playwright, once expressed regret that he spent less than 0.5 per cent of his life writing plays. But even in his most despairing, frustrated moments, he surely could not have hoped to spend more than, say, 10 per cent of his time writing plays.) Surely it would be presumptuous of me, patronising, as well as unrealistic, to think that all of us not only could, but should, be more philosophers than we are. After all, a central tenet of this book is that virtually everybody is a philosopher.

I grasp this solution with relief. But, being a philosopher, something still niggles me. What can it be? Well, suppose we are considering the case of an industrial chemist, who when he is off the job, is very clear that what he wants to do is have a ball. He earns good money, and that's what he is able and going to have, and he is certainly not going to sit around philosophising, or think that he should. Well, as I have tried to show earlier, no job will bypass philosophical problems. In his case he may be unable to avoid considering, say, the conse- quences of consuming non-renewable resources, or producing insecticides that will injure their users and produce resistant strains of whatever form of life he is employed to destroy or control. He may not like this part of his job, but avoid it he cannot; neither – surely – should he.

As to his leisure: how could I be contemptuous of, say, restoring vintage cars – they are beautiful and, I think, valu- able in ways other than the simply financial. But, and despite all this, honesty compels me to raise this last question: we have only one life. (A typical philosopher's platitude.) We live it from birth to death. (Another.) We have to make decisions, often in ignorance of their eventual outcome, and without the subsequent experience of life that might, in retrospect, lead us to wish that we had done differently. But all of us do know that, as our lives lead towards their close, we will, as we should, ask ourselves, 'Should I have lived my life thus?' And if we have spent it in getting and spending, in designing the most efficient internal-combustion engine, developing the most efficient and cheapest car-insurance company, manu- facturing the best ice cream that money can buy, we may feel that, yes, that was right for me. But, of course, we may feel differently and wish, if only our opportunities had been differ- ent, that we had lived a different life. What I think we cannot wish, and should not wish, is that *we were never exercised by such questions*, however puzzling and anguishing they may be. To wish that we had lived a completely unexamined, unreflective life is itself the product of reflection and self-examination, and to wish it away is, it seems to me, to wish for a kind of living death, a non-human life – a life which, as Plato said, is not worth living.

Readers who would like to question me about philosophical claims made in this book, or any philosophical issues raised by it, are welcome to write to me, c/o Darwin College, University of Kent at Canterbury, Canterbury, CT2 7NY. I will do my best to respond.

INDEX